The ★★★★ PATTON MIND

THE PROFESSIONAL DEVELOPMENT OF AN EXTRAORDINARY LEADER

Roger H. Nye

AVERY PUBLISHING GROUP INC.
Garden City Park, New York

Cover Design: Martin Hochberg and Rudy Shur

Library of Congress Cataloging-in-Publication Data

Nye, Roger H. (Roger Hurless)
    The Patton mind : the professional development of an extraordinary
leader / by Roger H. Nye.
        p. cm.
    Includes bibliographical references and index.
    ISBN 0-89529-428-1
    1. Patton, George S. (George Smith), 1885–1945—Knowledge
and learning. 2. Generals—United States—Biography.
3. United States. Army—Biography. I. Title.
E745.P3N94 1993
355'.0092—dc20
    [B]   92-10490
                                                                 CIP

Copyright © 1993 by Roger H. Nye

Printed in the United States of America

10 9 8 7 6 5 4 3 2 1

Contents

To my ever supportive family—
my patient wife, Nan;
our talented daughter, Elizabeth;
and our always perceptive son-in-law, Luigi Di Cataldo.

Foreword

M Y FATHER, George S. Patton, Jr., departed this life on 21 December, 1945, three days before my twenty-second birthday. At the time of his passing, I was a First Classman at West Point, preparing myself for the homestretch toward graduation with the Class of 1946 and a lifetime Army career.

From the time I entered West Point, in July 1942, until his untimely death, I saw my father but twice. The first time was during his visit to West Point for a few hours in October 1942, prior to his departure for Morocco and Operation Torch. The second occasion was on 7 June, 1945, when he landed in Boston, a national hero of World War II. Prior to 1942, we were frequently separated by the exigencies of his service, the constant turbulence of many moves and changes of station because of the coming war, and my attendance at preparatory school in Pennsylvania during 1938–1942.

I knew George S. Patton, Jr., as a loving father, avid horseman, yachtsman, game hunter, and conversationalist. During meals he would fascinate his three children with stories of his time and service at West Point and thereafter. He was a spellbinder, telling us of his associations with John J. Pershing, Leonard Wood, C. P. Summerall, Henry Stimson, Sereno Brett, and literally all of those great characters who moved across the stage of the pre- and post-World War I Army. During the late twenties and thirties, many of them took meals at our various homes in the Washington-Fort Myer area.

My lifelong friend and classmate, Roger Nye, has succeeded in bringing forward an aspect of George S. Patton, Jr., which clearly demonstrates his total professionalism and career dedication. As his son, I was quite aware of his reading and study of, for example, the Great Captains, the Civil War, and, most especially, the Napoleonic Wars. However, I was not totally cognizant of the tremendous effort he placed into those studies— the dedication, the research, and, most importantly, the time.

Many stories come to mind, such as the evening when my mother entered our quarters at Fort Shafter, Hawaii, and found her husband at his desk in the back study of the house. He was crying. He had been reading J.F.C. Fuller's *Generalship: Its Diseases and Their Cure*. The appendix to that great classic addresses the ages of 100 generals, from Xenophon to Robert E. Lee, at the heights of their careers. Of the total, only eleven were senior in age to Patton at that time. The fifty-year-old lieutenant colonel clearly felt that opportunity had passed him by.

One could not complete a foreword to a book about my father without mention of his wife, and my mother, Beatrice. She shared with him not only his love of horses and boats and soldiering, but also his love of books and conversation about them. They were devoted to each other. They often expressed their love in gifts of books; their letters often cited their reading as well as the writing and speaking projects they had undertaken as World War II became a reality. I have recently forwarded to the West Point Library a collection of her speeches and articles, to be placed with letters my father wrote to her during World War II.

Colonel Nye's effort is unique. It will do much toward the advancement of professionalism within the Corps of Cadets and, certainly, the Officer Corps of the Army. It will clearly demonstrate that the attainment of high rank in our most honorable profession demands eternal concentration and study, and the time to allocate to it. This volume is more than just a reference work of books and papers that G. S. Patton, Jr. studied during his lifetime. It is, of course, historically interesting to note what he studied. But the real message relates to the way a soldier prepared himself to achieve success in war and, at the close of his career, realized he had gained that success.

George S. Patton
Major General
USA–Retired

Preface

GREAT MOMENTS of American military leadership in World War II have become legend in the books and films about that vast global conflict of the 1940s: Patton's mercurial drive across France with the Third Army, and his smashing into the German flank in the Battle of the Bulge in the Ardennes; MacArthur's island-hopping across the Pacific, with only the skimpiest of forces, but driving the Japanese back to their homeland; Eisenhower's brilliance in projecting American national strategy in Marshall's office in 1941, and his deftness in keeping a coalition together through the invasion and taking of the European west lands; "Lightning Joe" Collins' mastery of the operational art in his command of VII Corps in Normandy and beyond.

And so on to "Hap" Arnold and Brehon Somervell and Omar Bradley and the host of military men who raised and fought the American ground, naval, and air forces around the world. Such a clustering of American military leadership had appeared only once before, in the later years of the Civil War, in the genius of Grant, Lee, Jackson, Sherman, and many of their colleagues.

Conditions in American life before World War II were not propitious for the nurturing of such military men. American society had long been intolerant of a military caste that might spawn military warriors as had happened in Europe and Asia. Americans were in an especially pacifist mood in the twenties and thirties, with a penchant to starve the Army of weapons, people, and training. War planning and fighting presumed the defense of the Americas, with technology geared to the horse, bayonet, and motorcar.

What, then, can account for the sudden appearance of those men of military greatness in a short span of a few years in the early 1940s? Winston Churchill attributed the quality of American World War II generalship to their training at the staff college at Fort Leavenworth. That, of course, does not account for why only certain Leavenworth graduates achieved excellence while many others did not. The fact that most of the World War II "greats" were commissioned from West Point might say something about a second theory—their selection and training at the United States Military Academy; but the knowledge and insights needed to lead corps and armies in worldwide coalitions had to be acquired long after their undergraduate experience.

A third theory is that those who achieved greatness did so outside of schools, through a very intense and lifelong self-study of their profession. It is the purpose of this book to explore the dimensions of that professional self-development theme.

In his memoir *At Ease*, Eisenhower wrote of his reading about the military profession with Brigadier General Fox Conner in the 1920s. Omar Bradley wrote that he and other junior officers "studied everything we could get our hands on." Douglas MacArthur read constantly, as did J. Lawton Collins, Maxwell D. Taylor, and Matthew B. Ridgway. However, we generally know little about the reading patterns of the officer corps between the wars. Many were not readers, while among those who were, the habit was so commonplace that the actual reading material was rarely recorded.

The great exception is George S. Patton, Jr. This man has been celebrated as a highly energized and profane man of action—a doer rather than a thinker, many said. But he left behind the most complete record of exhaustive professional study of any World War II general—or any general in American history, for that matter.

The Patton Mind sets out to explain how Patton acquired and used a military library for almost daily study of his profession and how he employed his system of marginal notes and file cards to develop his thinking about tactics, strategy, leadership, and military organization. Those thoughts were expressed in a stream of lectures, staff papers, and journal articles, and also in diaries, poetry, and finally in a classic book, *War As I Knew It*.

The focus of this book is on the Patton Collection of the United States Military Academy (USMA) Library at West Point, New York. Beginning in 1987, Major General George S. Patton, United States Army–Retired, began donating to West Point several hundred books from his father's library, asking the Friends of the West Point Library to assist in the process. This book is intended to serve as a guide to the Patton Collection and to provide an example of professional self-development as pursued by one of America's greatest soldier-leaders. It is hoped that through this publication, George S. Patton, Jr.'s successors will be inspired to develop their own patterns of professional study.

Documentation is based on the bibliography at the end of this book. "The Patton Library" refers to the collection of books and manuscripts in the home of George S. Patton, Jr., Beatrice Ayer Patton, and their heirs, in South Hamilton, Massachusetts, in the late 1940s. Many of those books are now in the USMA Library at West Point, New York. Most of the original manuscripts are in the Library of Congress, in Washington, D.C. Many manuscript copies are kept at West Point. The manuscripts consist primarily of letters between Patton and his wife, Beatrice; letters between Patton and his father; diaries; notebooks; and papers and speeches that he wrote.

The author has relied heavily on Martin Blumenson's two-volume *Patton Papers* (BPP) to guide the reader to the most accessible source. Wherever the author cites a different source he includes that author's name and the page number.

The author is deeply indebted to Major General George S. Patton and Ruth Ellen Patton Totten for their continuing advice on their patrimony. Martin Blumenson's *Patton Papers* provided continuing linkage between the reading habits of the budding World War II genius and his lifetime output of writing and lectures. David Holt of the Patton Museum at Fort Knox, Kentucky, was most generous in providing photographic support, and the staff of the Documents Division of the Library of Congress was particularly helpful in directing me to needed parts of their extensive holdings of the papers of General George S. Patton, Jr.

I also owe a debt of thanks to Colonel John A. Calabro and other members of the Council of the Friends of the West Point Library for their help on the manuscript. Also of great help were Joanne Holbrook Patton, Professor Carmine Prioli, Major Steve Dietrich, Mrs. Diana Snell, Mr. Edward J. Krasnoborski, the USMA Department of History, and the staff of *Armor* magazine. Finally, Gladys Calvetti, Marie Capps, Alan Aimone, and Judith Sibley of the USMA Library staff have been unstinting in their support of this study.

Roger H. Nye
Colonel
USA–Retired
The Rocks, Webb Lane
Highland Falls, New York

CHAPTER ONE

Foundations for a Military "Life of the Mind" 1885–1902

BEFORE WE EXPLORE the rich sources of the Patton mind, we should be clear on the greatness of the Patton *persona* that emerged in World War II. His professional skill and courage were never better demonstrated than on August 10, 1943, when he was driving the U.S. Seventh Army along the northern coast of Sicily, hoping to beat the British to Messina and capture Germans before they could escape to mainland Italy. (See map on page 171.)

He had ordered the 3rd Infantry Division to make an amphibious landing behind the German lines early on the 11th, but Major General Lucian Truscott phoned him the evening before to recommend calling off the operation as too risky. Patton also learned that II Corps commander General Omar Bradley agreed, and so did the U.S. Navy. Patton barked, "Dammit, the operation will go on," banged down the receiver and left for the 3rd Division headquarters.

In *Command Missions*, Truscott later wrote this:

> An hour later, General Patton came storming into my Command Post giving everybody hell from the Military Police at the entrance right on through until he came to me. He was screamingly angry as only he could be. "Goddamit, Lucian, what's the matter with you? Are you afraid to fight?" I bristled right back: "General, you know that's ridiculous and insulting. You have ordered the operation and it is now loading. If you don't think I can carry out orders, you can

give the Division to anyone you please. But I will tell you one thing, you will not find anyone who can carry out orders which they do not approve as well as I can."

General Patton changed instantly, the anger all gone. Throwing his arm about my shoulder he said: "Dammit Lucian, I know that. Come on, let's have a drink—of your liquor." We did. General Patton departed in his usual good spirits. (Truscott 235.)

Patton recorded in his diary a considerably different version of the discussion. He wrote that he had told Truscott: " 'If your conscience will not let you conduct this operation, I will relieve you and put someone in charge who will. Remember Frederick the Great—'L'audace, l'audace, toujours l'audace.' I know you will win and if there is a bottle-neck you should be there and not here.' I then told Truscott I had complete confidence in him, and, to show it, was going home and to bed, and left. On the way back I worried a little, but feel I was right. I thought of Grant and Nelson and felt O.K. That is the value of history."

He wrote to wife Beatrice the next day: "Yesterday I earned my pay. We were to put on a swimming operation, and it was all set. Then at 8:00 both Omar and Lucien [sic] called to say it was too risky. I told them to do it. . . . It worked, and now they think they thought of it. I had to get pretty tough and ask how they would like to have stars turn out to be eagles.

"I have a sixth sense in war as I used to have in fencing, and besides I can put myself inside the enemies head and also am willing to take chances. Last night I remembered Frederick 'L'audace' . . . and Nelson putting the glass to his blind eye and saying 'Mark well, gentlemen. I have searched diligently and see no signal to withdraw. Fly the flag to continue the action.' Also the other acts of victorious generals . . . those historic memories cheered me no end."

That episode from the World War II diary of General George S. Patton, Jr., and amplified in a letter to his wife, is but one snapshot among thousands of the mind of a great general in action at the peak of his career. But Patton's sources of strength and confidence and daring lie deep in history, in the legends of Frederick the Great and Horatio Nelson and Ulysses S. Grant. He began acquiring that faith, and the body of knowledge that could be summoned on his command, in his earliest years in California when his belief in his martial bloodlines and his very special education led him to seek his destiny as a soldier.

By the time he was sixteen, George Smith Patton, Jr., had determined that he would become a professional soldier. However, his special vision of himself as a soldier required him to pursue the education and training of a "military gentleman." His vision was also tied to his belief that he came from a distinguished ancestry and belonged to a social class that bore some responsibility for maintaining an orderly society. We know that primarily from two long papers he wrote, one in 1927 as a tribute to his father and one in 1913 in which he told about his ancestry as he remembered its being told to him as a boy. Both papers accounted for the firmness of his decision at sixteen to pursue a military career.

Patton's mother, Ruth Wilson, included among her ancestors Major David Wilson of the Continental Army in the American Revolution and later Speaker of the Tennessee House of Representatives. His son Benjamin fought Mojave Indians on the way to California and held a captain's commission in the Mexican War. In the 1830s, Benjamin Wilson built the house on the San Gabriel ranch in which his grandson George S. Patton, Jr., was raised after his birth on November 11, 1885.

Young Patton's paternal grandfather, the first George Smith Patton, graduated from the Virginia Military Institute in 1856 and was killed in the battle of Cedar Creek at Winchester, Virginia, in 1864 while commanding the 22nd Virginia Cavalry. His widow migrated with her children to California via Panama and married another 1856 VMI graduate, George Hugh Smith, a Civil War hero who young George admired until death separated them in 1915.

George's father, the second George Smith Patton, graduated from VMI in 1877 and became a lawyer in the Pasadena area of California. While he did not pursue a military career, he instilled in young George

Patton's parents (Ruth Wilson Patton and George Smith Patton), probably in the early or mid-1920s. (USMA Library photo.)

a great pride in his military ancestry and introduced him to guns, hunting, sailing, and military history. "Papa" duelled with the youngster with wooden swords, bought him ponies and taught him to ride, and saw that he caught more than his share of catfish and yellowtail, usually on Catalina Island, where one day the boy shot five wild goats. The character of the rugged outdoorsman was set.

The father sensed early, however, that his son was not developing normally as a student. The words the lad saw on a printed page had distorted letters, and reading became a chore to be avoided. Papa kept young George out of school, and instead launched him on a program of aural learning. Family members read to him until he was eleven years old, and he was required to memorize long passages from the classics, ancient history, and romantic poetry.

A half century later his wife wrote: "By the time the future general had reached the age of eight, he had heard and acted out the *Iliad*, the *Odyssey*, some of Shakespeare's historical plays, and such books of adventure as *Scottish Chiefs*, Conan Doyle's *Sir Nigel, The White Company*, the *Memoirs and Adventures of Brigadier Gerard, The Boys' King Arthur*, and the complete works of G. A. Henty." (Beatrice Patton, "A Soldier's Reading.") Meanwhile, George was encouraged to read more and more on his own, and in 1897 Papa decided it was time to send him to school.

Patton at age ten in a sailor suit. (Photo courtesy of the Patton Museum.)

Martin Blumenson, in his 1985 book, *Patton: The Man Behind the Legend, 1885–1945*, concluded that Patton suffered from "the dyslexis flaw" that makes printed letters appear upside down or reversed. He also pointed out that the psychological symptoms that accompany dyslexia include feelings of inadequacy, problems of concentration, and the need to compensate for impairments in the learning process with accomplishments in other areas. He suggested that Patton acquired a strong motivation to overcome this handicap and to allay his fears of inadequacy by demonstrating superiority in many walks of life. Certainly, Patton accomplished both in an amazing feat of will and endurance. He could read well by the late teens, although he never overcame his inability to spell words correctly. (Recent research has suggested that some persons with a history of dyslexia come away from the experience with certain advantages, such as an unusual way of perceiving problems and creating solutions.)

In the fall of 1897, George, Jr., was sent to Mr. Stephen Clark's School for Boys in Pasadena. Over the next six years he and the sons of elite southern California families studied a curriculum that emphasized mathematics, English, geography, drawing, four languages (Greek, Latin, French, German), and, particularly, ancient and modern history. During those years, both Patton's written exercises and the entries in his private journals reflect a deepening interest in military commanders

and their political roles. Miltiades, Epaminondas, Themistocles, Alexander the Great, and Julius Caesar were all subject to his commentary, as were their tactics, leadership qualities, and moral character. They provided background for written ruminations about his own future and the importance of patience, hard work, and continued study if he was to achieve the "destiny" he was beginning to define for himself.

The Patton, Ayer, and Banning families at a California outing, circa 1900. Patton is kneeling in the rear and wearing a light suit. (USMA Library photo.)

Before undertaking an extended study of Patton's development as a professional military man, two other phenomena about the Patton mind should be cited, both with roots in his earliest days. One was his continuing encounter with déjà vu, or as the psychologists use it, the illusion that one has previously had a given experience. The other was his remarkable retention of things he had memorized. Both had an important impact on the development of his personal philosophy of life and how he thought about his profession.

Evidence of Patton's encounters with déjà vu and of his remarkable memory comes from his very close associates and especially from his family. In addition to his parents, those most likely to have observed those phenomena in Patton were: Beatrice Ayer Patton, whom he married in 1910; daughter Beatrice Smith Patton, born in March 1911; daughter Ruth Ellen Patton, born in February 1915; and son George Smith Patton, born in December 1923. Also in this group should be a sister, Miss Anne Patton, generally known as Nita or Anita, and George's mother's sister, Miss Annie Wilson, generally known as Aunt Nannie, who travelled widely and contributed extensively to the growth of Patton's military library.

In August 1990, Ruth Ellen Patton Totten, the second daughter of George S. Patton, Jr., retold this story: She was a youngster when the family drove from Washington to visit one of the Civil War battlefields, taking along military attaché Friedrich von Boetticher in the full regalia of a German army officer. As usual the family was deployed to represent key figures in the battle. ("Mother always had to play the North.") Major Patton said he would play General Jubal Early and therefore would be located "right here" on the map. Von Boetticher protested that his book indicated that Early was located "over there." As the argument went on, a very old man in muttonchop whiskers hobbled up and listened; they thought he was attracted by the German uniform. But in time he said very firmly, "The major is right. General Early was right here. I was at this battle as a boy." Patton looked at the German and said, "Yes. I was here too." Von Boetticher changed Early's location on his map and the play continued.

Patton (right) at age sixteen, and his father, at home near San Gabriel, California. (Photo courtesy of the Patton Museum.)

Ruth Ellen recalled in 1990 other instances when her father told of his experiences with déjà vu, often in after-dinner talk around the dining table in the twenties and thirties. One was his memory of being carried on a shield by four Vikings. She was asked why there were no books on reincarnation or Buddhism in the Patton Library, which had been accumulated over decades. She replied that her father's "I was there" was born into him, not induced by listening or reading, although those activities might have provided some rationale for what was innate.

When asked to recall her father's earliest experiences with déjà vu, she told of his recalling when he was a small boy in California "playing war" with his cousins, the Browns. He loaded them in a wagon, had them cover themselves with barrelhead shields, and told them to fire arrows out between the shields when they reached the enemy. Then he pushed the wagon off the brow of the hill, and it hurtled its way down and careened through a flock of turkeys at the bottom. The Pattons would eat turkey for days. When someone bothered to ask Georgie how he had gotten the crazy idea, he said that in Bohemia centuries ago, John-the-Blind had done just that and won a great victory against the Turks. Where had he heard about it? "Oh," he told them, "I was there." Major Patton elaborated the story, explaining that the wagon in

Bohemia was the first instrument of modern armored warfare.

The sessions around the dining table often included poetry recitations that Major Patton had required the children to memorize. Ruth Ellen gave an example, starting with the first stanza of Alfred, Lord Tennyson's "The Revenge: A Ballad of the Fleet":

> At Flores in the Azores Sir Richard Grenville lay,
> And a pinnace, like a fluttered bird, came flying from far away:
> 'Spanish ships of war at sea! we have sighted fifty-three!'
> Then swore Lord Thomas Howard: ''Fore God I am no coward;
> But I cannot meet them here, for my ships are out of gear,
> And half my men are sick. I must fly, but follow quick.
> We are six ships of the line; can we fight with fifty-three?'

Her brother George joined her, and together they continued reciting many of the fourteen stanzas, telling how Sir Richard attacked the fifty-three galleons with his *Revenge:* "God of battles, was ever a battle like this in the world before? / For he said 'Fight on! Fight on!' / Though his vessel was all but a wreck." This poem that the family recited together concluded with the last lines, "And the little *Revenge* herself went down by the island crags / To be lost evermore in the main."

Ruth Ellen suggested that the Patton family's ability to remember that which had been learned in youth was more than just a matter of training. She said the funeral eulogy of a Patton killed at Gettysburg in the Civil War noted particularly the man's prodigious memory. She also set about to type four pages of her father's favorite poems and sayings as she remembered them generations later. One was the six stanzas of Sir Edwin Arnold's "After Death," taken from his translation from the Arabic in the 1883 *Pearls of the Faith.* (See inset on page 9.) Ruth Ellen noted that "When our grandfather died ["Papa" in 1927] GSPJr made my sister Bea and me memorize this poem." In it, the everlasting soul speaks from afar that the temporary body has been abandoned, but the separation from those left behind will not be long. This may be one of the few indications of the effect of oriental religion on Patton's thinking and probably came from his father's vast reading. Most remarkable was Ruth Ellen's losing only a few words and lines from her memory some sixty years later.

She also typed out a fragment of an ode that had been a Patton favorite. Again, the theme was the everlasting soul; it was the fifth stanza of William Wordsworth's "Ode: Intimations of Immortality," written between 1803 and 1806, and called by Ralph Waldo Emerson "the high-water mark reached by intellect in this age." Ruth Ellen's memory of it was without flaw, except for citing "his vision" rather than "the vision" in the sixteenth line. (See inset on page 8.)

Two of Patton's Favorite Poems

Below is the fifth stanza of William Wordsworth's "Ode: Intimations of Immortality," a favorite ode of Patton. The poem, which explores the everlasting soul, was memorized by the Patton family in the 1920s. This version was typed from memory by Patton's younger daughter, Ruth Ellen Patton Totten, in August 1990. To the right is a poem that Patton made his daughters memorize upon the death of Patton's father in 1927. It is Sir Edwin Arnold's translation from the Arabic of "After Death," and it, too, deals with the everlasting soul, and may indicate the influence of oriental religion on Patton's thinking. This translation comes from Cunliffe and Thorndike, editors, *The World's Best Literature*, Volume II, Knickerbocker Press, 1917.

```
          FRAGMENT: AN ODE

Our birth is but a sleep and a forgetting:
The soul that rises with us, our life's star,
Hath had elsewhere its setting,
   And cometh from afar.
   Not in entire forgetfulness,
And not in utter nakedness,
     But trailing clouds of glory do we come
     From God, who is our home.
Heaven lies about us in our infancy;
   Shades of the prison house begin to close
Upon the growing boy,
   But he beholds the light, and whence it flows
He sees it in his joy;
The youth, who daily farther from the east
Must travel, still is Nature's priest
And byhis vision splendid
Is on his way attended;
     At length the man perceives it die away
     And fade into the light of common day.

                              ---Wordsworth
```

After Death
from *Pearls of the Faith*
by Edwin Arnold

He made life — and He takes it — but instead
Gives more: praise the Restorer, Al-Mu'hid!

He who died at Azan sends
This to comfort faithful friends: —

Faithful friends! it lies, I know,
Pale and white and cold as snow;
And ye say, "Abdullah's dead!"
Weeping at my feet and head.
I can see your falling tears,
I can hear your cries and prayers,
Yet I smile and whisper this: —
"I am not that thing you kiss;
Cease your tears and let it lie:
It *was* mine, it is not I."

Sweet friends! what the women lave
For its last bed in the grave
Is a tent which I am quitting,
Is a garment no more fitting,
Is a cage from which at last
Like a hawk my soul hath passed.
Love the inmate, not the room;
The wearer, not the garb; the plume
Of the falcon, not the bars
Which kept him from the splendid stars.

Loving friends! be wise, and dry
Straightway every weeping eye:
What ye lift upon the bier
Is not worth a wistful tear.
'Tis an empty sea-shell, one
Out of which the pearl is gone.
The shell is broken, it lies there;
The pearl, the all, the soul, is here.
'Tis an earthen jar whose lid
Allah sealed, the while it hid
That treasure of His treasury,
A mind which loved Him: let it lie!
Let the shard be earth's once more,
Since the gold shines in His store!

Allah Mu'hid, Allah most good!
Now Thy grace is understood:
Now my heart no longer wonders
What Al-Barsakh is, which sunders
Life from death, and death from Heaven;
Nor the "Paradises Seven"
Which the happy dead inherit;
Nor those "birds" which bear each spirit
Toward the Throne, "green birds and white,"
Radiant, glorious, swift their flight!
Now the long, long darkness ends.
Yet ye wail, my foolish friends,
While the man whom ye call "dead"
In unbroken bliss instead
Lives, and loves you: lost, 'tis true
By any light which shines for you;
But in light ye cannot see
Of unfulfilled felicity,
And enlarging Paradise;
Lives the life that never dies.

Farewell, friends! Yet not farewell;
Where I am, ye, too, shall dwell.
I am gone before your face
A heart-beat's time, a gray ant's pace.
When ye come where I have stepped,
Ye will marvel why ye wept;
Ye will know, by true love taught,
That here is all, and there is naught.
Weep awhile, if ye are fain, —
Sunshine still must follow rain!
Only not at death, for death —
Now I see — is that first breath
Which our souls draw when we enter
Life, that is of all life centre.

Know ye Allah's law is love,
Viewed from Allah's Throne above;
Be ye firm of trust, and come
Faithful onward to your home!
"*La Allah illa Allah!* Yea,
Mu'hid! Restorer! Sovereign!" say!

He who died at Azan gave
This to those that made his grave.

Another Patton favorite came from Homer's *Iliad*—Achilles' prayer at Troy, probably translated from the Greek by Papa. As Ruth Ellen remembered it:

> O Father Zeus; save us from this fog and give us a clear sky
> so that we can use our eyes. Kill us in daylight if you must.

She also recalled this snippet from Sir Henry Newbolt's "The Island Race":

> To set the cause above reknown,
> To love the game beyond the prize,
> To honor, while you strike him down
> The foe that, comes with fearless eyes,
> To count the life of battle good
> And dear the land that gave you birth,
> And dearer yet, the brotherhood
> That binds the brave to all the earth.

Patton later finished his career praying to his God for better weather in which to fight the enemy he honored. (See inset on page 11.)

Patton (left) and his father sitting on the porch of their house, known as Lake Vineyard, in April 1901. (USMA Library photo.)

Ruth Ellen also remembered her father's love for a prayer by Socrates: "All-knowing Zeus; give me what is best for me. Avert evil from me though it be the thing I prayed for; and give me the good, for which, from ignorance, I did not ask."

The "Life of the Mind" that Patton took into his career and eventually passed on to his children was spawned in the house of his childhood, Lake Vineyard, near San Gabriel in California. It meant that once his formal education was finished he would take up the day-to-day study of an evergrowing personal library, accompanied by a torrent of writing. Both activities closely wove together his beliefs about his everlasting soul with his view of a fated destiny as a battle hero and military gentleman. All were necessary to account for the military genius he became.

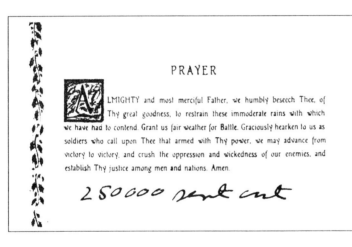

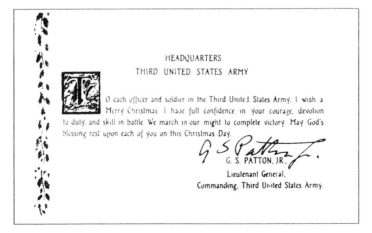

For Christmas 1944, Patton sent vest-pocket-sized cards to his soldiers. One side of the card contained a prayer, written by Chaplain James O'Neill, asking for better weather in which to fight. The other side contained a Christmas greeting from Patton. The "250,000 sent out" notation on this particular card was penciled by Patton. In holiday spirit, the large "A" and "T" were in red, the embroidering vine in green.

Patton in 1903, during his one year as a cadet at Virginia Military Institute. (Photo courtesy of the Patton Museum.)

CHAPTER TWO

Military Schooling
1903–1909

HAVING MADE the decision to become a soldier, and nearing graduation from Clark's school, Patton set himself the goal of admission to West Point, with its four-year course and Regular Army commission. United States Senator Thomas R. Bard of California was lobbied intensively to nominate George, Jr., in 1904, when the senator's one cadetship in the 500-man Corps of Cadets would become available to a new man. Meanwhile, George would study for a year at the Virginia Military Institute, following in the footsteps of his father and grandfather. VMI also offered the opportunity for another year's maturing, as well as a preview of the academy curriculum and military lifestyle. Furthermore, the academy entrance examination could be waived by certification that he had successfully completed a year of college study. Even if the academy appointment was not obtained, he could continue at VMI and seek one of the few Regular Army commissions awarded to outstanding graduates.

Papa delivered George, Jr., to the Lexington, Virginia, barracks and returned to California, where a letter soon reported reading problems. He replied to his son, in part: "That must have been pretty embarrassing when you could not read the 'no hazing pledge.' How did you get out of it? I hope you managed to pass it off. I do not see how you are going to over-come this difficulty except by practicing reading all kinds of writing. Do not give it up, but when you start to read any thing keep at it till you work it out. You mis-spelled hazing. The verb is 'to haze' and you should remember the general rule—to drop the final 'e' before 'ing.' "

Thereafter, Patton's reading problem virtually disappeared from his correspondence, although he continued to agonize over his spelling in letters to his father. He found that he could handle college-level work successfully; after five months he was ranked 9 out of a possible 10 in English, 9.1 in mathematics and drawing, and a perfect 10 in history. In the spring of 1904 he was examined for and won Senator Bard's nomination, and entered West Point that summer with VMI's certification of his academic ability.

Within a few months he found himself failing in English at West Point, but Patton did not blame his reading problems. He wrote his father, "I got an instructor who in an evil moment found out my utter lack of knowledge about English Grammar so he has been questioning me on it with much regularity and I with equal exactness have flunked; still it is not all his fault for I don't spend enough time even on the part I know about. . . . I know that I should study and I don't." By the end of his first year at West Point he stood well in English but had failed examinations in both French and mathematics and was told to repeat the entire year. Thus he joined the class that would graduate in 1909, and he would spend a total of six years in military schools, three as a lowly plebe. His dyslexic flaw was never mentioned in official correspondence nor in his private letters from West Point, although he often regretted his continued inability to spell.

In the summer of 1905, Patton took the first step in what would become a lifetime habit of keeping a journal or diary of his thoughts and activities. He wrote his address in the front of a small notebook and added, "$5.00 reward will be paied to any person finding this book if he returns it. G. S. Patton Jr." The first entry was: "Do your damdest always." A second notebook was started the next year. Entries in both tended to be military in nature, such as five principles of war, or paraphrases like, "Daring is wisdom it is the highest part of war. Napier."

An entry in 1906 reflected how far he had progressed in planning his reading and envisioning his library. It was headed "List of Books I Should Read" and appears here unedited.

Oman—History of the Art of War in the Middle Ages
DeWith—Three Year's War
Maguire, TM—Strategy and Tactics of Mountain Ranges
T. D. Pilcher—Some Lessons for the Boer War
Napoleon—Maxims de la Guerre
Krug, ed.—Adams' Great Campaigns
Hemley—Operations of War
Lloyd, Henry—Military and Political Memoirs
von der Goltz—Nation in Arms
Henderson—Science of War

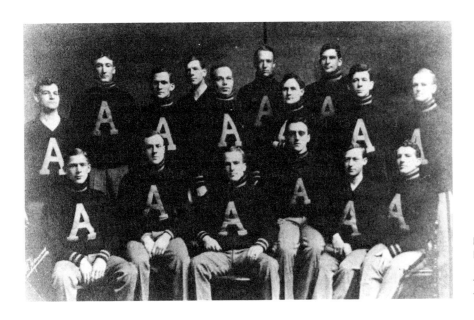

Patton played football at West Point. In this team photo from 1908 he's standing fifth from the right. (Photo courtesy of the Patton Museum.)

Rees, Hugh (pub)—Letters on Tactics
Jomini—Art of War and Dictionary of Battles
Green—Russian Campaigns in Turkey
Hohenlohe—Letters on Infantry, Cavalry, and Artillery
Upton—Armies of Europe and Asia
McClelland Campaigns of Stewart's Cavalry
Jomini—Life of Napoleon

Patton could not have been more than a twenty-year-old sophomore when he compiled that list. Twenty years later, the record would show that he had, indeed, read most of those books.

His notebooks indicated that he was reading Charles Oman in December 1906, although in the following year he told his father there was no time to read or do anything but study and play football. In a composition entitled "The Necessity of a Good Library at West Point," he wrote: "We are sorry to say that there are comparatively few men in the corps who realize the importance of military study and military history which is, as Napoleon says, the only school of war."

Support for his reading came more from home than from the academy. He acquired C. W. Robinson's *Wellington's Campaigns, Peninsula–Waterloo, 1808–1815* in 1907 when family members frequently visited West Point. In September 1908 he wrote to his mother, "I am awfully glad Aunt Nannie got those [military] books for I wanted them and I think that they are very good books and this practice march has more than ever convinced me of the value of book knowledge of war. It is the whole show and there are surprisingly few men who seem to

Patton at West Point circa 1908. (USMA Library photo.)

realize its importance." Also in 1908, George's father inscribed to Cadet Patton a volume of Major General Henry Lloyd's *The History of the Late War in Germany Between the King of Prussia and the Empress of Germany and Her Allies* that had been printed in London in the eighteenth century. It was the forerunner of Patton's significant collection of valuable antique books of a military nature. (See pages 165–167.)

Papa also continued to help George define his martial destiny. For example, in June 1905, when the son wrote of his disappointment in losing a hurdles race, the father wrote back: " . . . the real victor is he who strives bravely and *deserves* to win. There is even a sort of glory that crowns defeat—when it comes from no fault of the contestant. . . . you remember when we first read Kipling's poem 'The Destroyers'—there was a line we could not understand—'The choosers of the slain.' Well the other night I was reading one of Carlyles [Thomas Carlyle's] essays—and he explained the meaning of the term—It seems that in the Norse mythology—that of our ancestors the Vikings—the warriors who died in battle were accounted the real heroes—above those who survived—and before every battle the Valkyrie—or Valkyrs *chose* those who were adjudged worthy of death—and entrance into Valhalla—and these Valkyrs were thus called the 'choosers of the slain,' as the slain were called and esteemed 'The Chosen.' So in all Life's battles you can find the real heroes among the *apparently* defeated."

Young Patton seemed to accept into his philosophy the part of his father's counsel about heroic death, but not the part about heroic defeat. In the spring of 1908 he wrote into his notebook: "Remember that you have placed all on war. Therefore you must never fail. Hence if you attack—and you must never do anything else—put in every man and win or mark the high tide of your charge with your body. The world has no use for a defeated soldier and nothing too good for a victor. . . . If you die not a soldier and having had a chance to be one I pray God to dam you George Patton. . . . Never Never Never stop being ambitious. You have but one life. Live it to the full of glory and be willing to pay." In January 1909, he wrote to his parents: "I have got to—do you understand got to—be great—it is no foolish child dream—it is me as I ever will be. I am different from other men my age. All they want to do is to live happily and die old. I would be willing to live in torture, die tomorrow if for one day I could be realy great." (BPP I 142, 160.)

During his last year at West Point, Patton could satisfy his yearning to read and learn everything he could from military history, partly because The Military Art was included in courses in the Department of Engineering. His notebook writing was sprinkled with references to the Great Captains: "Napoleon at Jena made three mistakes in two days and won the battle." "Remember Frederick the Great how he said to his faultering men 'Come on men do you want to live for ever?' " "I believe

Cadet Adjutant Patton at West Point, probably in the summer of 1908. (USMA Library photo.)

Pictures taken circa 1908 show Patton preparing for and participating in USMA track meets.
Second photo from top shows Patton the hurdler.
In third photo, Patton is second runner from the right.
Bottom photo shows Patton (center) and two unknown classmates. (USMA Library photos.)

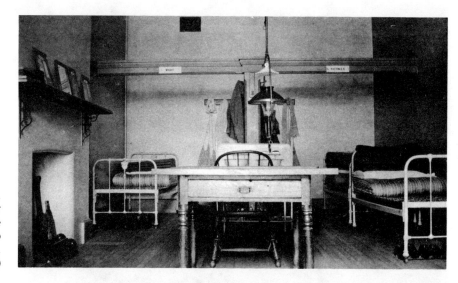

Patton's room at West Point, circa 1908. The bunk in the rear and to the right is Patton's. The bunk on the left belongs to Cadet John M. Wright. (USMA Library photo.)

that in order for a man to become a great soldier . . . it is necessary for him to be so thoroughly conversant with all sorts of military possibilities that when ever an occasion arises he has at hand with out effort on his part a parallel. . . . To attain this end I think that it is necessary for a man to begin to read military history in its earliest and hence crudest form and to follow it down in natural sequence permitting his mind to grow with his subject until he can grasp with out effort the most abstruce question of the science of war because he is already permiated with all its elements."

As the year went on, Patton's letters to Beatrice Ayer, whom he hoped to marry, conveyed more and more of his plans for professional reading. In a letter of March 25, 1909: "It has been raining all day so there was no drill and having nothing to do I read for about four hours until I could hardly see. . . ." In April: "I have been reading a german Translation on Tactics to night and it is a most saddening work for to be a good soldier one has to know so much and they seem to know it all and I know so little. How can I ever learn enough to fight with them yet I must." Finally, in May: "I hope that after I get out of here I shall find plenty to do for so many officers get in to that awful habit of being always busy and not doing any thing. . . . I am going to try . . . to read war for a certain number of hours each day and hope to have time to read other things too, also for society if there is any and for athletics."

Patton's academic requirements in the study of war enriched his library. Arthur Wagner's *Organization and Tactics* was published originally in 1897 at Fort Leavenworth, Kansas. Patton's copy is signed "George Patton, Cadet U.S.M.A. Nov 6, 1908" and is annotated as if associated with course work in military science in his First Class year. Branch selection was upon him, and he drew sidelines by a quotation on page 15: " . . . that army which has the largest proportion of cavalry

Cadet Patton (left) looks through a book with an unknown classmate during Cadet Training, circa 1908. (USMA Library photo.)

Patton amid other cadets
assembling for a parade at
West Point, circa 1908.
(USMA Library photo.)

Cadet Patton between his parents and in a comforter, at West Point circa 1908. (USMA Library photo.)

will win the next great war." (See inset on page 22.) He wrote extensively in the margins in a way that marked him as more advanced in military knowledge than other cadets at that time or even today.

In the spring of 1909, Cadet Patton studied *Elements of Strategy* by Lieutenant Colonel G. J. Fiebeger, USMA Professor of Engineering. It had chapters on strategic theory, preparation for war, mobilization (the Prussian system), the conduct of strategic operations (Napoleon, Henri de Jomini, Helmuth von Moltke), and the offense and defense in strategy (American Civil War). Patton's annotations were few, but he did inscribe on the closing page: "End of last lesson in Engineering. Last lesson as Cadet, Thank God." Further, he wrote in pencil inside the back cover the following:

Qualities of a Great General

1. Tactically aggressive (loves a fight)
2. Strength of character
3. Steadiness of purpose
4. Acceptance of responsibility
5. Energy
6. Good health and strength

"Patton" is inscribed in block letters on the cover, and he signed it "George Patton/Cadet U.S.M.A./April 29, 1909." Patton's copy of the textbook *Topographical Surveying and Sketching* by Thomas Rees was also signed, and he wrote into it the problems he was assigned to solve in a course.

In his last weeks as a cadet, Patton used two other books written by Colonel Fiebeger. One was *Campaigns of the Civil War*, in which Patton wrote his daily assignments on the back pages, along with the comment "Finished April 17, 1909. Stood first. Gen. average 2.997+ out of three. Remember to take field glasses to Gettysburg. Also notebook and camera." Before leaving by train on May 1, he and his classmates would read Fiebeger's *The Campaign and Battle of Gettysburg* and the administrative instructions issued with it.

Cadet Patton (foreground) reading at West Point summer camp, circa 1907. (USMA Library photo.)

On May 11, 1909, George wrote Beatrice from the Eagle Hotel in Gettysburg: "This evening after supper I walked down alone to the scene of the last and fiercest struggle on Cemetery hill. To get in a proper frame of mind I wandered through the cemetery and let the spirits of the dead thousands laid there in ordered rows sink deep into me. Then just as the son sank behind South Mountains I walked down to the scene of Pickett's great charge and seated on a rock just where Olmstead and two of my great uncles died I watched the wonder of the day go out.

"The sunset painted a dull red the fields over which the terrible advance was made and I could almost see them coming growing fewer and fewer while around and beyond me stood calmly the very cannon that had so punished them. There were some quail calling in the trees near by and it seemed strange that they could do it where man had known his greatest and last emotions. It was very wonderful and no one came to bother me. I drank it in until I was quite happy. A strange

The USMA polo team, circa 1909. Patton is fourth from the left. (Photo courtesy of the Patton Museum.)

Cadet Patton, within months of his commitment to the Cavalry Branch, made these sidelines, agreeing that cavalry would prove a decisive factor in winning the next great war. From Arthur Wagner's *Organization and Tactics*.

ject of the proper proportion of cavalry, Hohenlohe says: "Considering the great importance of the possession of a large mass of cavalry, and the immense advantage which a superior force of cavalry will give us at once over the enemy, in that it will blindfold him and open our eyes, will shut him in closely and give us all freedom, and will tie his hands while it will assist us to strike, we cannot have too many cavalry. The answer to the question is, therefore, simple: We must have as many regiments of cavalry as possible." With us the proportion should be such as to enable our cavalry speedily to overwhelm any to which it may be opposed, whatever the proportion may be to the other arms.* The extended use that may be made of cavalry in raids and in dismounted fighting would render it much easier to have the proportion too small than too large.**

SPECIAL TROOPS.

The troops of the Engineer and Signal Corps, the Medical Department, and the Quartermaster's Corps (if there be one) may be classed as special troops. To this classification belong also troops employed in the construction and management of military railroads; but in the service of the United States the duties performed elsewhere by these troops would probably be performed by the Quartermaster's Department, or by people in the employment of the railroad companies.

Engineers.—In the United States Army the engineers perform the duties of sappers, miners, and pontoniers.*** In

*The Mexican Army can put in the field 8,000 regular cavalry. This can be increased from the reserve of the permanent Army and the general reserve to 26,000. This is the largest force of cavalry that our armies seem at all likely to encounter.

**In a letter to the author, General James H. Wilson, the distinguished cavalry commander, says: "I do not doubt that a properly organized army should have one-third cavalry, or that, all other things being equal, that army which has the largest proportion of cavalry will win in the next great war."

***This refers, of course, to engineers with an army in the field. The engineers also serve in the sea-coast defense, and have charge of the torpedo system.

pleasure but yet a very real one.

"I think it takes an evening like that to make one understand what men will do in battle. It was a wonderful yet a very foolish battle." (BPP I 173.)

Patton graduated on June 11, 1909, number 46 in general order of merit among 103 in his class. He had written to his father of his debt to West Point: " . . . all that is left of the boy who entered here . . . are the aspirations. The rest is changed completely. . . ." He had acquired a sense of discipline and devotion to duty but had maintained his sense of individualism and uniqueness in the crowd about him. His reading handicap had been overcome, and he had programmed a lifetime of professional reading, recorded through a new habit of keeping journals and diaries. He had deepened his quest for military knowledge and for fame as a soldier, already focusing on attack, victory, and the meaning of courage and death in that quest. And he left the academy with the beginnings of a model professional and personal library that would nourish his ambition.

Patton the adjutant (left) and the three other members of his battalion staff in 1909. (USMA Archives photo, copied from the 1909 *Howitzer*.)

Patton in a photo probably taken in early 1909, shortly before his graduation from West Point. (USMA Archives photo.)

CHAPTER THREE

Combining Professional Study With Experience 1909–1917

I N SEPTEMBER 1909, despite hay fever attacks, Second Lieutenant George Patton paced through his first weeks of officership with K Troop, 15th Cavalry Regiment, at Fort Sheridan, Illinois, with competence and acceptance by all concerned. Captain Francis C. Marshall, his first troop commander, had known him at West Point and was rated by Patton as one of the few "gentlemen" on the post, having enough servants, uniforms, and manners to distinguish himself from other officers. Lieutenant Patton found delight in the two succeeding years of training and disciplining soldiers, caring for horses, supervising target ranges, inspecting, and, especially, leading tactical field exercises.

Patton began to combine such practical experience with professional study as soon as his trunks arrived at Fort Sheridan. His cadet texts had been supplemented by a West Point pamphlet, *British-Boer War*, which he signed but did not annotate. He wrote his name and the date and "15 Cav" in each of the eight volumes of François Guizot's *History of France*, published originally in the 1860s and reprinted in a handsome deluxe edition in America about the time Patton graduated from West Point. In November 1909, he acquired a deluxe edition of Volume I of Edward Gibbon's *The Decline and Fall of the Roman Empire*.

In a book inscribed "G. S. Patton, Jr. 1909," he later wrote in pencil: "The first military book other than memoirs and histories which I ever read." That book was *Modern Warfare or How Our Soldiers Fight*, written under the pseudonym "Ubique" but dedicated to the author's nephew, a lad named Lancelot Gordon. This book is a fantasy, describing a fic-

Lieutenant Patton at a map maneuver exercise in Fort Sheridan, Illinois, in 1910. Patton is second from the right. (U.S. Army photo courtesy of the Patton Museum.)

tional war that breaks out between the British and Germans in the summer of 1905, when the Germans attack France and Belgium and the British move an army to the Continent to face them. This prophecy of World War I is preceded by a detailed description of how British infantry, cavalry, and artillery units organize and fight, and it ends with a German defeat after four days of fighting. Patton did not mark the book, although his "R" for "have read" appears on the binding.

In January 1910, Patton wrote his father that he and "Mr. Cooke" in K Troop had started "a course of military study for the afternoons of four days a week which ought to be interesting and useful both." He started *Studies in Minor Tactics* on January 22, 1910, and subsequently wrote "Finished. Apr 19, 1910" on the last page. That manual, a 1908 product of the faculty of the Army School of the Line at Fort Leavenworth, used maps of Leavenworth terrain to present problems in patrolling, outposts, advanced guards, rear guards, attack, and defense. On page 193, Patton underlined, "It is not wise to risk victory in an attempt to surround the enemy completely." He then wrote a cautionary note in the margin, "A very common error. G."

During that period Patton also read *Tactical Orders and Decisions* by German Army Captain Albert Buddecke, a book translated and published in 1908 by the Army School of the Line at Fort Leavenworth. He wrote "George S. Patton, Jr. 2 Lt 15th Cav" on the title page of *American Campaigns,* based on the Leavenworth lectures of Major Matthew Steele and published as a War Department document in 1909. Patton's bluepencilled marginal notes are limited to the Battle of Chancellorsville, where he asks, "How did Lee time this?" (341)

On May 26, 1910, Lieutenant Patton married Beatrice Ayer in St. John's Episcopal Church near Beverly Farms, Massachusetts. They spent a month-long honeymoon in Europe, where he expanded his library. He wrote his name, unit, and "London, June 17, 1910" in the front of Colonel David Henderson's *The Art of Reconnaissance,* which he had bought at Hugh Rees, Ltd., Military and Naval Booksellers, Stationers, and Publishers.

When the honeymooners returned, George left for maneuvers in Wisconsin, carrying several books he had purchased in London. He wrote Beatrice: "Clausewitz is about as hard reading as any thing can well be and is as full of notes of equal abstruseness as a dog is of fleas." He had bought a 1909 *General Carl von Clausewitz On War* and wrote on the last page, "Finished August 15 1910/George S. Patton, Jr." The book was a translation by a Miss Maguire of perhaps one-quarter of Clausewitz's *On War,* with extensive notes by T. Miller Maguire, who listed himself in the London edition as a barrister-at-law and member of the Order of the Rising Sun of Japan. Although Patton's frequent side-

Beatrice Ayer Patton at the Bear Hotel in Hungerfords, England, in 1910, during her honeymoon with Patton. (USMA Library photo.)

lines and annotations reflected more interest in Maguire than Clausewitz, he paid close attention to complex ideas in the political and strategic aspects of statecraft. He would read Clausewitz more extensively in 1926.

Patton also bought from Hugh Rees an English translation of Freiherr Colmar von der Goltz's *The Nation in Arms,* which he heavily annotated. His note on page 52, "the trouble with militia," reflected an early Patton preference for regular, professional forces. This undoubtedly tied in with his reading in 1911 of F. N. Maude's *War and the World's Life* (which he reread in 1925, according to his annotations). On January 20, 1911, he recorded that he was reading a Leavenworth translation of Lieutenant General Georg von Alten's *Studies in Applied Tactics.* His copy of Thomas Baldock's 1898 *Cromwell As a Soldier* was not annotated. With those European authors he was mixing in Americans. His copy of *Home Letters of General Sherman* was inscribed "G S Patton Jr 1909," the year it was published. By 1910 he owned at least seven volumes of *Battles and Leaders of the Civil War,* edited by Robert Underwood and Clarence Buel for The Century Company; in one volume he wrote, "Bought in 1909 and 1910 at W. S. Lindon."

The parts of Patton's readings as a second lieutenant that would influence his thinking as a creative general would depend on how much his ideas were nourished or starved in the intervening years. Patton's expertise in World War II was in grand tactics, or the operational level of warfare—the movement, support, and sequential employment of large military formations in military campaigns. Much of Patton's reading by 1912 had been at this level of military activity. However, Patton was equally famous as a heroic leader who could inspire men with word and deed. Was there a connection between that aspect of his persona and his early study?

Before they were married, Beatrice gave Patton *The Crown of Wild Olive,* a book published in 1906 based on "Four Lectures on Industry and War," delivered by artist John Ruskin at the Royal Military Academy at Woolwich in 1865. Ruskin's arguments in glorifying war and the warrior are much like those used repeatedly by Patton in later years. (Some are reprinted in the inset on page 29.) Ruskin found that the human frailties of sensuality and selfishness were expressed in peace, but that in war the best qualities in men were brought to the fore—truth in word, strength in thought, unselfishness, and sacrifice for the common good. Ruskin stated that only in "the clear possibility of the struggle's ending in death" could those virtues of humanity come to the test. Patton was incorporating those ideas into his writing and speeches and poetry before World War I. Yet, in the copy that Beatrice gave him, there is no annotation, no "R" on the binding. In the 1930s, J.F.C. Fuller reprinted many of Ruskin's 1865 thoughts in his *Generalship:*

John Ruskin on War

A Lecture at the Royal Military Academy, Woolwich, 1865

You may imagine that your work is wholly foreign to, and separate from mine [as an artist]. So far from that, all the pure and noble arts of peace are founded on war; no great art ever yet rose on earth, but among a nation of soldiers. . . . [War] is the foundation of all the arts . . . [because] it is the foundation of all the high virtues and faculties of men.

The common notion that peace and the virtues of civil life flourished together, I found to be wholly untenable. Peace and the *vices* of civil life only flourish together. We talk of peace and learning, and of peace and plenty, and of peace and civilization; but I found that these were not the words which the Muse of History coupled together: that, on her lips, the words were—peace, and sensuality—peace, and selfishness—peace, and death. I found, in brief, that all great nations learned the truth of word, and strength of thought, in war; that they were nourished in war, and wasted in peace; taught by war, and deceived by peace; trained by war, and betrayed by peace; in a word, that they were born in war, and expired in peace. . . . [From wars of self-defence] have arisen throughout the extent of past ages, all the highest sanctities and virtues of humanity.

If you, the gentlemen of this or any other kingdom, choose to make your pastime of contest, do so, and welcome. . . . A goodly struggle in the Olympic dust, though it be the dust of the grave, the gods will look upon, and be with you in. . . . The great justification of this game is that it truly, when well played, determines *who is the best man*—who is the highest bred, the most self-denying, the most fearless, the coolest of nerve, the swiftest of eye and hand. You cannot test these qualities wholly, unless there is a clear possibility of the struggle's ending in death. It is only in the fronting of that condition that the full trial of the man, soul and body, comes out. You may go to your game of wickets, or of hurdles, or of cards, and any knavery that is in you may stay unchallenged all the while. But if the play may be ended at any moment by a lance thrust, a man will probably make up his accounts a little before he enters it. Whatever is rotten and evil in him will weaken his hand more in holding a swordhilt than in balancing a billiard cue.

—From *The Crown of Wild Olive: Four Lectures on Industry and War,* as quoted by J.F.C. Fuller in *Generalship: Its Diseases and Their Cure,* 24.

Its Diseases and Their Cure. Patton might have been reinspired to use those warrior themes in his World War II pep talks.

Patton had been reading inspirational military biographies since his teens. While attending VMI he was given Lord Roseberry's *Napoleon: The Last Phase;* it was inscribed "Geo. S. Patton Lexington, Va Sept 8–1903 from L. H. Strother." The West Point experience accented Napoleon's leadership. He wrote "G S Patton Jr 1909" in Herbert Sargent's *Napoleon Bonaparte's First Campaign* and proceeded to make entries such as these in the margins of the pages: "went with advance guard himself" (41); "he always hoped for luck and did what he could with what he had" (43); "great success can only be gained against a fool. . . . personal energy and fighting ability are greater than logic" (62); and "This campaign illustrates the predominance of *Man* over men and things; it shows the virtue of hard fighting and the determination to win or die. It shows at Mantua that if 20,000 men allow themselves to be contained by 8000 they deserve defeat." (95)

Lieutenant Patton must have let known his interest in Napoleon. In December 1910 he received the four volumes of Louis de Bouriennes' *Memoirs of Napoleon Bonaparte* from Ellen Banning Ayer, his mother-in-law. The birthday inscription in his two-volume *Napoleon I* by August Fournier was "George S. Patton, Jr. from Aunt Nannie/11 November, 1911." Patton's annotation in J. Holland Rose's *The Personality of Napoleon* was an underlining of "he was no ordinary brain. . . ." When he acquired Wayne Whipple's *The Story-Life of Napoleon*, he underlined "There ought to be two distinct classes of masters—one who should teach the pupils, another who should govern them." Patton then wrote, "Same applies to the type for staff officers and the type for commanders." Patton was reading Napoleon not only to learn how that French leader had commanded, but to think about how he himself should command.

In October 1910 Patton reported to Aunt Nannie the first of many future husband-and-wife joint intellectual exercises: "I am translating a French article for the General Staff. At least B is and I do the copying. I may be famous yet thanks to her." Nine months later he wrote Nannie: "[Translating] is not very hard but I am curious for B's revision of it. I may find some startling changes in my ideas." Later he sent his father a carbon copy of "The Danger of Morocco," an article he translated from *La France Militaire* which warned against assuming that victory against native armies meant prowess against European counterparts. (BPP I 212–219. For Patton's problems in translating German, see copy in margin.)

Boredom might have motivated Patton to delve deeper into writing. In 1911 he learned to use the typewriter and soon produced "Saddle Drill" for the use of K Troop. He then started, but never finished,

---

Lieutenant Patton Reads Treitschke

"Sources were his specialty, and as a bride I remember his handing me a copy of [a book by Heinrich] von Treitschke saying: 'Try and make me a workable translation of this. That book of von Bernhardi's *Germany and the Next War* is nothing but a digest of this one.' Unfortunately, my German was not of that caliber, and he had to make do until a proper translation was published several years later [*Treitschke, His Doctrine of German Destiny and of International Relations*, London, 1914]. He was, however, one of the first Americans to own that translation, as later he owned translations of Marx, Lenin and the first edition of *Mein Kampf;* believing that one can only understand Man through his own words and not from what others think he thinks."

—Beatrice Patton, from "A Soldier's Reading."

"National Defense," an appeal for military preparedness. He apparently found that he enjoyed the challenge of writing, a timely discovery in view of his transfer to the nation's capital in December 1911. Within two months of his arrival at Fort Myer, just beyond the Potomac River in Virginia, he wrote "Principles of Scouting" for use within his new unit, Troop A of the 15th Cavalry.

Patton's now unquenchable thirst for fame found new expression in 1912 when he learned he was being considered as an American Army challenger in the Modern Pentathlon competition in the 1912 Olympics in Stockholm. He had previous experience competing in all five events—riding, pistol marksmanship, swimming, running, and swordsmanship. He started to train in May, sailed to Europe with his family in June, and was the only American among forty-two Pentathlon contestants when competition started on July 7. He emerged fifth, behind four Swedes. He subsequently developed a Pentathlon Scrapbook and wrote an official report recommending changes in the Army's selection and training of athletes for the 1916 Olympics.

Before returning to the United States, he and Beatrice toured Berlin, Dresden, and Nuremberg, and then spent ten days in Saumur, France, where Patton took lessons in the dueling sword and saber from

The fencer on the right is Lieutenant Patton, displaying his swordsmanship in Stockholm, Sweden, in 1912. (USMA Library photo.)

Patton practicing his hurdling for the 1912 Olympics, held in Stockholm, Sweden.
(Photo courtesy of the Patton Museum.)

Monsieur l'Adjutant Cléry, master of arms at the French Cavalry School. His learning from Europe's master swordsman was also written into his official Olympics report, and then into a separate article in *The Army and Navy Journal* entitled "Use of the Point in Sword Play." His study with Cléry, and his writing about it, was to launch him on a new course of gaining recognition and favorable assignments in the coming years.

George's newfound writing ability came to the fore in his three-month assignment to the Office of the Chief of Staff of the Army in December 1912. General Leonard Wood was consolidating the power of the Chief of Staff during that time, and the Secretary of War, Henry L. Stimson, would continue to recognize Patton throughout Stimson's long career in public service, which would extend through World War II. In one of his first staff actions, Patton wrote to Representative John Q. Tilson that he could find examples of America's unpreparedness for war in Emory Upton's *Military Policy of the United States.* He did not bother to clarify why he had written "G.S. Patton Jr. 1909" in his copy of a fourth impression of Upton's book which was printed in Washington in 1912.

In a staff paper entitled "Notes on the Balkan Campaign to Include the First Peace Negotiations," Patton summoned up his reading in military history to comment on the plans and operations of the military forces then engaged in warfare in the Balkans. His comments referred to interior versus exterior lines of communication in the Napoleonic Wars, the strategy of Epaminondas in the fourth century B.C., the "oblique attack" of Frederick the Great in the eighteenth century, and the losses from artillery shrapnel in the current Balkans campaign.

Patton's most important work during those years appears to be in the new design for 20,000 Cavalry sabers that the Chief of Staff ordered into production in February 1913. Patton had studied the 1911 British Cavalry *Sword and Saber Notes* and the French Cavalry *Drill Regulations* and was circulating his draft article that would appear in the March issue of *Cavalry Journal* under the title "Form and Use of the Saber." His thesis was that a thrust of the point of a sword is deadlier than a blow from its edge. He cited Marshal Maurice de Saxe and Napoleon on the value of thrusting with the point, and he decried the heritage left by the Turks, who had to hack through layers of clothing to inflict damage on the enemy. He assailed the U.S. Cavalry for following the oriental approach and instead called for abandoning the curved scimitar in favor of the straight sword. He preferred training American recruits to thrust and stab, as with a bayonet, rather than furthering the American boys' habit of wielding the edge of a club or a bat. In March 1913, Patton was ordered to the Springfield (Massachusetts) Armory for three days to ensure that the new sabers, with straight blades, were being manufactured to his specifications.

Early in the summer of 1913, Patton received orders to report to the commandant of the Mounted Service School in Fort Riley, Kansas, to become the school's first Master of the Sword. He would design and teach a course in swordsmanship to officers and senior enlisted soldiers while being a student in the First Year Course of the School. He was authorized to delay en route in Saumur, France, for further instruction in the European method of teaching the drill of the straight sword to cavalrymen. While doing this, the Pattons toured extensively in the French countryside that he would fight through in 1918 and 1944.

During his two-year stay in Fort Riley, Patton wrote extensively. "Drill Regulations for the Cavalry Sword" was followed by "Sword Exercises, 1914," published by the Army Chief of Staff. He served on the editorial board of *The Rasp,* published annually at Fort Riley by and for cavalrymen. For the 1914 issue, he wrote "Mounted Swords-manship" and "Army Racing and Records, 1913," which contained a photograph of his second-place finish to a Lieutenant Rockwell in the Military Handicap at Belmont Park in Long Island. (347) By June 1, 1915, he had published *The Diary of the Instructor in Swordsmanship,* a manual that described the course Patton was teaching and used photographs of the author to illustrate proper sword techniques.

Second Lieutenant Patton in the charge saber position (left) for mounted instruction and in the guard-to-the-left saber position (right) for dismounted instruction at Fort Riley, Kansas, in 1913. (U.S. Army photos courtesy of the Patton Museum.)

His professional library continued to grow while at Fort Riley. He signed and read Homer Lea's *The Day of the Saxon,* a gift in 1913 from his wife, and the two volumes of *The Memoirs of Baron de Marbot,* printed in London in 1892. He also acquired a translation of Captain Martin Cerezo's *The Siege of Baler,* an account of that struggle in the Philippine Islands in 1898, and the 1912 Leavenworth translation of Major de Pardieu's *A Critical Study of German Tactics and of the New German Regulations.*

In April 1915 he wrote his wife that he had spent a Sunday reading for twelve hours and then working on two tactical problems: "I am ashamed to admit that they are the first ones I have done since early in 1912." Just a week before, however, he had written his name in the front of both volumes of *Tactics,* written by Colonel William Balck of the German Army in 1908 and translated by Lieutenant Walter Krueger at Fort Leavenworth in 1911. Only a few checkmarks in the index indicate Patton had read this complex work on the relationship between tactics and strategy and on the operating techniques and weaponry of the European armies. More current was his reading of Friedrich von Bernhardi's 1914 book, *How Germany Makes War.* The war in Europe was much on his mind, and he wrote his father in May 1915, "There is but one International Law—the best Army."

While a student at the Mounted Service School, Patton inscribed "M.S.S." into his copy of James Bryce's *The Holy Roman Empire,* probably used for reference purposes since he did not annotate it. Neither did he make notes in a publication that was to become important in American officer education in later years, Captain E. D. Swinton's "The Defence of Duffer's Drift." Swinton told how a British lieutenant in the Boer War had a sequence of dreams in which he managed to get his platoon repeatedly slaughtered as he tried to find the right answer to defending a lonely stream crossing; at last he got it right and dreamed no more. The Germans developed a similar tale, entitled "A Summer Night's Dream"; both were reprinted and bound by the British *United Service Magazine* by 1912, when Patton signed his copy. His might have been the only copy in the First Year Course, from which he graduated in June 1915.

While on summer leave Patton acquired a little-known book that may have set him on the path of developing the flamboyant public personality for which he would become famous in World War II. Gustave Le Bon's *The Crowd: A Study of the Popular Mind* was a London publication in 1896, and Patton inscribed a ninth edition in July 1915. In its early pages Patton read that individuals act abnormally when in crowds because they get a feeling of invincible power, are subject to the contagion of a collective will over the individual will, and lose their inhibitions upon hearing the suggestions of a few leaders with hypnotic messages. Lieutenant Patton wrote in the margin of page 35, "The will to Victory thus affects soldiers. It must be inculcated. G."

At the end of chapter one Patton scribbled, "The individual [leader] may dream greatly or otherwise, but he must infect the crowd with the idea [in order] to carry it out." On page 57 he put three sidelines alongside: "Given to exaggeration in its feelings, a crowd is only impressed by excessive sentiments. An orator wishing to move a crowd must make an abusive use of violent affirmations. To exaggerate, to affirm, to resort to repetitions, and never to attempt to prove anything by reasoning are methods of argument well known to speakers at public meetings." Echoes of that were to appear in the Patton oratory in years to come.

Three sidelines also appeared on page 61, next to: "Crowds exhibit a docile respect for force, and are but slightly impressed by kindness, which for them is scarcely other than a form of weakness. Their sympathies have never been bestowed on easy-going masters, but on tyrants who vigorously oppressed them." While Patton could not be accused of being an easy-going master in his speeches as a senior officer, he drew respect for his forceful manner of demanding discipline and hard training. As for his wearing spectacular uniforms whenever addressing large crowds, Patton wrote in the margin of page 84 of Le Bon: "Advantage of a peculiar dress."

Next to a discussion of religious leaders Patton wrote on page 85: "Miracles of Christ [were] very potent to influence the crowd." Within three years he was to produce miracles of bravery for his men in World War I. (See page 47.) In addressing his troops he would use the ideas he had marked with a sideline on page 132: "It is not by reason, but most often in spite of it, that are created those sentiments that are the mainsprings of all civilization—sentiments such as honour, self-sacrifice, religious faith, patriotism, and the love of glory." And when he emerged from World War I with enormous personal prestige, he had acted in conformance with what he had earmarked on page 148: "Prestige is the mainspring of all authority. Neither gods, kings nor women have ever reigned without it." In the margin he had written: "Hence, it must be acquired." (See Patton's annotations inset on page 37.)

In the summer of 1915, Patton heard he would probably be ordered to rejoin the 15th Cavalry on its way to the Philippines. He hurried to Washington, D.C., where he secured a transfer to the 8th Cavalry, which was being moved from the Philippines to Fort Bliss, Texas. Recognizing that he would be on border duty much of the time, he shipped his nine polo horses and three hounds to his father in San Gabriel, California, and arrived in El Paso in late September. There he was told he was eligible for promotion to first lieutenant if he passed an examination before a board of officers in October. He later wrote to Beatrice, "I have done

Patton Annotations: reactions to Le Bon's *The Crowd*

GENERAL CHARACTERISTICS OF CROWDS 35

activities of his spinal cord, which the hypnotiser directs at will. The conscious personality has entirely vanished; will and discernment are lost. All feelings and thoughts are bent in the direction determined by the hypnotiser.

Such also is approximately the state of the individual forming part of a psychological crowd. He is no longer conscious of his acts. In his case, as in the case of the hypnotised subject, at the same time that certain faculties are destroyed, others may be brought to a high degree of exaltation. Under the influence of a suggestion, he will undertake the accomplishment of certain acts with irresistible impetuosity. This impetuosity is the more irresistible in the case of crowds than in that of the hypnotised subject, from the fact that, the suggestion being the same for all the individuals of the crowd, it gains in strength by reciprocity. The individualities in the crowd who might possess a personality sufficiently strong to resist the suggestion are too few in number to struggle against the current. At the utmost, they may be able to attempt a diversion by means of different suggestions. It is in this way, for instance, that a happy expression, an image opportunely evoked, have occasionally deterred crowds from the most bloodthirsty acts.

We see, then, that the disappearance of the conscious personality, the predominance of the unconscious personality, the turning by means of suggestion and contagion of feelings and ideas in an identical direction, the tendency to immediately

[handwritten margin note, vertical]: The will to Victory thus affects individuals. It would be modeled. ?

36 THE MIND OF CROWDS

—to deliver the tomb of Christ from the infidel, or, as in '93, to defend the fatherland. Such heroism is without doubt somewhat unconscious, but it is of such heroism that history is made. Were peoples only to be credited with the great actions performed in cold blood, the annals of the world would register but few of them.

[handwritten note]: The individual may dream greatly or otherwise but he must infect the Crowd with the idea to carry it out.

Probably gods way of guiding the world is by making them amenable to his instrument of the moment.

THE LEADERS OF CROWDS 141

§ 2. THE MEANS OF ACTION OF THE LEADERS: AFFIRMATION, REPETITION, CONTAGION

When it is wanted to stir up a crowd for a short space of time, to induce it to commit an act of any nature—to pillage a palace, or to die in defence of a stronghold or a barricade, for instance—the crowd must be acted upon by rapid suggestions, among which example is the most powerful in its effect. To attain this end, however, it is necessary that the crowd should have been previously prepared by certain circumstances, and, above all, that he who wishes to work upon it should possess the quality to be studied farther on, to which I give the name of prestige.

When, however, it is proposed to imbue the mind of a crowd with ideas and beliefs—with modern social theories, for instance—the leaders have recourse to different expedients. The principal of them are three in number and clearly defined—affirmation, repetition, and contagion. Their action is somewhat slow, but its effects, once produced, are very lasting.

Affirmation pure and simple, kept free of all reasoning and all proof, is one of the surest means of making an idea enter the mind of crowds. The conciser an affirmation is, the more destitute of every appearance of proof and demonstration, the more weight it carries. The religious books and the legal codes of all ages have always resorted to simple affirmation. Statesmen called upon to defend

[handwritten margin note]: Wilson looks it.

148 THE OPINIONS AND BELIEFS OF CROWDS

these sentiments are its basis, but it can perfectly well exist without them. The greatest measure of prestige is possessed by the dead, by beings, that is, of whom we do not stand in fear—by Alexander, Cæsar, Mahomet, and Buddha, for example. On the other hand, there are fictive beings whom we do not admire—the monstrous divinities of the subterranean temples of India, for instance—but who strike us nevertheless as endowed with a great prestige.

Prestige in reality is a sort of domination exercised on our mind by an individual, a work, or an idea. This domination entirely paralyses our critical faculty, and fills our soul with astonishment and respect. The sentiment provoked is inexplicable, like all sentiments, but it would appear to be of the same kind as the fascination to which a magnetised person is subjected. Prestige is the mainspring of all authority. Neither gods, kings, nor women have ever reigned without it.

The various kinds of prestige may be grouped under two principal heads: acquired prestige and personal prestige. Acquired prestige is that resulting from name, fortune, and reputation. It may be independent of personal prestige. Personal prestige, on the contrary, is something essentially peculiar to the individual; it may coexist with reputation, glory, and fortune, or be strengthened by them, but it is perfectly capable of existing in their absence.

Acquired or artificial prestige is much the most

[handwritten margin note]: + how it must be acquired.

nothing at all except study," which was apparently enough to pass the test in cavalry drill regulations, field service regulations, and applied tactics. He was promoted to first lieutenant on March 23, 1916. Between trips to the Mexican border with Troop A, Patton kept up his writing, informing Beatrice that "Adventure magazine has not accepted my story so I will try some other, probably the Wide World Magazine."

When Lieutenant Patton heard that his regiment would not be a part of Brigadier General John J. Pershing's Punitive Expedition into Mexico, he asked to be assigned as an aide to Pershing. They left Fort Bliss together on March 13, 1916. During the next year, the American press found a hero in Patton for killing Villista captain Julio "General" Cardenas and two of his "banditos," but the year dragged on into long months of tedium. He asked his father to provide books and his sister Nita to send Pershing a copy of Harry Wilson's 1903 *Lions of the Lord: A Tale of the Old West*. He published an article in *Cavalry Journal* entitled "Cavalry Work of the Punitive Expedition." The article was a paean to Pershing's training methods but also expressed Patton's tactical opinions, such as extending the advanced guard farther ahead of an advancing main body than was normally done.

As 1916 in Mexico came to an end, he took out his frustration on Beatrice by sending her his "gastly" poems and writing: "I have been reading the Book of Morman and it is the darndest rot I have ever run into." Then, on December 20: "Darling Beat: It is just about a year since we had that wind storm at Sierra Blanca and you cried and wished I would resign. It has been awful here for the last two days. I have never seen such dust. And it made me wish I was out of it. If I could only be sure of the future I would get out. That is if I was sure that I would never be above the average army officer I would for I don't like the dirt and all except as a means to fame. If I knew that I would never be famous I would settle down and raise horses and have a good time. It is a great gamble to spoil your and my own happiness for the hope of greatness. I wish I was less ambitious, then too some times I think that I am not ambitious at all only a dreamer. That I don't realy do my damdest even when I think I do."

But Patton's mind was hardly ready for retiring and raising horses. He wrote his father ten days later: "Only in epochs where the state is dominent has men advanced. Individualism is the theory of decay. . . . Individual man has habitually failed to run himself for himself. He must be run. Germany has the only true idea. The few must run the many for the latters good. To Hell with the people. Asto your jocular assertion, that the central powers are on the point of ruin, even the after effects of Christmas cannot justify such a belief. The allies are on the point of rupture and another year of war will see their shadow policy an utter failure." In those words Patton revealed harbingers of his mind

Lieutenant Patton in Mexico in 1916 while serving as an aide to Brigadier General John J. Pershing. (Photo courtesy of the Patton Museum.)

of the future: an abiding respect for German military and political thought; a distrust of democratic institutions, which he believed compromise pure ideas and waste human and material resources; and great misgivings about the ability of alliances of nations to bring about victory in war.

He was, however, learning the craft of military command from Pershing, who Patton would label his "favorite general" in dinner conversations for the rest of his life. He explained in a notebook titled "Dublan, Mexico" how Pershing conducted an inspection of a troop unit and then: "Nothing is too minute to escape him. A button shirt not fastened a loose spur. . . . Every arm is inspected intensely and so far as possible personally by Gen. Pershing. It is this personal care which gets the results and only this *personal* care will." Later he wrote to Beatrice: "I had to open all the horses mouths in four regiments of cavalry which is some job. . . . The [black] 10th Cav. had the best equipments and altogether put up the best show. . . . I have learned more useful soldiering while in Mexico than all the rest of my service put together." He later provided Pershing with a typed copy of his "Mexican Diary," which he kept religiously during their sojourn south of the Rio Grande.

During the year he had also successfully defended his straight saber from attacks by traditionalists, first with a six-page paper to the President of the Cavalry Equipment Board and finally with another *Cavalry Journal* article, entitled "The Present Saber—Its Form and the Use for Which it is Designed." Again he turned military history to his purpose, citing Cyrus the Great in the sixth century B.C., soldiers in the American Civil War, and soldiers in the twentieth century Chinese army for having survived blows from the edge of a curved sword.

Pershing maintained his association with Patton after the Punitive Expedition was discontinued. He visited the family in California, spurred by a romantic interest in George's twenty-nine-year-old sister Nita (formally Anne); for several years she assembled a scrapbook of his exploits in Mexico and France, as well as press speculations on their possible engagement to be married. When Pershing was told he would command the American Expeditionary Force in Europe, he caused Patton to be ordered to join him on the H.M.S. *Baltic* as it sailed for Liverpool on May 28, 1917.

CHAPTER FOUR

To War With the First Tank Brigade 1917–1920

WHILE ON LEAVE in Massachusetts, Patton was promoted to captain. His initial duty as Commanding Officer, Headquarters Troop in General Headquarters, American Expeditionary Force (GHQ,AEF) was to take charge of the sixty-seven enlisted men who would serve as drivers and clerks. He modified their uniforms, saw that they studied French, and was billeted with them in the Tower of London for the week that Pershing conferred with the British. George sent to Papa a copy of what he called the "oratory" he was required to present during the many gala affairs arranged for the American contingent. Upon arrival in Paris he assembled a fleet of vehicles for the headquarters and learned that his conversational French was sufficiently precise and fast to converse with French military and civilian contacts. His reading began to include works in French; he reported to Beatrice that he was reading Alexandre Dumas' "The Three Muskateers" [sic] in its original tongue. But he soon became bored with the headquarters routine, despite writing a plan for setting up a military police system for American soldiers in France, and despite his first airplane flight, piloted by Colonel William "Billy" Mitchell, later to be court-martialed for his persistent advocacy of air power.

It may have been this boredom that tipped Patton toward the career in tanks which would bring the fame he sought. He wrote Beatrice on September 19, 1917, "There is a lot of talk about 'Tanks' here now and I am interested as I can see no future to my present job." Only two months before, he had written in a staff memorandum that the tank was "not worth a damn." In early October he wrote a letter to the Commander in

17592

Lieutenant Colonel Patton stands in front of a Renault tank at the American tank school in Bourg, France, in the summer of 1918. Patton built the school and trained its officers. (Photo courtesy of the Patton Museum.)

Chief of the American Expeditionary Force. It began, "I understand that there is to be a new service of 'Tanks' organized and request that my name be considered for a command in that service." Two weeks later he accepted the challenge of starting an AEF School for Light Tanks near Langres, France. Taking this assignment went against the recommendations of AEF Chief of Staff General James G. Harbord and Patton's closest adviser, Colonel Fox Conner, both of whom thought he should become an infantryman and command a battalion in combat rather than specialize in an untried field.

Tanks were not a part of any armed force when the Great War broke out in 1914, but within a year the British were building a heavy tank and the French a light one. By September 1917, Pershing was projecting a need for 375 to 600 heavy tanks and 1,200 to 1,500 light tanks to support the twenty combat divisions he was forming in France. He would start by having Patton train American soldiers on light tanks obtained from the French Renault works.

On November 30, 1917, the British achieved a stunning breakthrough of German lines at Cambrai, France, by massing 300 tanks—the first major employment of tanks in military history. By January 1918, Patton was writing Beatrice, " . . . I feel sure that tanks in some form will play a part in all future wars." Could this be the destiny he had sought?

As Patton built the American tank school at Bourg, France, his mind absorbed massive amounts of detail on requisitioning land, constructing buildings and tank training areas, selecting and training officers and men to handle the new technology, designing organization and communications systems for mechanized warfare, requisitioning supplies and spare parts for a tank battalion (calculated down to a mechanic's need for replacement nuts and bolts), and employing the machines in combat once they had been transported by rail to the appropriate sector of the front. As the first member of the American Tank Corps, Patton naturally borrowed ideas from the French and British, but he melded these notions with ideas from the American military system to create a blend that would set the pattern for U.S. mechanized forces in World War II.

Major Patton started learning about tanks by visiting the French center of tank training at Chamlieu and Renault tank manufacturing in Paris; this was interspersed with conversations with men of tank experience, such as the Chief of Staff of the British Tank Corps, Colonel J.F.C. Fuller, who had participated in the breakthrough at Cambrai and would lead the development of tank doctrine and organization in the years between the World Wars. By December 12, 1917, Patton had written "Light Tanks," a fifty-eight-page report with four attachments that described the Renault tank, prescribed organization of tank units, recommended tank force tactics, and outlined methods of instruction and drill for soldiers who would be selected to become tankers. Years later, Patton would write across the top of the report: "This paper was and is the basis of the U.S. Tank Corps. I think it is the best Technical Paper I ever wrote. GSP, Jr."

On January 23, 1918, Patton gave his first lecture on tanks, to fifteen senior officers at GHQ,AEF; he emphasized that the purpose of the new machines was to cross trenches and destroy barbed wire and machine guns so the infantry could advance to where the bayonet could kill the enemy. Tanks could restore movement to the battlefield and save lives, but first the infantry would have to learn the teamwork of how to use them. That theme became the core of his writings and lectures for the next six months; it was amplified with his drafting the drill regulations for the tank service and his writing eight single-spaced typed pages on the principles of training the Tank Corps. He wrote Beatrice in March 1918, "I have a stupendous job and little time and none of my officers are worth a damn. I have to instruct all of them in every thing under heaven except

World War I tank school group in Bourg, France, in 1918. The group includes Major
Sereno Brett (second from left), Lieutenant Colonel Joseph Viner (fourth from left), and
Colonel Patton (right). (Photo courtesy of the Patton Museum.)

infantry drill and I have to check them up at that. I have to teach maping,
Visual training, Aiming, gas Engines, signaling, reconnaissance,
Intelligence, and some other things that I cant recall. I send them out to
teach classes and have to watch them make mistakes." In late April he
had trained enough men and received enough tanks to organize the 1st
Light Tank Battalion; Lieutenant Colonel Patton was its commander.

When Patton perceived confusion about the design of future tanks,
he wrote that priority for tank features should go first to "mobility of
strategic employment" and "speed and radius of action on the battlefield"; following this, designers could pay attention to "ease and cheep-
ness of construction, command for the guns and vision, and ability to
cross trenches." (BPP I 526.) In June 1918, he expanded his thinking with
"Brief Notes on the Tactical Employment of Tanks" and considered their

use in counterattack and exploitation of success; in a forecast of his operations in World War II he wrote, ". . . boldness is the key to victory. The tank must be used boldly. It is new and always has the element of surprise. It is also very terrifying to look at as the infantry soldier is helpless before it."

In the summer of 1918 he became both student and instructor at the Army Staff College course at Langres, where he wrote four more papers—on tank drill regulations, reconnaissance, tank driving, and the tank platoon leader. In his faculty role he lectured on tanks and often put on demonstrations of how they should be used in attacking "the Bosch." His student *Notebook for the General Staff Officer* was signed "G. S. Patton, Jr. Col. Tank Corps, Graduate, Army Gen. Staff College." He would repeat a much more thorough course at Fort Leavenworth five years later, but the Langres course provided the skills needed to assure that his tank units would mesh with the activities of infantrymen, artillerymen, signalers, airmen, and logisticians.

In the year that Patton the innovator had prepared to unleash a new form of American warfare, he had also nourished the strains of character that would assure his leading his troops courageously in combat—he had kept alive his vision of the historical military leader and had refurbished his inner belief that death or victory are the only noble choices of the professional soldier in combat. The best of those thoughts were expressed in poems, often written when he could not sleep at night. He mailed the poems to Beatrice, cautioning her not to lose them. His diary reflected that his historical reading remained prodigious—"read a book" in Paris in January, "up until after midnight reading Mark Twain" in Langres, "read a book B gave me *The Kingdom of the Blind*" in Chaumont, and "sat up until 12 reading French history from 1814 to 1914." He used his knowledge of military history to confound the censors about where he was located—to Beatrice he suggested Langres as being founded by Marcus Aurelius, and Chaumont as the site of the signing of the treaty of 1814. His lectures were peppered with historical examples, such as Alexander's using movable towers to overcome the walls at Tyre—"today we overcome inverted walls with the tank." (BPP I 553.)

To prepare his men for combat, Patton drew on all his historical resources to convince them that absolute discipline and obedience were essential for their survival and victory. In a lecture to all new arrivals at the tank center, he praised the Germans, who since 1805 had bred the quality of discipline in themselves "as we breed speed into horses." He cited the armies of Philip of Macedon and Alexander the Great, as well as the Roman legions, for being highly disciplined. "You must get it likewise: instant, cheerful, and automatic discipline, so that when we the quarterbacks give the signal of life or death in the near day of battle, you will not think and then act, but will act and if you will, think later—after the war. It is by discipline alone that all your efforts, all your patriotism, shall not have been in vain. Without it Heroism is futile. You will die for nothing. With DISCIPLINE you are IRRESISTIBLE." (BPP I 500.)

Other subjects in his lectures also were to become hallmarks of the Patton legend. Duty: "This imperious sense of obligation is the mark of the thoroughbred in men as in horses. . . . The thoroughbred man does not argue. He goes until his duty is done or he is dead." Attack: "The object of all training is to create a 'Corps d'Elite,' that is a body of men who are not only capable of helping to win a war, but are determined to do so. It cannot be emphasized too often that all training, at all times and in all places, must aim at the cultivation of the OFFENSIVE SPIRIT in all ranks. . . ." (BPP I 500.) Soldierly deportment: Patton had insisted that his AEF headquarters' troops dress like model soldiers, and he wrote Pershing a memo, "Military Appearance and Bearing," which decried the slovenly dress and saluting of junior officers. He noted frequently in his diary that he was continually correcting others. He wrote Beatrice that he suspected some of the reserve officers wanted to poison him and that, like Louis XI, he would have to eat only eggs. He even reported a lieutenant for profanity and stopped his officers from gambling when he thought individual losses were too great. His tankers were held to such a high standard of dress and deportment that they were praised throughout the AEF as model soldiers, even though their motto was "Treat 'em Rough, Boys." (BPP I 439, 472, 556.) In all this attention to dress and conduct, Patton saw a linkage between pride in self and victory on the battlefield— a soldier who does not shave every day cannot build the self-esteem and confidence necessary to fight well in war. He would apply those principles repeatedly in World War II.

In early August 1918, Patton's tank force had 900 men, 50 officers, and only 25 Renault two-man tanks. He was told that by the end of the month he would have 144 tanks and that he should form a second battalion and create a headquarters that would become the 1st Tank Brigade, to be commanded by Patton. This transpired August 24, and he then planned and led the brigade in the first American wartime tank action, in the battle of St. Mihiel on September 12. His battalions, augmented by French Army tank groups, supported the U.S. 1st and 42d Infantry Divisions.

His diary entries, letters to Beatrice, and after-action reports recount how all objectives were taken in the face of a general German retreat, how Patton met Brigadier General Douglas MacArthur during the day, how he bravely led tanks across a bridge that might have been mined, how the tanks outdistanced the infantry and had to come back, and how he generally spent the day with the forward elements braving machine-gun fire rather than being at a headquarters position where higher command could reach him. For this he was later criticized, but he had gained great stature with his troops. Also, he had learned that tanks fighting in mud consume gasoline so quickly that they are immobilized by mid-afternoon and must be resupplied before dawn in terrain without roads; he had already built the tank-towed sled to accomplish that.

By the time Patton took the tank brigade into the Meuse-Argonne Operation on September 26, he had 345 tanks (including French Army units), and had worked out a successful scheme where he could be in the front lines while maintaining communications with his rear command post by means of pigeons and a group of six to ten runners. This time his two battalions operated with the 28th and 35th Infantry Divisions but had little time to train with them before the attack. German resistance was intense, and Patton found it necessary to expose himself continually to machine-gun and artillery fire while he kept tanks moving across obstacles and rallied infantrymen back into the attack. He was virtually alone and within forty meters of enemy machine guns when he was hit in the leg; his orderly, Private First Class Joseph T. Angelo, dragged him to a shell hole. When tanks caught up with them, Patton directed them where to attack, and some twenty-five German machine-gun nests were destroyed. Patton, whose actions that day earned him the Distinguished Service Cross for extraordinary heroism, was evacuated, operated on, and hospitalized for a month.

The brigade, meanwhile, fought on for fourteen days, until it virtually ran out of tanks and men. Six of seven captains were hit in the first three days, as were thirty lieutenants out of thirty-five. Of the 834 officers and men of the 1st Tank Brigade who fought in the Meuse-Argonne Operation, only eighty were able to fight fourteen days later.

While in the hospital, the thirty-two-year-old Patton was promoted to full colonel. As he returned to command the remnants of the brigade, Patton wrote his father, "An officer is paid to attack not to direct after the battle starts. You know I have always feared I was a coward at heart but I am beginning to doubt it. Our education is at fault in picturing death as such a terrible thing. It is nothing and very easy to get. That does not mean that I hunt for it but the fear of it does not—at least has not detured me from doing what appeared to be my duty." (BPP I 631.)

The men of the 1st Brigade knew he was back in command when he issued his first order "Concerning dress, comportment and discipline of this command." Then, he turned to "Notes, Entraining and Detraining at Night," followed by "Practical Training, Tank Platoon." In a more complex paper, "German and Allied Theory of War," he traced the development of tactics through World War I. In "Tank Tactics" he developed a new lecture for the tank center. As part of his research he had been reading German documents about tanks, and he reported to Beatrice that "they under estimated the tank and it cost them the war perhaps. At least it hurried the end." His lecture at the Army General Staff College at Langres was entitled "Light Tanks in Exploitation" and was favorably received. His audience did not know that he had prepared a more radical version but had decided not to use it; this version called for conventional breakthrough at first, but then using the speed and shock action of the tank for deep penetration into the enemy rear areas, in a forecast of what Patton would do in World War II. (BPP I 659.) Patton's imagination had been triggered by the first tests of controlling tanks by wireless radio.

On November 11, 1918, Patton celebrated his thirty-third birthday along with the armistice by writing what he called "a poem on peace" and sending it to Beatrice. The poems continued to express the more firmly developed aspects of his mind. For example, the last stanzas of "The End of War," written in France in 1917, reflected his belief that pacifists would bring on the next war. (See inset on page 49.)

Patton's father was less than enthusiastic about George's poetry and manner of speech. He wrote on February 29, 1919: "You are now 34 [33] and a Col and the dignity going with your rank invests what you say with more importance so I hope in your speeches you will be very careful & self restrained—for your own good & your future—Another gift you have developed I really regret—and that is the ability to write verse upon vulgar and smutty objects. That is very dangerous. . . . All the really big men I have known—abstained from repeating vulgar stories—and all who were facile in speech—cultivated great reserve. . . . I dont want to preach and will say no more but I am sure your own judgment—upon reflection will agree with mine." (BPP I 686.) Throughout his career Patton rarely, if ever, did agree.

Through the winter, Patton campaigned to be sent home with the tank brigade rather than join occupation forces in Germany. He also worked on a manuscript for a book he titled "War As She Is," which had chapters on The Soldier, The Line Officer, The Staff Officer, Generals, and Combat. The manuscript argued for a year's military training for all American male youth, more military academies for the officer corps, and the selection of generals from those who have devoted their lives to ceaseless effort at the military profession. "The road to high command leads through a long path called 'The History of War.' . . . To be useful in battle, military knowledge, like discipline, must be subconscious. The memorizing of concrete examples is futile for in battle the mind does not work well enough to make memory trustworthy. The officer must be so soaked in military lore that he does the military thing automatically. The study of military history will go far towards producing this result; the study of mathematics will not. But the above study must continue after entry into the service and last until the day of retirement. . . ." (BPP I 676.)

On February 26, 1919, Patton entrained 65 officers and 1,475 enlisted men of the tank brigade and headed south for Marseilles, where they boarded the S.S. *Patria*. The port commander praised Patton for the discipline of his troops. But after a stop in Gibraltar, Patton wrote in his

"There is no end to war," wrote Patton in "The End of War," a poem he wrote during World War I. The poem professed that pacifists would bring on the next war. From the Patton notebook "Selected Poems: 1916–1925," in the USMA Library.

#14.

THE END OF WAR.

When the hairy apes of long ago
Battled for days, to see
Whether the tails of future apes,
Should straight or curly be,

Other apes whose hair more sparsely grew,
And the shes who were great with child,
Hung from the branches up side down,
And sighed and gibbered and smiled.

They said "Such sights are hardly nice
"For tails are what they are",
"They said" Tis savage and like the wolves,
"This must be the end of war".

When the painted savages of the swamps,
Slew the clay daubed men of the brae,
In order to settle by flint and club,
Which clan might draw mammoths on clay,

The craven lake-folk, smeared with fat,
Crouched on their rafts and said,
"Though insects bite us through our grease,
"Tis better than being dead."

"Our cultured smell makes us despised,
"We live a mildewed life,
"But we are the people of brotherly love,
This must be the end of strife".

The gentle Persian fled before
The warlike men of Greece;
The Phalanx broke their masses,
So they advocated peace.

They praised the purple coated fop,
Whose hands were white and slim;
They loathed the sweaty brute in bronze,
And, loathing, fled from him.

While huddled in their harlots arms,
Their land in flames they saw,
Yet kissed the painted odalisques,
And cried "Tis the end of War".

When Carthage conquered far off Spain,
And all but conquered Rome,
She suffered from the lethargy,
Of fighting far from home.

She deified domestic quiet,
Her youth would no more fight;
Till Bloody Zama's fatal day,
Destroyed for e'er her might.

For having conquered Spain, she thought,
Like countless fools before,
That having gained her peace by strife,
There would be no more war.

'Twere idle further to recount,
The folly of mankind,
Who gaining all by battle,
To future wars grows blind.

The folly of the slogan,
Down all the ages rings,
The ruins of republics,
The funeral dirge of kings.

"At last all strife is ended,
"Battles shall rage no more,
"The time of perfect peace has come,
There can be no more war".

Still, like the foolish revellers,
in Babylon's banquet hall,
They'll take their ease while mocking
The writing on the wall.

They will disband their armies,
When this great strife is won,
And trust again to pacifists,
To guard for them their home.

They will return to futileness,
As quickly as before,
Though Truth and History vainly shout,
"THERE IS NO END TO WAR".

~~Langres~~ France Dec. 30, 1917.

This is an effort to express my prevailing idea in verse. I had the notion for over a year but the result is not up to the effort.

diary, "I hope nothing stops us until we get in. Hardly any young officers can be trusted to obey orders." By March 15 they had closed into Camp Meade, Maryland, home of the Tank Corps, now composed of three tank brigades, armed with 218 Renault and 25 British Mark V tanks brought from France, and hundreds of Renault copies just off the assembly lines in the United States. After discharging his veterans, Patton's renumbered 304th Tank Brigade was down to one company, but he was so successful in recruiting through the coming year that it was back to the authorized thirteen companies by mid-1920.

Patton travelled extensively on his return to the States—California, the tank manufacturing centers in Illinois and Massachusetts, horse show sites, and West Point. When he learned that Army Chief of Staff General Peyton C. March wanted to reduce the West Point curriculum to three years in order to graduate more classes, he wrote Pershing: "What West Point makes is a soul. We the graduates are efficient because we can't help it. We dont run away because we are a lot more afraid of our conscience than we are of the enemy. The Soul cannot be built in one or two years. It would be much better to have several West Points." (BPP I 700.) Pershing would soon testify before Congress that he would not have come to West Point if it had not been a four-year course. It remained a four-year course. Patton would try over the next two decades to become the Commandant of Cadets at the Military Academy, but he would not succeed.

As Colonel Patton settled into his Camp Meade command he resumed his professional studies. He had brought from Europe a 1919 typescript of Sun Tzu's *The Art of War,* translated in 1910 by Lionel Giles of the British Museum. He annotated the forty-five-page manuscript with approving comments about capturing and living off the enemy's supplies, changing one's tactics rather than repeating them, and (strangely enough, in light of Patton's later writings) leaving the enemy an escape route, especially in the pursuit. He wrote on the last page, "A very good Field Service Regulations GS Patton Jr."

Patton learned that a heavy tank battalion, which had moved from Camp Colt, Pennsylvania, was commanded by Lieutenant Colonel Dwight D. Eisenhower. They began to collaborate on writing about the future of the tank. Patton obtained *Seventy Problems: Infantry Tactics, Battalion, Brigade, Division,* which had been written under the direction of John F. Morrison during the five years he headed the Military Art Department at Fort Leavenworth. Patton and Eisenhower would compare their solutions to problems with the "approved solutions" from the Leavenworth faculty. Then they would rework each problem while adding tanks to one of the forces involved—and they were always delighted whenever the force with tanks would win. Patton's extensive marginal notes indicate a more fundamental disagreement with Morrison's 1914 solutions, usually on the grounds that they were "too

The U.S. Tank Corps at Camp Meade, Maryland, in 1919. In the second row from the bottom are Colonel Patton (fifth from right) and Lieutenant Colonel Dwight D. Eisenhower (fourth from right). (Photo courtesy of the Patton Museum.)

cautious." (144) "The solution of this, as of most of the preceding, is too timid. Time is waisted." (118) Morrison ended his preface to the book by noting, "Such practice, combined with knowledge of human nature and common sense, is what makes the tactician." Patton referred to the sentence and wrote, "Qualities lacked by Gen. Morrison. G.S.P."

In September 1919, Patton undertook a series of lectures at the Camp Meade tank center, beginning with "The History, Employment, and Tactics of Light Tanks." He reiterated that tanks were simply an auxiliary arm to assist the advance of the infantry, although he forecast tank versus tank battles, which might take on aspects of naval battles. He lectured more boldly in "The Effect of Tanks in Future Wars," for he perceived that since the war had ended, soldiers had begun to doubt that tanks would be used again—when in reality the new designs were much more effective and would be extremely useful in upcoming wars, which Patton said would be fought in the backward regions of Asia, Africa, and the Americas, especially Mexico. He pointed out that other armies were retaining their tank corps as separate entities, rather than grafting them onto infantry, cavalry, or artillery branches "like the third leg of a duck, worthless for control, for combat impotent." (BPP I 720.)

Turning to other subjects, Patton lectured on "The Obligations of Being an Officer," in which he reminded his audience that through the ages military men had ennobled their calling by adopting customs and traditions that "render beautiful the otherwise prosaic occupation of being professional men-at-arms: Killers." (BPP I 723.) His list of do's and don'ts was exhaustive; it included not telling smutty stories, not swearing in the mess, and reading military subjects three and a half hours per week.

While the lecture series ran, Patton dispatched memoranda on tank design and manufacture to a variety of tankers, ordnance officers, and senior officials. He read J.F.C. Fuller's *Tanks in the Great War* and made seven pages of notes; he concluded, however, that Fuller's "entire views are extreme and though sound will not be realized in our generation." (BPP I 736.) Patton summarized his own thoughts in "Tanks in Future Wars," which appeared in the May 1920 issues of both the *Infantry Journal* and the *Cavalry Journal.*

The three years' experience with tanks had been good for Patton. He won the Distinguished Service Cross with only five days in combat. He was subsequently awarded the Distinguished Service Medal for creating and leading the Bourg tank center and the 1st Tank Brigade. He received the fame he sought in the many headlines about his feats, and he achieved the rank of colonel at age thirty-two.

But in one important way, he had contributed to the demise of that experience. He was so outspoken on the philosophy that tanks exist to support infantry that ranking generals such as Pershing believed him, and so did important congressmen. The National Defense Act of 1920, passed on June 2, abolished the Tank Corps and assigned all tank units and personnel to the Infantry Branch. This dissolution took place despite the simultaneous creation of new branches such as the Air Service, the Chemical Service, and the Finance Department.

The act also established new personnel policies; Patton was returned on June 30 to his Regular Army rank of captain of Cavalry but was promoted to major the next day. Although he remained in command of his tank brigade, he asked for relief from that assignment and for a return to duty with the cavalry. He reasoned that he did not want to transfer to the infantry and that his brigade had completed its reformation. On September 30 he turned over command of the brigade to his successor and returned to Fort Myer, Virginia, to take command of the 3d Squadron of the 3d Cavalry. The experience with tanks would fast become a memory.

CHAPTER FIVE

Patton's School for Professionals 1921–1925

T HE PATTON SCHOOL for officers and soldiers reopened on his return to Fort Myer, this time for students who were cavalrymen rather than tankers. As at Bourg and Meade, he started with the fundamentals of discipline and individual skills and progressed up the ladder to platoon and troop and more advanced combat techniques of the offensive and defensive. In the process he trained his officers to be trainers. He was very explicit about which paragraphs of *Cavalry Drill Regulations* he wanted them to teach to their troopers, and he later questioned the men to see if they had learned.

In a single month he scheduled twenty-two lectures and lessons for his officers, sixteen of which he delivered himself, to include marches, orders for the attack, outposts, rear guards, and a variety of subjects on the care of the horse. He prepared for some lessons by typing on five-by seven-inch cards, noting his own ideas and identifying those of others. One set of seven cards gave him a ready reference to "Quotations from Soldiers," with a strong emphasis on Napoleon, Frederick and later German leaders, and American Civil War generals. (Patton's description of the cavalryman as a warrior-scholar is set forth in the margin copy.)

In 1921, Patton challenged his officers with a series of exercises and maneuvers in the Virginia countryside, demanding that they come up with solutions to problems he posed. His emphasis was on initiative, speed of decision-making, and bold use of cavalry mobility. The field exercises culminated when Patton conducted a tactical ride that pitted

**Excerpts From
"The Cavalryman,"
a Lecture to Officers, 1921**

"[The cavalryman has] a thorough knowledge of war by reading histories, lives of cavalrymen, by the study of the tactics of his arm and by the constant working of problems. . . . He must train himself into the possession of a GAMBLER'S Courage.

". . . the successful cavalryman must educate himself to say 'CHARGE.' I say educate himself, for the man is not born who can say it out of hand. . . .

"Civilization has affected us; we abhor personal encounter. . . . We have been taught to restrain our emotions, to look upon anger as low, until many of us have never experienced the God sent ecstacy of unbridled wrath. We have never felt our eyes screw up, our temples throb and had the red mist gather in our sight.

"And we expect that a man . . . shall [suddenly throw off] all caution and hurl himself on the enemy, a frenzied beast, lusting to probe his foeman's guts with three feet of steel or shatter his brains with a bullet. Gentlemen, it cannot be done—not without mental practice. . . .

"Therefore, you must school yourself to savagry. You must imagine how it will feel when your sword hilt crashes into the breast bone of your enemy. You must picture the wild exaltation of the mounted charge when the lips draw back in a snarl and the voice cracks with passion. . . .

"When you have acquired the ability to develop on necessity momentary and calculated savagry, you can keep your twentieth century clarity of vision with which to calculate the chances of whether to charge or fight on foot, and having decided on the former, the magic word will transform you temporarily into a frenzied brute. . . .

"To sum up, then, you must be: a horse master; a scholar; a high minded gentleman; a cold blooded hero; a hot blooded savage. At one and the same time you must be a wise man and a fool. You must not get fat or mentally old, and you must be a personal LEADER."

—Patton Collection, Library of Congress and USMA Library. (A more complete version is in Blumenson's *Patton Papers* I 757.)

Troop A defending a line against an attack by the rest of the squadron.

Three books in the Patton library assisted him in designing those exercises: General von Verdy du Vernois' *A Tactical Ride,* Lieutenant Colonel William H. Waldron's *Tactical Walks,* signed by Patton in 1921, and Farrand Sayre's *Map Maneuvers and Tactical Rides,* which he inscribed "Maj 3d Cav Ft Myer Va 1921." Patton's program of tactical rides for officers might also have been inspired by a fourth book, a 1907 London publication by Major General Douglas Haig entitled *Cavalry Studies, Strategical and Tactical,* describing five training rides Haig had conducted for cavalry officers in India. Patton made careful notes in that book, but it is unclear whether he did so before or after World War I.

To force his officers to think about future warfare and the art of command, Patton apparently drew heavily on books such as *The War of the Future* by German General Friedrich von Bernhardi, which he dated "Feb 9, 1921" and marked extensively in the margins. (See inset on page 56.) Patton probably used it in preparing his paper "Tactical Tendencies" in November of that year. (BPP I 747, 758.) But if Patton found in Bernhardi an advocate of a war of movement, he also found and underlined passages on leadership. For example, next to "Even the youngest officers must be required to look after the material welfare of their men," Patton wrote in the margin, "When the first men of the Tank C[orps] came to Langres we had hot coffee for them. One of them, later commissioned, said to me after the war that this act had a profound effect." (202) In another place, Patton underlined: "These two elements, automatic obedience and unshakable confidence in the superior, form the basis of discipline." Then he drew an arrow to "automatic" and wrote, "I used that word in a lecture in May, 1918. Till then discipline had never been defined in the U.S.A." (199) In 1931, Patton would reduce the von Bernhardi book to eight 3- by 5-inch note cards for his ready reference.

Patton's extensive study of the German military thinkers had picked up after the war with his reading at Camp Meade of F. W. Longman's *Frederick the Great and the Seven Years' War.* His note cards of "Quotations from Soldiers" contained a phrase from Frederick that Patton would use throughout World War II: "Ride the enemy to death. L'Audace—L'Audace!—Tout jour L'Audace!!!" He also borrowed from Frederick, "He who tries to protect everything will protect nothing," and "Don't haggle," about which Patton wrote, "Meaning it is better to act resolutely, even in an erroneous manner . . . than to remain inactive or irresolute." This injunction to act quickly rather than debate and lose the initiative became basic to Patton's philosophy, from his dictum to attack immediately when occasioning upon a meeting engagement with the enemy to his suspicion of civilian war councils and great staffs that studied problems endlessly without coming to decisions. It would not

Major Patton (foreground, right) commanding 3rd Squadron, 3rd Cavalry Regiment, at Fort Myer, Virginia, in 1921. (Photo courtesy of the Patton Museum and originally donated by Master Sergeant Gordon W. Staples, the squadron bugler, who is pictured astride the horse nearest the spot marked "X.")

preclude him, though, from meticulously planning anticipated campaigns in World War II.

In addition to Frederick, Patton sought German ideas from Freiherr Colmar von der Goltz's *The Conduct of War,* published in 1896. Patton's "Quotations from Soldiers" note cards cited von der Goltz: "The statesman who knowing his instrument to be ready and seeing war inevitable, hesitates to strike first is guilty of a crime against his country." Patton dwelled on that theme after the Allied victory in 1945, concluding that the all-powerful American army should be turned on the exhausted Soviet army before the latter could recover enough to win the inevitable war between the two powers. In *Portrait of Patton* Harry Semmes quotes Patton: "We are going to have to fight them sooner or later; within the next generation, I am sure, maybe a whole lot sooner.

Patton Annotations: reactions to von Bernhardi's *The War of the Future*

126   THE WAR OF THE FUTURE

vorable weather, and are as good as useless for this purpose at night or in dense fog.

At night, movements by railway and, in some circumstances, the position of villages and camps are all that aëroplanes can usually distinguish. It is only when flying very low and at short distances that it is possible for aëroplanes to light up the area they wish to reconnoiter. On the other hand, in good weather aëroplane reconnaissance is often able to show better results than cavalry could ever have done. The whole area occupied by the enemy can be photographed from the air. This makes it possible to fix the position and organization of the enemy's system of defenses in the greatest detail. Further, it is possible to observe and photograph from the air the movements of trains, the position of stations and rolling stock, aërodromes, the size and approximate capacity of camps, magazines and ammunition depots, the emplacements of hostile batteries and the presence of tanks (either directly or by distinguishing their tracks on the roads).

Of course the enemy will do his level best to conceal all these establishments from aërial observation, but if the reconnaissance is really careful and systematic it will often be possible

not in war of movement so pictures will be ancient history before they are developed.

200   THE WAR OF THE FUTURE

the highest standard of efficiency have been laid. Unfortunately, these qualities by themselves are not enough to protect the troops against injurious influences from home. Of course the influence of officers who enjoy the confidence of their men will be able to do a great deal in this respect, but it is necessary that the troops shall be kept apart from the home country in a certain sense, and feel that their interests are not the same although they are a genuine national army.

They must develop a proud feeling of professional detachment towards the civil population. Such a feeling is absolutely justified. While the civil population at home, who are not directly touched by the war, have to bear a few, though serious, privations, the soldier is offering his life and facing countless dangers, often when suffering the greatest physical torments and trials. In many cases he has left his family behind in want and anxiety. There he is in the field, living in wet trenches or exposed shell-holes, far from friends and relations who might be giving him moral support, though often enough they only worry and torment him with their faint-heartedness and tendency to exaggerate their trouble. Undoubtedly he has the right to regard himself as a

F.

The first men crippled permanently in a war should be well pensioned at once and the first advertised.

THE SOURCES OF POWER   201

being apart, the sole real representative of the nation and the Fatherland, and to look down with pride on those at home, who live in safety under his protection, and yet all too often grumble and groan and pay him back with words only, not with deeds.

The officers must devote themselves to cultivating this sentiment of soldierly self-conscience and keeping the troops alive to their own high calling. This is relatively easy in the case of old and famous regiments who have a great tradition, for in that case there is historic fame on which to build. It is far harder, however, in a war which, like the last war, summons the whole nation to arms, compels the formation of many new regiments, scatters the old solid officers' corps and fills their places with young and inexperienced officers of the reserve; a war which everywhere disturbs the old order, keeps all units in a state of flux and never permits the maintenance of higher units of fixed constitution. All this means that the higher officers, who have all had a long period of regular service and thus acquired a wealth of experience, must devote themselves unceasingly to teaching and helping their subordinates to influence the men in the right direction.

Here the paramount necessity of sending wounded men back to their own units at any sacrifice of expense. A. E. F. failed in this, It would probably have been corrected.

THE SOURCES OF POWER   203

to this psychological factor. The moral attitude of men is frequently influenced by their physical feelings. Hunger, overstrain, or being kept continuously in the danger zone under the effects of the nerve-shattering thunder of the guns and the shells falling and bursting about them, have an influence which cannot be prevented and in the long run paralyze their moral powers.

Lastly, we must consider the influence which the commander in chief may have on the whole army. Just as the spirit of a regiment depends on the influence of the regimental C.O., the spirit of an army depends on the personality of its leader, which does not always make itself felt in victory only. There are subtle threads woven between the commander in chief and his subordinates. They cannot be seen, but they work with wonderful power. It is the unconscious force of suggestion of a great man which asserts itself here. This subtle influence is originally the effect of victory, but when once it has been firmly established it will survive even the heaviest disasters. After Kolin and Kunersdorf Frederick the Great's men worshiped him just as much as after his first brilliant victories, and the halo which Napoleon won on the battlefields of 1796 existed in the

Why not do it now while our Army is intact and the damn Russians can have their hind end kicked back into Russia in three months? We can do it ourselves easily with the help of the German troops we have, if we just arm them and take them with us; they hate the bastards." (271)

For his note cards on training, Patton drew extensively from Lieutenant General Hugo von Freytag-Loringhoven's *Deductions From the World War,* printed in London in 1918. He also studied carefully the writings of Erich von Falkenhayn, whose *The German General Staff and Its Decisions, 1914–1916* was published in New York in 1920. Patton extracted for his note cards, "The soldier who is well disciplined, has his heart in the business, and has learned to attack is equal to any situation in war." Von Falkenhayn's triple theme became the core of Patton's lectures.

In 1922 Patton underlined heavily Volume I of General Erich von *Ludendorff's Own Story, August 1914–November 1918,* including passages such as "discipline is not intended to kill character, but to develop it," and a commander "must carry out most punctiliously the plans of General Headquarters which were opposed to mine, rather than my own." (183) During World War II, Patton might have recalled some of that Prussian thinking when he wrote in his diary scathing disagreements with the way his superiors, including Eisenhower, Bradley, and many Allies, were conducting the war; but in practice he generally obeyed their orders.

Ludendorff was also the source for this 1922 entry Patton made in a set of twenty-three note cards entitled "World War": "Tactics should be placed above mere strategy. Without tactical success strategy could not be accomplished. Strategy which does not think of tactical success is condemned at the start to failure. Numerous examples of this were furnished by the attacks of the Entente in the first three years of the war." Patton recognized Ludendorff's allusion to the tens of thousands of Allied casualties in the battle of the Somme and the futility of the strategy of attrition when tactics were so narrowly limited to the frontal attack. Patton became a devotee of the open war of movement, where unlimited tactical possibilities could lead to great strategic gains. When he would speed across Europe with the Third Army in World War II, his mind would always be on Berlin.

But perhaps Patton's strategic sense came more from the British than the Germans. His "Quotations" note cards also carried this entry: "Henderson: The tide of warfare ebbs and flows on an ocean which is studded with STRATEGIC objectives." Patton had been reading G. F. Henderson's *The Science of War: A Collection of Essays and Lectures, 1891–1903,* published in 1919. Reading Henderson also inspired him to write that the day of the cavalry charge might be over. He cited page 274 of Henderson when he wrote on a note card entitled "War of

Patton Annotations:
reactions to Balck's
Development of Tactics

1866–67," "It seems to me probable that Henderson was thinking of a Cav. which is extinct when he mentions European cav. That in view of rifled small arms, the charges we saw in the Civil War are about all we will get in the future. The history of the opening and closing of the W[orld] W[ar] bears me out. G.S.P." He had great respect for Henderson, the author of his favorite biography on Stonewall Jackson.

Patton studied the 1922 English translation of William Balck's *Development of Tactics—World War*, a two-volume update of the German officer's prewar writings. Patton wrote on the last page: "This is the best book on the interior economy of war, that is of *how* and not *when* men fought, that I have ever read." (See copy in margin.) Patton was again influenced by the sense of professionalism of the Germans. He cited Balck in his note cards on World War I: "Speaking of the retrogression of the quality of men and especially of officers, Balck says, P. 261, 'However, the infantry had a far different value than had the infantry with which we executed the offensive at the opening of the World War. Battalions and companies were commanded by young . . . officers who probably had had by then experience in the field, but who lacked those qualities which had formed the strength of our officers in peace. Thoroughly trained to meet all situations, indefatigable in the CARE of their subordinates, an example in danger as in the enduring of fatigue and hardships, our old officer corps was the best proof of the correctness of our peace training.' " Patton then observed: "I noted among the new [U.S.] officers in France this same lack of caring for men and of the feeling of responsibility to show courage and stand fatigue—regulars, no matter how worthless, have this." Then he cited General Washington's plea that a U.S. military academy be founded.

Thus Patton found between the Prussian concept of military professionalism and the needs of the American democratic society a linkage: conditioning young men for courage and sacrifice, drilling them in the knowledge of their calling, motivating them to perform with dedication, and creating many West Points to carry out the plan.

From Fort Myer Patton sent General John J. Pershing a copy of R.M.P. Preston's *The Desert Mounted Corps* and wrote, "It is the greatest military book I have ever read." (BPP I 762.) In his own copy he wrote, "This is the third copy I have owned." His interest in desert warfare was also reflected in his counting all the cavalry charges in the official report of Great Britain's Egyptian Expeditionary Force, *The Advance of the Egyptian Expeditionary Force, July 1917 to October 1918.* The commander, General Sir Edmund H. H. Allenby, had signed Patton's copy. During this period he also acquired W. T. Massey's *The Desert Campaigns* and H. S. Gullet's *The Australian Imperial Force in Sinai and Palestine, 1914–1918,* published in Sydney in 1923. And he read thoroughly *The Life of Sir Stanley Maude,* a biography by Charles Callwell about a lieutenant general who participated in the major campaigns in the Middle East in the Great War. Patton commented on the last page, "Except for his addiction to paper work—a very grate soldier."

To further his study of the Middle East campaigns in World War I, Patton acquired the Indian Army's *Notes of the First Indian Army Corps, From October, 1917 to November, 1918,* which has been reprinted at Fort Leavenworth with an extensive set of maps, and he read *Four Years Beneath the Crescent* by Rafael de Nogales of the Turkish Army. In 1926 he studied Volume II of *The Campaign in Mesopotamia, 1914–1918,* which had been compiled by F. J. Moberly for the Historical Section of Great Britain's Committee of Imperial Defence; when he read on page 318 that General Keary disagreed with his superior's plan of attack, Patton wrote in the margin, "Should have been *relieved!*"

In reading von Bernhardi and other authors during the early twenties, Patton frequently wrote an "F" in the margins, apparently to earmark ideas he wanted to file for use in his lectures and articles on the future of warfare. He also used "Q," "D," and "P." The Q designated a quotation he wanted to save; the D and P remain mysteries.

Historical memoirs that Patton did not sign or date, but probably read during the early twenties included the autobiographical *Days and Events, 1860–1866* by Thomas Livermore of the 18th New Hampshire Volunteers, with its running accounts of the battles of Chancellorsville and Gettysburg. Patton's underlinings in the book were mostly in passages describing the positive and negative attributes of Civil War commanders. The mystery of that book is the signature "R. P. Patterson" on the flyleaf, indicating it might once have been owned by the future U.S. Secretary of War. Patton also indicated he had read *The Autobiography of Sir Harry Smith, 1787–1819,* printed in London in 1910; although Smith wrote personal accounts of the Peninsular Campaign against Napoleon, the burning of Washington in 1812, and the fighting at Waterloo, Patton made no notes in the book.

Many books that Patton read in the 1921–1925 period reflect his strong interest in strategic and operational history. He annotated William Naylor's *Principles of Strategy* with many F's for his file on the future of warfare. He signed and read, but barely annotated, A. T. Mahan's *The Influence of Sea Power Upon History, 1660–1783.* Herbert Sargent's *The Strategy on the Western Front* received this comment in 1925: "Too strong a believer in diplomatic strategy. Fails to see that the only end of war and strategy is the destruction by battle of the enemy army." Patton read and put on note cards his thoughts on the views of Marshal Ferdinand Foch, both from *Precepts and Judgments* and *The Principles of War.* Patton's notes taken from Field Marshal Douglas Haig's *Features of the War* (1919) appeared on note cards labeled "Training." In his study of the Great War, Patton also made annotations in his copies of Field Marshal John French's *1914* and Major General Henry Allen's *My Rhineland Journal.*

Perhaps Patton acquired more books than he could read in that busy time. Left without annotations were James Williamson's *Mosby's Rangers,* given to him by "B Jr.," and Sir John Froissart's *Chronicles of England, France, Spain and the Adjoining Countries,* given to him by his father in 1921. John Maynard Keynes' 1920 *The Economic Consequences of the Peace* was left without annotation, as was Sir David Henderson's *The Art of Reconnaissance.* Perhaps C. T. Brady's *Indian Fights and Fighters* did not need careful reading, nor its sequels, *Northwestern Fights and Fighters* and *Border Fights and Fighters.* On the other hand, James Bryce's *The American Commonwealth* received closer attention, and all three volumes of Sir George Arthur's 1920 *The Life of Lord Kitchener* were marked with the I-have-read "R" on the binding. Another 1921 gift from Papa, a translation of Marcus Aurelius' *Meditations,* had the same marking but was left without annotation.

Meanwhile, Patton's Napoleonic collection, much of it left unsigned and undated, burgeoned to include: Baron Menéval's *Memoirs Illustrating the History of Napoleon I,* L. E. Henry's *Napoleon's War Maxims,* Thomas Watson's *Napoleon: A Sketch of His Life, Character, Struggles, and Achievements,* Alexander Kiesland's *Napoleon's Men and Methods,* M. Watson's *A Polish Exile With Napoleon: Letters of Captain Piontkowski,* and F. L. Petre's *Napoleon's Last Campaign in Germany, 1813.*

The postwar years also brought growth to the Pattons' social standing. With a key role in the eastern polo establishment, and many close friendships in Washington military and civilian society, the Pattons' leisure doings saw print in the *Army Navy Journal* and the Washington, New York, and Boston newspaper columns. George wrote Beatrice on July 4, 1922, "I have been dining and lunching with Belmonts, Harrimans, Penn Smiths, Stoddards, Brice Wings, etc. to a great extent. These are the nicest rich people I have ever seen." While operating his school for officers and soldiers, Patton would also see that he would be noticed by men and women of importance. But the societal aspect of the Pattons' lives diminished greatly in December 1923 when they moved out of Quarters 5 at Fort Myer and headed west for the Army schools on the plains.

At Fort Riley, Kansas, Patton spent five months completing the Field Officers Course of the Cavalry School. In September 1923 he entered the one-year course at the Command and General Staff College at Fort Leavenworth and emerged as an Honor Graduate the following June. Finishing twenty-fifth out of 248 students, he was praised by the commandant as "one of the ablest and best officers of his grade in the service." The Chief of Cavalry, Malin Craig, later Chief of Staff of the Army, wrote him: ". . . you have added additional prestige to our

Major Patton on the field obstacle course at Fort Riley, Kansas, in May 1923.
(Photo courtesy of the Patton Museum.)

branch of the service." (BPP I 778.) Patton's typed "Notes" on the Leavenworth course had an index of 100 items and measured an inch in thickness. (See page of "sacred truths" on page 62.) In later years he asked Dwight Eisenhower to return his set of those notes; he typed on a copy: "Every user of these notes has graduated from the Command and General Staff School in either the Honor or the Distinguished Group." Eisenhower was the first man in his Leavenworth class in 1926.

Patton's next set of orders took him to Boston to serve on the 1st Corps Area Headquarters staff as G-1, Personnel. During his brief eight-month stay there he undertook two projects that showed the tanks-ver-sus-horse-cavalry bifurcation in his professional thinking. He wrote

Patton's *Sacred Truths* from "Notes" on the Command and General Staff College Course, 1923–1924.

SACRED TRUTHS. #1.

1. Determine MISSION after making brief written ESTIMATE-WRITE MISSION OUT AND LOOK AT IT.
2. Based on above come to and WRITE OUT DECISION.
3. Check back to see that all TROOPS and all RE-QUIREMENTS are accounted for.
4. BE SIMPLE-RECONNOITER.
5. Attack that flank which offers the best protection to your own troops.
6. Support attack of main blow by ALL available fire power and by action of holding attack.
7. When STRATEGY and TACTICS disagree TACTICS GOVERNS.
8. If enemy Div. is on front of 7200 yds or more PENETRATE.
9. ALWAYS PROVIDE FLANK PROTECTION.
10. Designate PC's of next lower unit to include Battalion.
11. Use FA Brig and AS Sqn of Reserve Divs to support front line units in attack.
12. Flank Guard is always less than estimated strength of enemy, it should be strong in artillery.
13. Never be contained by a force smaller than yourself.
14. The lines of the enveloping and the direct attack intersect in rear of the position of the enemy reserves, the envelopment is often directed at the reserves.
15. That part of enemy front not attended to by direct or enveloping attack must be covered by fire.
16. In taking up a defensive position or in placing an outpost always define LINE OF RESISTANCE.
17. In forcing a river crossing throw as many bridges as possible and don't choose the easiest place as the enemy will have made special plans to defend it.
18. Boundaries should be clearly defined TERRAIN features.
19. Avoid having enveloping attack OVERLAP much of main position.
20. Show in the "Order" the direction of the main effort of both the holding and the main attack.
21. Covering force is used in defensive when it has ROOM to maneuver in delaying ACTION. Otherwise use outpost alone. Outpost Covering force, and Cavalry may all be used at once.
22. In ACTIVE DEFENSE hold out large reserve of one tactical unit. In passive defense large reserve not needed.

"Armored Cars with Cavalry," published in the *Cavalry Journal*, envisioning a future Major General Alonza G. Gasoline in his command car. A screen presented him with a video image, projected from an overhead helicopter and showing a battlefield populated with tanks fighting gun duels. Aircraft were bombing with liquid fire. Admitting that improved cross-country tracked vehicles were still in the distant future, he advocated as a transitional step the armor plating of commercial two-ton trucks and their integration with horse cavalry.

He delivered a lecture in Boston on "Cavalry Patrols," which began with his argument that most future wars would be fought in terrain without the road network they had experienced in Western Europe. In such terrain cavalry patrols must find the enemy, fight to get information, and get it back to the commander. His ending: "Get around if you can't get through. . . . IT IS THE DUTY OF CAVALRY AND SHOULD BE ITS PRIDE TO BE BOLD AND DASHING." (BPP I 783.)

Patton's physical examination in 1925 revealed the history of his injuries and wounds in pursuit of that ideal, mostly from polo playing and automobile accidents. 1905–1909, as a cadet: fractures of arm, nose, ankle, ribs. 1910: hand fracture. 1912: lacerated head. 1914: concussion with partial paralysis of right arm. 1915: lacerated head. 1916: lacerated and burned head and neck. 1917: lacerated head and neck. 1918: gunshot wound, left thigh. 1921: fractured hipbone. 1922: lacerated head and upper lip. 1924: broken ribs, lacerated head, sprained knee. (BPP I 783.) In the Patton mind, one could not be bold and courageous in war unless he practiced those qualities regularly in peacetime sports and military exercises.

Patton's war experience clarified his youthful reflections on the necessity for officers to conquer fear, and after he visited West Point in 1919 he wrote that all commissioning systems should institutionalize sustained training to accomplish that end. His 1920 note cards on "Training" postulated that many West Points be established, with military history the core of the program, to "evolve a tradition which shall be stronger than fear or fatigue." (See margin copy on this page.)

Also in 1920 he wrote a poem entitled "Fear" (reproduced on page 64). A generation later, Patton's ruminations on controlling fear served as the opening for his talks to American soldiers going into battle for the first time. The poem was published in *Cosmopolitan* magazine in March 1945. In his 1990 *Lines of Fire*, Professor Carmine Prioli reproduces "Fear" and some ninety other poems by Patton; he demonstrates that nearly half were written between 1917 and 1925, when Patton was pondering his war experience and was training and motivating his officers to become the military leaders of the future.

Patton's personal method for handling fear in the face of death stemmed from a steadily growing belief in a form of reincarnation, one

Patton on West Point (From note cards entitled "Training," circa 1920)

All officers should go through West Point or new West Points. We have many splendid officers who have not done so; this does not affect the issue. We want a higher average, not splendid individuals. Cadets at such institutions should be lectured on the traditions of the service. They should be made to memorize and recite on the many citations for courage in our army. By constant reiteration they should be taught that the sole purpose of an officer is to serve his country; if such service requires death, it is but a great chance for immortality.

Too much attention is devoted at West Point to means to an end. Not enough to the end, i.e., the ability to lead men in battle. This ability presupposes knowledge of human nature. It is gotten by the study of the profession. They must see this and strive for it or in the drab reality of battle they will falter. The road to high command leads through a long path called the history of war. Like all long roads the scenery is not always interesting; there are desert stretches of prosaic facts. But now and again the traveler reaches eminences where he sees the most sublime panoramas ever vouchsafe to mortal—the deathless deeds of the great who have passed to Valhalla, which is death but not oblivion.

To be useful in battle, military knowledge like discipline must be subconscious. The memorizing of concrete examples is futile for in battle the mind does not work well enough to make memory trustworthy. One must be so soaked in military lore that he does the military thing automatically. The study of history will produce this result. The study of algebra will not.

—From the Patton Collection, Library of Congress. (Corrected for typing errors.)

In March 1945, *Cosmopolitan* magazine published "Fear," a poem written by Patton in 1920. Patton would often talk of the importance of controlling your own fear and instilling fear in the enemy. From Patton's *Selected Poems, 1916–1925*, USMA Library.

FEAR.

I am that dreadful,blighting thing,
Like ratholes to the flood,
Like rust that gnaws the faultless blade,
Like microbes to the blood.

I know no mercy and no truth,
The young I blight,the old I slay.
Regret stalks darkly in my wake,
And Ignominy dogs my way.

Sometimes,in virtuous garb I rove,
With facile talk of easier way,
Seducing where I dare not rape
Young manhood,from its honor's ### sway.

Again,in awsome guise I rush,
Stupendous,through the ranks of war,
Turning to water,with my gaze,
Hearts that,before,no foe could awe.

The maiden,who has strayed from right,
To me must pay the mead of shame.
The patriot who betrays his trust,
To me must own his tarnished name.

I spare no class,or cult,or creed,
My course is endless through the year.
I bow all heads and break all hearts,
All owe me homage--I am FEAR.

G. 26 Apr.'20.

*One of my favorites
It was published in
W.W.II. BRP*

in which his warrior soul would continue to return to Earth in a variety of fighting roles. As early as 1905 he was aware of the Norse legend of the Valkyrie choosing the bravest in battle to enter Valhalla and continue to train to fight the battle of the giants for the god Oden. (See page 16.) In time he would write "the sole purpose of an officer is to serve his country; if such service requires death it is but a great chance for immortality." Moreover, the future officer should read "the deathless deeds of the great who have passed to Valhala which is death but not oblivion."

One of the strongest indications of Patton's faith that he occasionally had departed and returned to Earth is found in his 1917 poem "Memories Roused by a Roman Theater." It portrays him sitting in a tank in the Roman ruins at Langres, France, musing that "more than once have I seen these walls" and "now again I am here for war/ Where as Roman and knight I have been/ Again I practice to fight the Hun/ And attack him by machine."

While it is difficult to find Patton's belief in reincarnation in his prose writings or lectures, one poem indicates the range and depth of his feeling. "Through a Glass, Darkly" (see boxed poem on this page and on page 66) was composed in 1922 at Fort Myer, Virginia; the title comes from the Bible's First Epistle of Paul to the Corinthians (13.12). The poem states that Patton's many lives might have been initiated as a caveman hunting for meat and that he might have been a soldier who stabbed Christ on the cross. He remembers having fought alongside the Greeks and Alexander at Tyre and with the Roman legionnaires. He was a pirate, a cavalryman with Napoleon, and finally a tanker in World War I. He always suffered horrible deaths. God determined when he would return and fight again. The poem explores the heart of the warrior soul or warrior spirit that Patton referred to in so many of his speeches and writings. Few in his audiences realized how much those simple terms were bound to concepts of eternity and reincarnation in his complex mind.

Through a Glass, Darkly

Through the travail of the ages,
Midst the pomp and toil of war
Have I fought and strove and perished
Countless times upon this star.

In the forms of many peoples
In all panoplies of time
Have I seen the luring vision
Of the victory Maid, sublime.

I have battled for fresh mammoth
I have warred for pastures new,
I have listened to the whispers
When the race trek instinct grew.

I have known the call to battle
In each changeless changing shape
From the high souled voice of conscience
To the beastly lust for rape.

I have sinned and I have suffered,
Played the hero and the knave;
Fought for belly, shame or country
And for each have found a grave.

I cannot name my battles
For the visions are not clear,
Yet I see the twisted faces
And I feel the rending spear.

Perhaps I stabbed our Savior
In His sacred helpless side.
Yet I've called His name in blessing
When in after times I died.

In the dimness of the shadows
Where we hairy heathens warred,
I can taste in thought the life blood—
We used teeth before the sword.

While in later clearer vision
I can sense the coppery sweat
Feel the pikes grow wet and slippery
When our phalanx Cyrus met.

Hear the rattle on the harness
Where the Persian darts bounced clear,
See their chariots wheel in panic
From the hoplite's leveled spear.

See the goal grow monthly longer,
Reaching for the walls of Tyre.
Hear the crash of tons of granite,
Smell the quenchless eastern fire.

Still more clearly as a Roman,
Can I see the legion close,
As our third rank moved in forward
And the short sword found our foes.

Once again I feel the anguish
Of that blistering treeless plain
When the Parthan showered death bolts,
And our discipline was vain.

I remember all the suffering
Of those arrows in my neck.
Yet I stabbed a grinning savage
As I died upon my back.

Once again I smell the heat sparks
When my Flemish plate gave way
And the lance ripped through my entrails
As on Crecy's field I lay.

In the windless blinding stillness
Of the glittering tropic sea
I can see the bubbles rising
Where we set the captives free.

Midst the spume of half a tempest
I have heard the bulwarks go
When the crashing, point-blank round shot
Sent destruction to our foe.

I have fought with gun and cutlass
On the red and slippery deck
With all Hell aflame within me
And a rope around my neck.

And still later as a general
Have I galloped with Murat
When we laughed at death and numbers
Trusting in the Emperor's star.

Till at last our star had faded,
And we shouted to our doom
Where the sunken road of Ohein
Closed us in its quivering gloom.

So but now with tanks a clatter
Have I waddled on the foe
Belching death at twenty paces,
By the starshell's ghastly glow.

So as through a glass and darkly
The age-long strife I see
Where I fought in many guises,
Many names—but always me.

And I see not in my blindness
What the objects were I wrought.
But as God rules o'er our bickerings
It was through His will I fought.

So forever in the future,
Shall I battle as of yore,
Dying to be born a fighter
But to die again once more.

G.S.P.
May 27, 1922

CHAPTER SIX

Staff and Study
1925–1928

DISASTER STRUCK Patton's library in March 1925, when his household goods were ravaged by fire and water in the hold of the S.S. *Grant* en route to Hawaii, Patton's newest assignment. At least one of the book boxes "was burned all to pieces," and the others burst open when water from the firehoses swelled the contents. Since 75 percent of the remaining books had lost their covers, Patton undertook a massive rebinding process in Hawaii. (BPP I 784.) Today, those books are identified by straw-colored buckram covers, hand-printed titles and names of authors, and the occasional "R" indicating Patton had read them. For example, Patton's copy of William Ganoe's *History of the United States Army* was bought in 1924, damaged in the 1925 fire, and rebound in 1926.

Patton now began to make lists of his professional reading since being commissioned in 1909. In the summer of 1926 he read *The Direction of War: A Study of Strategy* by British Major General W. D. Bird. The front of the book presents Bird's long "List of Books Consulted," above which Patton wrote in red pencil, "I have read the books checked." (See inset on page 68.)

During Patton's stay in Hawaii, from 1925 to 1928, his reading seemed focused on strategy and the broader aspects of the conduct of war. Many of his marginal notes in Bird's *The Direction of War* referred particularly to Japan and generally to wars arising from rivalries over trade and natural resources. That fitted his role as G-2, intelligence officer, of the Hawaiian Division. Soon after he arrived in Hawaii he started

Patton Annotations: reactions to Bird's *The Direction of War*

I have read the books checked
GSP August 16 1926

LIST OF BOOKS CONSULTED

STRATEGY AND GENERAL PRINCIPLES

Correspondance militaire de Napoléon I. 1858–70.
La guerre napoléonienne. Lt.-Col. Camon. 1903–7.
Dictionnaire-Napoléon. D. Hinard. 1854.
Napoleon as a general. Yorck von Wartenburg, trans. 1902.
Napoleon. Lt.-Col. T. A. Dodge. 1904–7.
Préceptes et jugements de Napoléon. Lt.-Col. Picard. 1913.
Despatches and supplementary despatches of the Duke of Wellington.
  Lt.-Col. J. Gurwood. New edition, 1852.
Correspondance militaire. Von Moltke. French translation, 1903.
On war. Von Clausewitz, trans. Col. F. N. Maude. 1908.
Précis de l'art de la guerre. Genl. A. H. Jomini. Revised edition, 1894.
The operations of war. Genl. Sir E. B. Hamley. Fifth edition, 1889.
The conduct of war. Lt.-Genl. von der Goltz, trans. Maj. G. F.
  Leverson. 1899.
The nation in arms. Lt.-Col. von der Goltz, trans. P. A. Ashworth.
  New edition, 1899.
L'Esprit de la guerre moderne. Series, Genl. H. Bonnal. 1904–12.
La guerre moderne. Genl. Derrécagaix. 1890.
The development of strategical science. Genl. von Caemmerer. 1905.
The science of war. Col. G. F. R. Henderson. 1905.
Letters on strategy. Prince Kraft zu Hohenlohe-Ingelfingen. 1898.
Stratégie. Col. Blume. French translation, 1884.
Études stratégiques. Comdt. Mordacq. 1910.
Politique et Stratégie. Comdt. Mordacq. 1912.
Clausewitz. Lt.-Col. Camon. 1911.
The elements of strategy. Tovey and Maguire. 1904.
The balance of power, 1715–89. A. Hassall. 1908.
Minor tactics. Maj.-Genl. C. F. Clery. Thirteenth edition, 1896.
The art of naval warfare. Adml. Sir C. Bridge. 1907.
The influence of sea power upon the French revolution and empire.
  Adml. A. T. Mahan. 1892.

CAMPAIGNS

Cromwell. T. Carlyle. Centenary edition, 1897.
Cromwell as a soldier. Col. T. S. Baldock. 1899.
England in the Mediterranean, 1603–1713. Julian S. Corbett. 1904.
England in the Seven Years' War. Julian S. Corbett. 1907.
Frederick the Great. T. Carlyle. 1894.
Victoires, conquêtes, désastres, etc. des Français, 1792–1815.
  1817–21.
History of Europe from 1789 to 1815. A. Alison. 1839–42.
History of the British Army. Hon. J. W. Fortescue. First
  edition, 1899–1914.

History of the war in the Peninsula. Maj.-Genl. Sir W. F. P. Napier.
  Chandos classics, 1890.
History of the Peninsular War. C. Oman. 1902–11. *G*
Notes sur la Prusse dans sa grande catastrophe, 1806. Von Clause-
  witz, trans. Capt. Niessel. 1903.
The Canadian war of 1812. Sir C. Lucas. 1906.
Jena to Eylau. Genl. von der Goltz, trans. C. F. Atkinson. 1913.
Neuf mois de campagnes à la suite du Maréchal Soult. Col. Dumas.
  1909.
La campagne de 1814. Comdt. Weil. 1891–6.
The campaign of Waterloo. J. C. Ropes. Third edition, 1903.
The Waterloo campaign of 1815. Capt. W. Siborne. 1844.
La campagne de 1815 aux Pays Bas. De Bas et de Wommersom.
  1908–9.
Précis politique et militaire de la campagne de 1815. Genl. A. H.
  Jomini. 1839.
The war in Afghanistan. Sir J. W. Kaye. 1851.
The history of the Sikhs. W. L. MacGregor. 1846.
The Sikhs and the Sikh wars. Gough and Innes. 1897.
The invasion of the Crimea. A. W. Kinglake. 1863.
The war in the Crimea. Genl. Sir E. B. Hamley. Fifth edition, 1892.
The history of the Sepoy war. Sir J. W. Kaye. Second edition,
  1875–6.
The 2nd Afghan war, 1878–80. Abridged official account. 1908.
The decisive battles of India. Col. G. B. Malleson. 1885.
Military history of the campaign in Egypt, 1882. 1887.
History of the Soudan campaign. 1889.
The story of the Civil war. J. C. Ropes. 1898–9.
Stonewall Jackson. Lt.-Col. G. F. R. Henderson. New impression,
  1900.
The Prussian official account of the Austro-Prussian war, 1866. 1872.
Sadowa. Genl. H. Bonnal. 1901.
Campagne de 1866 en Italie. Capt. Lemoyne. 1876.
Campagne de 1866 en Allemagne et en Italie. Capt. H. Barthélemy.
  1880.
The Russian army and its campaigns in Turkey. Maj.-Genl. F. V.
  Greene. 1879.
The official history of the war in South Africa, 1899–1902. 1906–10.
The official history of the Russo-Japanese war. 1910–14.
1914. Viscount French. 1919.
Forty Days in 1914. Maj.-Genl. Sir F. Maurice. 1919.
General Headquarters, 1914–16, and its critical decisions. Genl. von
  Falkenhayn. 1919.
Out of my life. Marshal von Hindenburg. 1920.
The march on Paris and the battle of the Marne, 1914. Genl. von
  Kluck. 1920.
Life of Lord Kitchener. Sir G. Arthur. 1920.
The Marne campaign. Maj. F. E. Whitton. 1917.
Nelson's history of the war. J. Buchan. 1914–18.
"Times'" history of the war. 1914–18.

MISCELLANEOUS

John Manners, Marquis of Granby. W. E. Manners. 1899.
A history of England in the 18th century. W. E. H. Lecky. 1892.
Life of W. Pitt, Earl of Chatham. B. Williams. 1913.
War speeches of W. Pitt, the younger. R. Coupland. 1915.
Life of Pitt. Earl Stanhope. 1861–2.
W. Pitt and the great war. J. H. Rose. 1911.
The rival powers in Central Asia. J. Popowski, trans. 1893.
Alimentation et ravitaillement des armées en campagne. Peyrolle.
  1898.
Les services de l'arrière à la grande armée. Capt. G. Lechartier.
  1910.
Fifteen decisive battles of the world. Sir E. Creasy. 1877.
Bacon's Essays. n.d.
Physics and politics. Walter Bagehot. 1887.
The finance of war. E. Crammond. 1910.
Finance and war. Capt. R. S. H. Grace. 1910.
Study of sociology. H. Spencer. Library edition, 1880.

"I have read the books checked," wrote Patton atop this list from W.D. Birds *The Direction of War*, published in 1920 and read by Patton in 1926. He had begun making lists of his professional reading back in 1909.

Prinz Kraft zu Hohenlohe-Ingelfingen's *Letters on Strategy* and William Robertson's *From Private to Field Marshal*. When the latter referred to the allied Supreme War Council as a political rather than a military body, Patton wrote, "Hence, not worth a damn."

Some of Patton's most predictive comments on strategy were made in Hector C. Bywater's *Navies and Nations*, which General Fox Conner gave him for Christmas in 1927. When the author wrote "the half garrisoning of Singapore is invitation to enemy capture," Patton scribbled "same true of Hawaii." (94) When the author wrote that Singapore could be made impregnable, Patton pencilled in "Pearl Harbor." (96) Patton's anti-British bias, which would come to the fore in World War II, was foretold when Bywater wrote of a British oil depot in Jamaica and Patton wrote "surely against us." (84) When the author discussed naval disarmament, Patton wrote: "Apparently Britain wants limitations so that if she can't win, at least all the rest will lose. GSPJr." (278)

Included in his reading sweep of high-level military affairs those years were Sir Frederick Maurice's *The Last Four Months: How the War Was Won*, Sir William Robertson's *Soldier and Statesmen 1914–1918*, and Lieutenant Colonel Philip Neame's *German Strategy in the Great War*. He also acquired, but did not annotate, *Chemical Warfare* by Amos Alfred Fries and Clarence J. West, *Training Management* by Alfred William Bjornstad, and the U.S. War Department's *Reports of Military Observers Attached to the Armies in Manchuria During the Russo–Japanese War*. He did, however, heavily annotate Chief of the German General Staff General von Hoffman's *The War of Lost Opportunities*, writing on page 29, "notice forward position of an army commander," and underlining three times Hoffman's reference to the American president as "the crack-brained Wilson." (246)

Among the books bound in Hawaii were Volume II of Herbert Sargent's *The Campaign of Santiago de Cuba*, Arthur Conan Doyle's 1902 *The Great Boer War*, and Volume II of *The War in South Africa* by the Historical Section of the Great General Staff in Berlin in 1906. Each of those had an "R" on its binding and generally discussed the higher levels of military affairs.

Meanwhile, Patton had kept up his study of tactics and operations, such as in Andrew A. Humphreys' *The Virginia Campaign of '64 and '65*. In October 1925 he acquired but did not annotate General Hunter Liggett's *Commanding an American Army: Recollections of the World War*, nor did he do more than put an "R" on the cover of his copy of the final *Report of the U.S. First Army Commander, General John J. Pershing From 10 August to 15 October, 1918*.

He had brought to Hawaii his copy of Helmuth von Moltke's *The Franco–German War of 1870–71* with notes about "bad staff work" and "bad orders." In January 1926, he started a thorough annotation of

Major Patton in 1926. (USMA Library photo.)

H. M. Johnstone's *A History of Tactics,* quarreling with the author on a variety of issues. In April and May he read *Warfare: A Study of Military Methods Since the Earliest Times* by Oliver Spaulding, Hoffman Nickerson, and John Wright; after thoroughly annotating 572 pages, he pronounced it "A good book." In July he read *Three Years War* and concluded that Christiaan DeWet—the Boer War commander and author of the book—had a desire to fight but had separated his forces. In October 1926, he began to annotate his copy of *Military Operations, France and Belgium, 1914,* compiled by J. E. Edmonds for the British Official History of the Great War. Also during 1926 he inscribed but did not annotate Edward Lyman Munson's *The Principles of Sanitary Tactics,* Charles D. Rhodes' *History of the Cavalry of the Army of the Potomac,* and Jacob Dolson Cox's *The March to the Sea: Franklin and Nashville.* For Christmas 1926 his wife gave him Henry Swainson Cowper's 1906 *The Art of the Attack.* In 1927 he studied *The Transformation of War* by Commandant J. Colin of the French War School and noted that the frontal attack was "useless in war in 1870." (41)

Although Patton read a large number of books in Hawaii, it is his intense study in 1926 of General Carl von Clausewitz's *On War* that most commands our attention. He rebound the version he had read in 1910, but he had also acquired a three-volume edition published in 1918 by E. P. Dutton and Company, translated by Colonel J. J. Graham, and with notes by Colonel F. N. Maude. Patton's thoroughness in studying the first volume is indicated by his listing on the flyleaf the pages of importance to him, especially Clausewitz's definitions of military terms such as strategy and tactics. The card headed "Clauserwitz" in Patton's card file paraphrased the famous dictum: "War is only a continuation of state policy by other means." Patton also annotated the second volume heavily. He did not indicate he had read Volume III, however, and had therefore missed Clausewitz's *Attack* and *Plan for War,* two of the six books in the three-volume set.

Patton did not always agree with Clausewitz. On page 31 of the first of the Graham volumes, Clausewitz suggested that if the object of combat is not destruction of the enemy force, but merely shaking the enemy's feeling of security, "we go only so far in the destruction of his forces as is sufficient." Patton wrote in the margin, "*Bunk*—always go the limit." On page 39, Clausewitz explained how "a whole campaign may be carried on with great activity without the actual combat playing any notable part of it." Patton wrote, "This would be a useless campaign." He was in the same mood on page 40 when he wrote, "War means fighting and fighting means killing."

Agreement was virtually total, however, when Patton underscored the key words in the third chapter of Clausewitz's Book I, *The Genius for War.* Courage, resolution, obstinacy, and imagination appealed to

Patton. He may have started using the phrase *coup d'oeil*—a glance of the eye—as he underlined Clausewitz's definition on page 50: "... it simply amounts to the rapid discovery of a truth which to the ordinary mind is either not visible at all or only becomes so after long examination and reflection." Throughout his reading of Clausewitz, he annotated certain ideas, such as boldness (186–189) and the need for great energy in commanders (291).

On numerous occasions Patton commented on the applicability of Clausewitz's teaching to current affairs. On page 5 of Graham's first volume, for example, Clausewitz said, "The worst condition in which a belligerent can be placed is that of being completely disarmed." Patton wrote, "U.S. now." On page 6 of Graham's second volume, Patton noted that the small German Army was gaining a combat edge in 1926 by becoming very efficient.

In reading Patton's copy of Clausewitz, one is struck by the anti-intellectual tone of some of the annotations. Through most of his life Patton had declared himself an anti-intellectual, but privately he had engaged in a lifetime of vigorous intellectual enterprise. The seeming contradiction in personality appeared particularly strong after the library fire of 1925. In November, for example, he wrote in the flyleaf of F. N. Maude's *The Evolution of Modern Strategy* these cryptic lines: "A good account of the superiority of energy over brains. To Stink (with sweat), not to Think—wins." But on page 127, when Maude extols ditch-digging for soldiers because "what is needed is strong back-muscles and horny hands," Patton wrote in the margin: *"Bull."*

Months later, Patton was in the same mood when he read this description of genius in Clausewitz's *The Genius for War*: "Every special calling in life, if it is to be followed with success, requires peculiar qualifications of understanding and soul. Where these are of a high order, and manifest themselves by extraordinary achievements, the mind to which they belong is termed *genius*." Patton underlined "soul" and replaced "mind" with "person." In the next paragraph he read "we must ... understand by 'genius' a very high mental capacity for certain employments"—and promptly crossed out the word "mental." (I, 46) A few pages later, however, Patton was noting that coup d'oeil is not available to ordinary minds and that imagination is one of many mental faculties needed by the commander. On page 187 he wrote, "Regulations govern masses; thoughts govern generals."

Patton's study of Clausewitz was far more penetrating than his reading of Niccolo Machiavelli's *The Prince*. Patton's copy was published at Oxford in 1897 and rebound after the 1925 fire. He printed "R" on the binding, but the only annotations were sidelines before page 10; he turned down the corner of page 78 and probably never returned to the book.

While in Hawaii, Patton's reading often turned to the historical or philosophical roots of learning. He consumed a 700-page textbook on ancient history, James Breasted's 1926 *The Conquest of Civilization*, in which his marginal notes were as much about government and taxes as about war. He sampled the William Stearns Davis text *Europe Since Waterloo*, focusing on the sections on the Revolutions of 1848 and Otto von Bismarck; he also read Charles Oman's *England Before the Norman Conquest*. His copy of Edward Creasy's *The Fifteen Decisive Battles of the World* was dated June 1926 but was left entirely unannotated—perhaps it was a replacement copy for one lost in the ship fire. Patton's Christmas reading in 1926, Sir William Muir's *The Life of Mohammad*, reflected his historical and philosophical eclecticism.

Throughout his Hawaiian tour, Patton never sacrificed his love for Civil War biographies. In the months before leaving Boston he had read both volumes of the *Memoirs of General William T. Sherman*, and upon arriving in Hawaii he rebound his copy of John Allan Wyeth's *Life of Nathan Bedford Forrest*. On page 648 of the latter, he noted Forrest's novel use of cavalry as dismounted infantry, with the comment, "Alexander the Great beat him to it." After settling in at Schofield Barracks he read both volumes of James Longstreet's *From Manassas to Appomatox*; in early 1926, he read General John Gordon's *Reminiscences of the Civil War*, in which he wrote of the last paragraph, "Papa read this to me when I was about 12. It must have appeared in a magazine. I remember it perfectly." Next he turned to Jacob Cox's *Atlanta* in Scribner's series on American Civil War campaigns, and then to General François de Chanal's 1894 *The American Army in the War of Secession*, which Patton noted was "a good account," given that it was by a Frenchman. His Christmas reading of 1926 was General Horace Porter's *Campaigning With Grant*; and as he departed Hawaii, he was writing in Charles Marshall and Frederick Maurice's *An Aide-de-Camp of Lee* that it was "a very good account, but it seems to stress that in actual battle, Lee lacked drive."

During his prodigious reading in the Hawaii staff assignments, Patton organized his learning on a series of typed four- by six-inch note cards. For example, fifteen cards were devoted to Napoleon, nine to Frederick the Great (see inset on page 74), twenty-one to the American Civil War, and fifteen to what Patton labeled the "War of 1866–67" in Germany. He cited the authors from whom he drew his notes, some perhaps from books in the Army library at Schofield Barracks.

When he noted, "At all times the French cavalry carried too much," he cited a now barely known *History of Cavalry* by Colonel George Denison. (See inset on page 74.) When he noted the arrival in 1841 of the German needle gun, he cited Ernest Lloyd's *History of Infantry*; he further noted that "the advent of this weapon emphasized the need for

**Patton on Controlling Fear
(From his 1925 lecture
"On Leadership")**

"Few men are by nature devoid of physical fear. The blistering heat of battle withers many a building reputation when the poor shrinking flesh fails to sustain the soul midst the myriad forms of dissolution in which the reaper seems to stalk the field. To combat this it behooves us to develop an anti-toxin to fear and with it to inoculate our men. The best virus is a mixture of race consciousness, a mind saturated with former deeds of heroism, an abundant sense of obligation and an insatiable desire for present distinction and posthumous celebrity, so that in the fateful hour he may subdue his weaker self with that mighty potion—fear of fear.

"Like a cold bath the first plunge is the hardest. Later, if he live, custom, fatigue, fatalism and pride will make him master of his emotions, for devoid of fear no normal man can ever become. Once on the morning of battle an officer asked Turenne if his knees shook from the cold and the veteran replied: 'No, my friend, they shake from fear but if they knew where I shall this day take them they would tremble more.' . . .

"We do not stress enough the necessity for personal exposure and rash boldness on the part of our officers. Man loves life and too often yields to the sophistry of the subtle demon Fear, when he whispers, oh, so temptingly: 'Your men need you, you must save yourself for them,' forgetting that the inspiration of an heroic act will carry men to victory . . . forgetful too that the blood of heroes like the dragons teeth will sprout new leaders to replace his loss."

—Patton Collection, Library of Congress

Patton organized his learning by typing key points onto note cards. Immediately below and left is the first of nine note cards he devoted to Frederick the Great. Patton wrote it in the 1920s. Patton devoted fifteen note cards to Napoleon. The eighth card, immediately below and to the right, was written in the 1920s and covers points from *History of Cavalry* by Colonel George Denison. Patton's first point on the depicted note card (top of next page) covering the German War of 1866–67 is that the advent of the German needle gun emphasized the need for target practice beyond what was needed in Napoleon's time. Patton was so taken by Ardant du Picq's *Battle Studies* that he typed 138 notes over twenty-six cards, agreeing with the author on many points: the quality of soldiers is more important than their quantity; regulated drills no longer reflect battle conditions; and skulkers should be shot. Note cards 7, 8, 10, 16, 20, and 24 are reprinted here. All note cards come from the Library of Congress.

                    Frederick the Great

  1. In 1768, Frederick wrote: "Battles are won by fire
      superiority."

  2. In general, his method of attack consisted in crushing a
      hostile flank by concentrated fire of artillery and
      infantry, delivered from an oblique direction.
      Protecting his other flank by refusing it.

  3. Precision and quickness of movement enabled him to
      maneuver even on battle-field.

  4. Frederick used cavalry for rear or flank attack after
      infantry and artillery had broken enemy.   (LUTHEN)

  5. His army capable of marching 20 kilometers a day.

  6. Prussian battalions formed in three ranks; other nations
      in four. Prussians fired by platoon successively, or
      by odd and even numbered platoons; other nations fired
      by rank.

                                   Napoleon, 8.
                    History of Cavalry,Denison.

  1. As early as 1766 French Cav, formed in two ranks
      with a distance of 12 paces¢ Under Nap. this was
      closed to 4)Interval between Sqns. ¼ Sqn front.

  2. At all times the French cavalry carried too much.

  3. Movement by fours invented about 1790.

  4. At beginning of Revolution French Cav numbered
      24000 more than half heavy Cav.

  5. After F. Prussian Cav.retrogaded,due to old and
      inferior generals rather than to poor men.

  6. By 1793 there were 22000 Chasseurs and 11000
      ￬￬￬/￬￬/ Hussars in French Army.However these troops
      were seperated into small units with Inf.Divs.

  7. In 1795 French Cav. captured Dutch fleet frozen in

                                        Du'Picq.7.
  35. Fire arms make the coordinated actions of large
       bodies more and more difficult. Individual VALOR of the
       soldier and of small groups will be decisive.
       VALOR IS MADE BY DISCIPLINE. 104.

  # 36. Since man cahnges little and we are interested in m
         man astudy of the past is useful in order to predict
         the future. 104

  37. The movement of troops prior to combat are necessary
       but WHOLY different from the fight. 105

  38. Great soldiers have known what their men would do
       how to inspire and how to use them. 105.

  39. #" Before gunpowder small forces beat greater-the sam
       is possible to day".105.

  40. #" Military men usually devise tactics to suit
       the characteristics of an ideal race under normal

---

       emotional conditions. It is necessary to consider man
  in battle(under emotion) and battle its self.
       Science changes many things in war but the HEART of
  man remains unchanged.Greater than discipline or tactics
  is the HEART OF MAN AS IT WORKS IN THE HEAT OF BATTLE"

War of 1866-67   History of Infantry   (Lloyd)

1. German needle gun invented 1841. Rate of fire, 7 shots per minute. Maximum range 1,000 yards. Effective range 500 yards. The advent of this weapon emphasized the need of target practice which had not existed at the time of Napoleon I.

2. Prussian artillery in 1866 was breechloading; Austrian artillery muzzle-loading.

3. In 1866, Prussian company columns broke into skirmish line: not to avoid losses but to get to a place where they could inflict them.

4. Austrains aware of their inferior rifle and muzzle-loader trusted to shock administered by columns. The ratio of losses was 5 to 1, Austrians leading.

Du Picq. 8.

41. We spend time on making deadly weapons more deadly and terror provoking.They are harder to face. We must train men to face them.(This surely points straight at selected regulars) 110

42. MUTUAL ACQUAINTANCE ADDS TO COURAGE. 110

43. The effect of new inventions on war is transitory because nations soon all get them.The determining factor of war is ,leaving aside genius and luck, the quality of the troops.Good troops must have training,confidence,nad mutual acquaintance,their success must clearly depend on the collective action of small groups.   110.

44. The study of battle shows that troops-rarely- will fight unless forced to do so by discipline. Modern war makes this coertion difficult. Man is still unchanged 200000men only half of whom will fight are of much less value than 100000 all of whom will because they must be fed. 111.

Du Picq. 10.

50. "ANCIENT BATTLE RESEMBLED A DRILL.There is no such resemblence in modern battle. This leads to confusion.(Since drill is regulated and battle is not drill is res a detriment as now taught. WE SHOULD HAVE ONLY DRILLS FOR FIGHTING.) 112

51. Man can stand only so much terror. Now he gets it sooner(the approach) and in more appauling forms. Also fire makes dispersion necessary discipline and dispersion are opposed.Hence we need it more and have more trouble in getting it. It must spring from long acquaintance with comerades,trust in officers who must be present and from (FEAR OF PUNISHMENT AND HABIT)

52. In former times man fought against man now he fights FATE in the form of blind bullets. He seems to be alone it is easy to skulk.(Squads should have rollcalls at objectives and the skulkers should be dealt with by the m men) (HOW CAN NATIONS IN ARMS U.S.MODEL DO THESE THINGS?

Du Picq. 16.

80. COMBAT AT CLOSE QUARTERS DOES NOT EXIST.At close quartersoccurs that ancient carnage when one side strikes the other in the back. 149.

81. At Wagram out of 22000 1500 to 3000 reached the position,there were 7000 casualties the rest skulked. 150

82. Due to the fact that the necessary dispersion of modern battle leads to loss of control . It is necessary to start the fight as late as possible.(Approach by stealth.) 152.

83. A thin line(or a line of groups of detachments) must have high discipline to advance,it rests on pride, habit and fear.154

84. It was the pride and discipline of the guard which saved the French at the BERESINA and HANAU. 155.

85. If cavalry cannot charge unshaken infantry what can infantry moving at a fourth the speed do???

Du Picq. 20

104. If the infantryman can walk under fire cannot the cavalryman gallop under it??181

105. The infantry cannot act alone more than ever it will need cavalry to make diversions and threaten flanks and rear. " HE WHO KNOWS HOW TO USE CAVALRY WITH AUDACITY WIL INEVITABLY BE THE VICTOR". 181

106. Cavalry has failed when it has lacked real cavalry generals. 182.

107. Cavalry should be organic in every infantry dif. 184

108. A cavalry action more even than in the case of infantry is an affair of morale.

109. In a charge cav against Cav 49 times out of 50 one side will turn before the contact.THE ESSENTIAL FACTOR IS DETERMINATION. 186.

Du Picq. 24.

128. ROMANCE is the emotion which sways the populace to war. Yet the actors in it;heros in the eyes of the crowd are:" only poor fold torn between, fear, discipline and pride.

129. Since we can not have Draconian discipline like the romans we must have cohesion,assured by MUTUAL ACQUAINTANCESHIP.Punishments for skulking should be adjudged and administered by the soldiers them selves. In 1859 there were 25000 SKULKERS in the Army of Italy. all got the campaign medal. Company courts should determine who gets it.

130. Napoleon regarded the rifle and bayonet as the most powerful weapon that man possesses. 232.

131. Cartridges-Gustavus::Iron Ram Rods-Fredrick-:: Improved vent(Load by hitting but on ground) republic and empire:: Breech loader-Sadowa:Magazine -PLEVNA? Smokless powder -Spanish War;;M.G. In numbers *W.W.

**Patton on Military Punishments
in Wartime
(From his 1927 lecture
"Why Men Fight")**

"Due to maudlin sentimentality
it is not possible to cause the
mass of a nation to view military
punishments from their proper
angle, namely as administrative
rather than judicial acts, whose
purpose in wartime is not to
wreak vengence on the guilty
but rather to restrain the
innocent.

"For example, the idea back of
the death sentence for such acts
as desertion, sleeping on post,
skulking, etc., is not inherent in
the offense itself. Desertion has
perhaps no extenuation, but the
other offenses usually have.

"The poor tired boy who sleeps
on his post is more to be pitied
than blamed insofar as his individual case is concerned. But the
act, harmless in itself, may have
exposed scores or hundreds of
his equally deserving comrades
to capture, wounds and death. It
is for their sake, not his fault,
that the final penalty should be
exacted of him.

"A man may, under the influence of fatigue, so forget his
obligation as to chance a term of
imprisonment against a
moment's oblivion, but he will
think several times before he
makes the same gamble with the
certainty of death, his own
death, not that of his comrades.

"So with the skulker. . . . he cuts
the very root of military virtue,
which is based on mutual
confidence.

"The execution of the skulker is
necessary, not for his sin but for
his betrayal of his comrades.
Judas is execrated for the
betrayal of One, should he who
betrays hundreds escape?"

—Patton Collection,
USMA Library

target practice which had not existed at the time of Napoleon I." (See inset on page 75.) The note cards on Napoleon and the Civil War some-times cite the *Encyclopaedia Britannica,* but the bulk of those notes cited Patton's own library—J. Colin, George Henderson, William Balck, H. M. Johnstone, and Sir Evelyn Wood's *Achievements of Cavalry.*

The note cards give us a rare insight into the Patton professional mind. There is his close attention to minute detail, such as the range of weapons, both maximum and effective, and its impact on tactics. We find his continued focus on nomenclature as a key to doctrine: "One of the lessons learned by the Germans in 1860 as to the use of artillery is indicated by the change of name from 'reserve artillery' to 'corps artillery.' " (Note card 4, "War of 1866–67.") We also find his sweeping generalizations: "Napoleon made no improvement in equipment dur-ing his wars." (Note card 1, "Napoleon.")

The book that may have influenced the Patton mind more than any other is Ardant du Picq's *Battle Studies.* Written mostly in the 1860s and published after his death in the Franco–Prussian War, du Picq's book was discovered by American officers in France during World War I and translated into English in 1921. Patton had heard of du Picq as early as 1911 when he quoted him in an unfinished paper entitled "National Defense": "Man ingages [sic] in battle for the purpose of victory not for the purpose of fighting." (BPP I 220.) Patton read the 1921 edition, typed 138 notes on twenty-six cards, and used the book to help solve the problem of getting infantry to advance through enemy artillery fire. Patton wrote to Eisenhower on July 9, 1926, with this recommendation: "First read Battle Studies by Du Picque (you can get a copy at Leaven-worth) then put your mind to a solution."

Du Picq was most expressive on man's being more important than machines in warfare and that generals who understood that principle had the best chance of success. Warfare, therefore, had not changed through the ages, despite technological advances. Discipline had always been important to make a higher percentage of troops actually engage the enemy. (See du Picq cards 7, 8, 10, 16, 20, and 24, inset on pages 74 and 75.)

While Patton faithfully quoted du Picq on the note cards, many of the notes were more reflective of his own thoughts on reading du Picq. A typical example is his note 50, on drills, which should be compared with one of Patton's later lectures on the subject. (See margin copy on page 78.) In the same vein, Patton might have derived from du Picq many of his thoughts about men who would not fight; his note 92 reads: "Place officers . . . behind the charging line to shoot men who skulk." He dwelt on the subject in notes 81 and 129 and in his later lecture "Why Men Fight." (See margin copy on this page.) In the mid-1920s the Patton mind, inspired by du Picq, was set against skulkers; years later when he would search World War II hospitals for malingerers, as betrayers of their comrades who fought bravely, du Picq would still be his inspiration.

Patton also made extensive notes on du Picq's comments on the use of cavalry. But even those led back to the human factor. He improved on du Picq's "The essential factor is determination" by writing on the next card that the success of a cavalry charge was determined by "R cube—R being RESOLUTION." In the 1980s, American historians such as Barbara W. Tuchman would write that resolution is the first quality needed by a successful American general.

The lectures and papers Patton produced in the mid-1920s did not draw extensively from the technical information on his note cards. Rather, they reflected his reading about the human factor in warfare, starting with his November 1925 lecture at Schofield Barracks "On Leadership." (BPP I 789.) He first established that the foremost trait of the leader is a "superiority complex." He added that habit should induce a sense of responsibility so strong that it would be "impossible for him to fail to discharge his trust." Patton's leader must also have "personality," made up of "charm, reserve, tact, consideration and aggressiveness in combat," all producing an "aura of authority." The "command personality" is a better "rider, shot, scout, cook, etc., than any of his men" and has "the ability to make quick and sound tactical decisions." Above all, Patton's leader must be able to conquer fear (see margin copy on page 73), for "courage, as in the day of our neolithic ancestors, is the greatest and most prized of virtues; lacking it, a shoulder full of stars is impotent to make a leader." With the possible exception of "tact," Patton had fairly accurately described the traits for which he would become famous in World War II.

Patton linked his thoughts on leadership with his earlier beliefs in the transcendent warrior's soul in his March 1926 lecture "The Secret of Victory." He raised the question of what made the Great Captains of history victorious, and then he belittled the writers who had attributed it to "the result of mathematical calculation and metaphysical erudition" or to knowledge they never had and plans they never made. "Disregarding the personality of Frederick [the Great] we attribute his victories to a tactical expedient, the oblique order of battle. . . . Yet the history of war is the history of warriors; few in number, mighty in influence. Alexander, not Macedonia conquered the world. Scipio, not Rome destroyed Carthage. Marlborough, not the allies defeated France. Cromwell, not the roundheads dethroned Charles. . . . "

Patton went on to assure his audience that professional study is important: "We require and must demand all possible thoughtful preparation and studious effort possible. . . . Our purpose is not to discourage such preparation but simply to call attention to certain defects

Patton on the Warrior Soul (From his 1926 lecture "The Secret of Victory")

"War is conflict, fighting an elemental exposition of the age-old effort to survive. It is the cold glitter of the attacker's eye, not the point of the questing bayonet, that breaks the line. It is the fierce determination of the driver to close with the enemy, not the mechanical perfection of a Mark VIII tank that conquers the trench. It is the cataclysmic ecstasy of conflict in the flier not the perfection of his machine gun which drops the enemy in flaming ruin. . . .

"In war tomorrow we shall be dealing with men subject to the same emotions as were the soldiers of Alexander; with men but little changed . . . from the starving shoeless Frenchmen of 1796. With men similar save in their arms to those who the inspiring powers of a Greek or a Corsican changed at a breath to bands of heroes all enduring and all capable. . . ."

—Patton Collection, USMA Library

in its pursuit. . . . In acquiring erudition we must live *on* not *in* our stud-ies. We must guard against becoming so engrossed in the specific nature of the roots and bark of the trees of knowledge as to miss the meaning and grandeur of the forests they compose. . . . "

Patton then announced his theme: "The secret of victory lies not wholly in knowledge. It lurks invisible in that vitalizing spark, intangi-ble, yet evident as lightning—the warrior soul." He described the war-rior soul with examples from history and from his own imagination. (See margin copy on page 77.) Following a discussion of the importance of a leader's loyalty to his men, he advised his officers to model them-selves in his image: "A man of diffident manner will never inspire con-fidence. A cold reserve cannot beget enthusiasm. . . . There must be an outward and visible sign of the inward and spiritual grace. It then appears that the leader must be an actor and he certainly must be. But . . . he is unconvincing unless he lives his part."

He closed with his basic message: "The fixed determination to acquire the warrior soul and having acquired it to conquer or perish with honor is the secret of victory."

Patton's October 1927 lecture, "Why Men Fight," began by listing the motivations that had gotten primitive man to fight: "hunger; sex and its simpler derivatives; unity of action, due to unity of impulses; biologically produced leaders; greed; the need for protection; ambition; romance; monotony and HABIT." He poked fun at the code of chivalry of the Middle Ages: "Truly the knightly belt and golden spurs with the aura attaching to them have never been surpassed as a means of raising man above himself to deeds of selfless heroism. But we must not forget that broidered belt and gilded iron were but as worthless dross save when the eyes of lovely demoiselles flashed on those tinsled gauds, the glory of their age-old blandishments. And medals of today derive their potency from just that source—sex."

Pointing out that "men were abundant who could take a day off to storm a cave, but were less numerous who could take a year off to cap-ture a city," Patton traced the rise of standing armies and the drills needed to habituate them to the exigencies of battle. He doubted, how-ever, that such drills were needed for men to fight well in modern armies. (See margin copy on this page.)

He then addressed the variety of measures needed "to keep man to his gruesome task in the terrible presence of death, and prevent him, particularly in his early experiences, from yielding to panic which ever hovers menacing about the best of troops." He cited first the "mental torture" that should be directed toward the pride of the soldier who fails in his duty. "Unfortunately, undue consideration for individuals, fear of estranging potential voters, and a silly censorship prevented the people at home from ever knowing whom to honor and whom to blame. Few units would have failed to reach their objectives had their members been sure that next morning the girls at home would have known. . . . It is interesting to recall that during the Russo–Japanese War a Japanese regiment which failed at 303 Meter Hill, if our memory serves us, was degraded, formed into a labor unit and the facts promptly published."

Patton demonstrated a similar frame of mind when he discussed the need for harsh punishments for soldiers who desert, skulk, or otherwise evade their duties and obligations. "Why Men Fight" foretold the philosophy that in World War II would lead to his purposefully slapping two soldiers hospitalized with possible battle fatigue.

The lecture also addressed the need for appeals to "National Patriotism," although Patton warned that the lack of "racial homogeneity" in American society often worked against this. He suggested that the appeal to patriotism would be improved, especially in case of invasion, "if pacifist moves were treated with less tolerance. The prompt shooting of some scores of conscientious objectors would go far towards removing bellicose inhibitions."

Moving to positive incentives to make men fight, Patton discussed at length the importance of awarding medals, and criticized the Army's medals program in the Great War: "Fearful that one unworthy might be decorated, we examined, hesitated and hectored our heroes, utterly forgetful of the fact that a coward dressed as a brave man will change from his cowardice and, in nine cases out of ten, will on the next occasion demonstrate the qualities fortuitously emblazoned on his chest. . . . We must have more decorations and we must give them with no niggard hand." During World War II, Patton carried a cache of medals with him and awarded them on the spot, telling his aides to follow up with necessary paperwork.

Patton closed the lecture by returning to his theme on the importance of leadership in getting men to fight. He suggested that American society could always have a large number of trained officers "by increasing greatly the number of graduates from the Military Academy and discharging the surplus after a year's service with troops. . . . " He recommended the same for graduates of the Reserve Officers' Training Corps colleges, such as the Virginia Military Institute and the Citadel. But he opposed the wartime practice of taking young men with exceptional educational backgrounds but insufficient military training and commissioning them lieutenants. Rather, officer commissions should be given to combat-experienced soldiers who show special bravery and competence. (See margin copy on this page.)

Buried within Patton's thirty-page speech "Why Men Fight" was this story of a soldier who on being called before his captain for fighting a comrade excused himself by saying: "Well, sir, it was this way. I was

---

Patton on Wartime Commissioning of Officers (From his 1927 Lecture "Why Men Fight")

"We must commission only brave and energetic men. As the only means of carrying out this notion, it is submitted that there be no training camps, that all commissions after the first battle go to soldiers of proven combat ability, and that all replacements be in the grade of private. In making this assertion it is evident that we are abandoning our thesis as to the advantages derivable from hereditary class distinctions. Such is exactly the case. It is futile to consider conditions which for us cannot exist. What we must do is to go back a thousand years or so and reconstitute in our armies the aristocracy of valor in which all aristocracy originated.

"Men commissioned and promoted in accordance with this plan will have as a start the aura of proven courage; they will have further the prestige of battle experience. Promotion so gained will arouse in them pride and a sense of obligation to be worthy of the honors conferred. Finally we will develop a hierarchy of courage and infinite solidarity since the junior will owe to himself his ability and to his superior its recognition; for, captured objectives, not mildewed diplomas, will mark the road to preferment. If confirmation for these remarks is necessary, it exists in two statements made by the master of war, Napoleon. 'Better,' he said, 'an army of stags led by a lion than an army of lions led by a stag.' And again, 'Every French soldier carries in his knapsack the baton of a Marshall of France.' "

—Patton Collection, USMA Library

cleaning the latrine and this guy comes by and says to me 'What are you going to tell your children when they ask you what you did in the great war?' So I hit him." A generation later Patton would use a similar story, elaborating on the joylessness of shoveling horse dung in Louisiana, to inspire his Third Army soldiers to fight their way across Europe.

CHAPTER SEVEN

The Balancing Act— Horses and Tanks 1928–1931

I N EARLY 1928, Major Patton learned that his next assignment
would return him to Washington for duty in the Office of the Chief
of Cavalry, at the time headed by Major General Herbert B. Crosby.
Patton's experience in mechanization would serve him well, Crosby
wrote, implying that Patton's wartime tanker voice would help ward
off the critics of horse cavalry. That probably stirred Patton to turn his
mind to a favorite theme that might be useful in Washington: the future
of warfare.

During his last few months in Hawaii, Patton prepared a long paper
misnamed "Drills for Fighting," which in fact was his vision of future
combat. He forecast that the next war would be waged by mass armies
rather than small professional ones. The United States would need to
adjust. Patton called for increasing the killing power of American units
by augmenting firepower while reducing manpower, thus improving
maneuverability. In the process he suggested eliminating headquarters,
integrating arms at lower levels, concentrating tanks in special units,
and putting aviation in direct support of moving ground units—all of
which foretold the Army reorganization that would take place on the
eve of World War II and the manner in which Patton would shape his
armored forces in that war.

Patton next focused on the balancing act between tanks and horses
that he would have to carry off in Washington, and he expressed some
of this in a lecture delivered at Schofield Barracks just before he departed Hawaii. Entitled "Tanks Past and Future," the lecture began with an

historical recounting of the forerunners of the tank, from the Trojan horse to unfinished notes by Leonardo da Vinci. Citing the British and American World War I experience, he advocated that in tank-infantry attacks the tanks should follow the infantry in the initial phases, and then pass through to lead the assault on machine guns and pillboxes; that would become standard procedure in World War II. (BPP I 836.) His lecture then forecast a negative future, saying he doubted the American army would ever have enough dependable tanks to support a new kind of warfare. He criticized the mindset of "the whole military profession" as too unimaginative to create a new concept of warfare, and he predicted the next conflict would revert to trench warfare, with only a limited role for tanks.

Patton left Hawaii with this efficiency report endorsement from his commanding officer, Major General Fox Conner: "I have known him for fifteen years, in both peace and war. I know of no one whom I would prefer as a subordinate officer." He also left with a personal and professional library of 321 books, most of them heavily annotated. One was signed "Georgie from Fox" and seemed appropriate for their years of discussions about military affairs—*The Indecisiveness of War: And Other Essays* by J. Holland Rose.

For his work in the Cavalry office, Patton drew on his library and on a long paper he had drafted much earlier, "A Study of the Combat of Cavalry up to and Including the World War." Beginning with descriptions of cavalry units in ancient armies, the typed version ran 249 single-spaced pages; excerpts would appear in many of his articles and speeches in the coming years.

Patton's cavalry library included manuals prepared at the Mounted Service School at Fort Riley, Kansas, such as the 1909 *The Army Horse in Accident and Disease* and the 1910 *Notes on Equitation and Horse Training*. Also included were Frank Gordon Churchill's 1912 *Practical and Scientific Horseshoeing*, Antoine de Brack's 1893 English version of *Cavalry Outpost Duties*, the 1917 American *Manual of Pack Transportation*, and even *The Manual of Equitation for the French Army, 1912*. Patton's copy of M. von Poseck's *The German Cavalry: 1914 in Belgium and France* had survived the ship's fire and was rebound in Hawaii. That is where Patton had bound *Employment of Cavalry*, the typescript version of Training Regulations 425–105 of the U.S. Chief of Cavalry; Patton's editing appears on every page.

While in Hawaii, he heavily annotated *Letters on Cavalry*, written in 1911 by Prinz Kraft zu Hohenlohe-Ingelfingen; at the end, Patton wrote, "All the principles here in seem sound to me. GSP Feb 17 1927." He also acquired Count Gustav Wrangel's *The Cavalry in the Russo–Japanese War*, which had been translated and published in London in 1907. During that period he also studied General Sir Evelyn Wood's 1897 *Achieve-*

ments of Cavalry, and he underlined this thought: "Let us not forget that in the employment of cavalry on a battlefield, the characteristics and skill of the leader are more important than either numbers or training, but the necessary aptitude is seldom found in man, and is always capable of improvement by study." (39)

Patton, who devoted much of his life to the cavalry and cared greatly for horses, is shown here on horseback. Date and location unknown. (Photo courtesy of the Patton Museum.)

While in Washington, Patton kept his cavalry library up to date, adding *Cavalry Training* from the British War Office in 1929 and the *Cavalry Journal*'s new *Basic Cavalry Manual* in 1930. Aunt Nannie later sent him Major General J.E.B. Seeley's memoirs, simply entitled *Adventure;* Patton annotated heavily the British general's descriptions of the use of cavalry in the 1916 Battle of the Somme, finding interest in the suvivability of the horse on the World War I battlefield.

Patton's first writing exercises for the Chief of Cavalry grew out of his duties as a member of a board of officers chosen to determine the suitability of the Christie caterpillar chassis for a mechanized cavalry vehicle. Patton had worked with Walter Christie just after the Great War, when the inventor's unique suspension and drive system gave

hope for the first truly American tank. In 1928, Secretary of War Dwight
F. Davis directed that an armored force be created at Camp Meade. The
Cavalry branch, mindful of its strictures prohibiting tanks, responded
by designing armored cars that could have tracks and carry guns but,
with less armor protection than tanks, would still move fast enough to
carry out cavalry missions. Secretary Davis approved their proposal to
obtain a Christie chassis and equip it as an armored car.

Patton wrote about the advantages and disadvantages of such vehicles and about their possible missions, such as conducting raids, adding
firepower and shock to maneuvering horse units, covering with-
drawals, and constituting powerful mobile reserve forces. In "Tactical
Employment of Armored Cars, Experimental," Patton wrote of the
necessity for the vehicles' having complete liberty of action, moving by
bounds, and conducting fire fights at close range. He warned against
making the armored cars too big and too heavy; he cautioned against
arming crewmen with individual weapons, which would tempt them to
fight like infantrymen. He then turned to designing the organization of
a mechanized cavalry regiment, in which armored cars would operate
with horse cavalry units.

In his next paper, "Cavalry in the Next War," Patton extolled the
value of the horse in terrain where roads barely existed, such as Mexico.
Not only could horses be used in reconnaissance, raids, and resupply,
he wrote, but in getting into the enemy's rear and launching the mounted charge. He related his experiences with tanks in World War I, ran
through a list of their limitations, and denounced their lack of depend-
ability in battle. Those shortcomings were so great that he felt that cavalry could make war on mechanized forces by attacking only at night,
destroying fuel supplies and bridges, and giving them no rest. In a 1929
conference on the impact of mechanization on cavalry, he elaborated his
view about the weaknesses of mechanized forces, to include the
inevitable congestion of deteriorating roads, the impossibility of high-
speed cross-country movement, the dependence on large volumes of
critical supplies such as fuel and ammunition, and the great difficulties
in command and control of dispersed moving forces.

In August 1929, the *Washington Post* printed a picture of Patton
standing in front of a tank in France, but he offered the view that the
tank and motor vehicle would not supplant all animals in a nation of
twenty-one million horses and four million mules. He later offered the
observation that horses require no experimental or developmental
costs, and that horses for a four-man patrol cost $600, but a tank for the
same purpose might cost $15,000. (BPP I 859.)

In his next paper, "The Value of Cavalry," Patton explained the
importance of cavalry by citing the testimony of experts such as
Pershing, Harbord, Summerall, Liggett, Parker, Haig, Allenby, French,

Patton and his family were excellent and enthusiastic riders. Left to right: son George, wife Beatrice, daughter Ruth Ellen, daughter Beatrice, and Patton. (Photo courtesy of the Patton Museum and originally taken by E. Morgan Savage of Boston.)

Foch, Petain, Weygand, von Hindenburg, Ludendorff, von Kluck, von Seeckt, and others. He then attacked the British visionaries of armored warfare who were denigrating the usefulness of cavalry (see margin copy on this page), and he listed the limitations of mechanical forces in future warfare. He noted that the cavalry was already augmenting its firepower with more automatic weapons and armored cars and that it soon expected to have tracked armored cars that would form strong mobile maneuver forces. He concluded, "The limitation inherent in . . . vehicles, such as their [in]ability to operate at night, to live off the country, or to penetrate woods and mountains indubitably stamp them as auxiliaries and not as supplanters of Cavalry. The individual mobility of cavalry and its universal adaptability are unaltered."

In October 1929, Patton was detailed to Fort Bliss, Texas, to umpire the 1st Cavalry Division maneuvers. His final critique disconcerted his audience by equating the attacking Brown forces with the Etruscans and the White forces with the defending Romans. He told of the Etruscans' crossing the Apennines into the Po valley in the 6th century B.C. He had been reading David Randall-MacIver's *The Etruscans*, published in 1927. The substance of his written reports, however, dealt with his increasing concern about command and control of mobile and dispersed units. He reflected views that foretold how he would control armored forces in World War II in ways vastly different from his experience in World War I. He wrote to Major General Crosby, "So far as I can

Patton on Cavalry's British Critics (From "The Value of Cavalry," 1929)

"There is not a single known statement of any soldier of combat reputation which is derogatory to Cavalry. Surely the remarks of Colonel J.F.C. Fuller (British Army) who during the course of four years' war replete with opportunities attained only the rank of Lieutenant-Colonel, the opinions of such a hack-writer as Captain Lyle [Liddell] Hart seem puerile when compared with the forceful statements of the elite of the military world. Despite this fact the effects of often repeated misstatements and halftruths are so far reaching and so readily swallowed by a gullible and motor minded public that a critical examination of the value of cavalry as compared with or modified by so-called scientific arms is necessary in order to reach a definite conclusion."

—From the Patton Collection, Library of Congress

see control and mobility are inimical. We should admit this and . . . let the two principal elements work independently. . . . " Later he reported, "There was much comment by all observers upon the lack of control in action. . . . As a matter of fact, in war we shall have much less control than at maneuvers. The sooner we accommodate ourselves to this fact and arrange our methods of war so that they will function despite lack of information, the better we'll be off.

"Due to the ill-advised attempt to make World War conditions of static combat applicable to cavalry, staff command [empowering staff officers to give orders and demand reports from subordinate commanders] was overstressed. . . . Much time was wasted. The essence of cavalry combat as has been demonstrated by all successful cavalrymen, of whom there are a very limited number, depends upon spontaneous cavalry leadership. Attempts to smother and delegate authority and

The Patton Family at Fort Myer, Virginia, in 1929. Left to right: wife Beatrice, Patton, daughter Beatrice, and daughter Ruth Ellen. Son George is kneeling in front of his father. (Photo courtesy of the Patton Museum.)

staff command is fatal." (BPP I 866.) In those last two sentences, Patton was drawing not on his Great War experience, but on his professional reading about the command of cavalry forces, which he later would apply to large mechanized formations.

For the next year, Patton continued to perform his balancing act between horses and mechanization. A lecture at the Pennsylvania National Guard convention: "An unfed motor stops; a starved horse takes days to die." A speech to the American Remount Association: "The horse is not useless; neither is the machine. What is wanted is better types of both run by men who know their powers and limitations and who instead of decrying each others capacities aid one another." A rebuttal to a study recommending six U.S. tank divisions: "The expenditure of twenty seven million [dollars] on lightweight .50 caliber machine guns would probably do much more toward the winning of the next war than will the expenditure of two hundred and seventy million on tanks." A "Mechanization and Cavalry" paper that appeared in the June 1930 *Infantry Journal*: "The fighting machine is here to stay, and if our cavalry has not lost its traditional alertness and adaptibility, we will frankly accept it at its true worth. If the 14th Century Knight could adapt himself to gunpowder, we should have no fear of oil, grease, and motors." A lecture on "Modern Cavalry" at the Marine Corps School: "In closing let me say that the greatest ill-luck I can wish those who think cavalry is dead, is to be against us in the next war. They will be the corpses, not we." (BPP I 872–880.)

Patton also carried his message in private conversations—to Secretary of State Henry L. Stimson, who rode Patton horses stabled in northwest Washington; to ex-Vice President Charles G. Dawes, who was invited to the Polo Ball in 1931; and, through his travels on the polo circuit, to numerous other men of substance and power. That he played his balancing act well was signaled by General Crosby's March 1930 efficiency report on Patton: "While an outstanding horseman he is also outstanding as an authority on mechanization due to his varied experience in France with the Tank Corps and to his continued interest in and study of the subject of mechanization."

Patton's prediction that tank divisions were but dreams for the far-distant future proved prophetic. Although Chief of Staff General Charles P. Summerall had established a multibranch mechanized force at Fort Eustis, Virginia, his successor, Douglas MacArthur, abolished it within a year; the Army budget had been slashed in the wake of the Depression, and no funds were available to sustain special forces. MacArthur ordered that each branch do what it could to mechanize further with its own resources. In 1933, after Patton had left the Cavalry Office, the experimental 1st Cavalry Regiment became mechanized at Fort Knox, Kentucky, where Colonel Daniel Van Voorhis and Lieutenant

The Argentine Polo Cup being presented to four members of the winning team. U.S. War Department polo teammates in the 1931 tournament included (left to right) Major John Eager, Lieutenant Gordon B. Rogers, Major Patton, and Major Jacob L. Devers. (Photo courtesy of the Patton Museum.)

Colonel Adna R. Chaffee, not Patton, began to provide direction to the growth of American armored forces.

As he went through his balancing act, Patton expanded his cavalry library to include mechanization. He acquired Major Basil Dening's *The Future of the British Army* and reviewed it for the *Cavalry Journal*. The book contributed to his thoughts about congestion in mechanized warfare; he noted on page 34, "movement difficult due to numbers and consequent lack of mobility." He partially read Lieutenant Colonel Giffard Martel's *The First Fifteen Years of Mechanization in the British Army* and Colonel H. Rowan-Robinson's *Some Aspects of Mechanization*. He reviewed Captain B. H. Liddell Hart's *The Remaking of Modern Armies* for the *Cavalry Journal* and doubted the author's claims about the effectiveness of air power.

He continued to acquire books on the modernization of warfare, such as *The Warfare of Today*, a series of lectures presented by French Lieutenant Colonel Paul Azan. In 1929 he heavily annotated J.F.C. Fuller's *The Foundations of the Science of War*; when Fuller predicted the discovery of a new weapon "that cannot be resisted," Patton wrote, "Bull," barely fifteen years short of the first atomic bomb explosion.

In the late twenties Patton expanded his Napoleonic collection. Louis St. Denis' *Napoleon From the Tuileries to St. Helena*, a gift from Aunt Nannie, was added, as were Louis Cohen's two-volume *Napoleon Anecdotes* and G. C. D'Aguilar's translation of General Burnod's

Napoleon's Maxims of War. Patton underlined much of Emil Ludwig's 1926 *Napoleon,* and on page 63 he wrote "ruthless" and on page 377 "thinks he is a thinker." Patton did not annotate two books he acquired in 1928: Maurice Barrès' *Memoirs of a Napoleonic Officer* and Herbert Sargent's *The Campaign of Marengo.* But when Sir Charles Oman's *Studies in the Napoleonic Wars* appeared in 1930, he found reason to comment frequently, such as: "History is the study of a few; the people serve for scenery." (26); "*Personality of one man!*" (28); and "Someone must run the show. The strongest will, whether he be politician or soldier." (36)

While assigned to the Chief of Cavalry, Patton kept up his reading in military biography. The books he read on Americans included *Lincoln or Lee* by William E. Dodd, *The Services of Supply: A Memoir of the Great War* by General Johnson Hagood, and *The Generalship of Ulysses S. Grant* by J.F.C. Fuller. His many marginal notes in the Fuller book foreshadowed the Patton persona of World War II: "Grant's flare for war"; "willing to fight"; "mislead the enemy"; "guts"; "rear attack"; "will to fight"; "act as you can, but *act*"; "strength of will"; "tenacity"; "superiority complex"; and "He was willing to take chances." On page 121 Patton wrote "the true art" next to Fuller's discussion of Grant's ability to hold the enemy's front while striking his rear simultaneously. And he made a special note near a footnote on page 108 about the wisdom of a commander's mentally cutting estimates of enemy strength in half to get to the truth rather than be overawed.

Other military biographies acquired by Patton in the late twenties were: *Julius Caesar and the Grandeur That Was Rome* by Victor Thaddeus; the *Diary of Frederick Mackenzie,* an officer in the Royal Welch Fusiliers in the American Revolution; *Xenophon* by L. V. Jacks; *A Greater Than Napoleon, Scipio Africanus* by B. H. Liddell Hart; *Great Captains Unveiled,* also by Liddell Hart; *Caesar's Conquest of Gaul,* translated by T. Rice Holmes; *Charlemagne* by Charles Russell; *Turenne* by General Max Weygand; and *Soldier, Artist, Sportsman: The Life of General Lord Rawlinson of Trent* by Sir Frederick Maurice, which Patton reviewed for the *Cavalry Journal.*

Patton's notes from 1928 in *McClellan's Own Story* reflected his belief that General George McClellan failed because he always "took counsel of his fears." Patton noted the same theme earlier that year by writing "Fear of THEY" (fear of the unknown enemy) in a discussion of General Nathaniel Banks on page 149 of Allen Tate's *Stonewall Jackson: The Good Soldier.* In 1930 he heavily annotated his all-time favorite, G.F.R. Henderson's *Stonewall Jackson and the American Civil War,* in which he wrote on page 497 of Volume II, "Papa read me this book first when I was about 12," thus explaining why he wrote "1899" on the flyleaf; another note indicates he reread Henderson's *Jackson* in 1935.

Nor did he ignore the Germans in the twenties. He acquired F. W. Longman's *Frederick the Great and the Seven Years' War* in 1926 and used it to express several favorite themes. When the author observed that Frederick's predecessor had a reputation that nothing would induce him to go to war, and therefore his battalions were ignored in statecraft, Patton wrote in the margin "U.S. too," reflecting his disdain for pacifistic politicians. When the author criticized Frederick, however, "because his habitual severity in cases of failure paralysed the wits of officers, and made them court disaster by literal obedience to his orders," Patton wrote in the margin "Too much Command."

On April 3, 1928, just before he sailed from Hawaii, Patton typed note cards on "Armies of Today," a paper by General Hans von Seeckt, who had retired as Commander-in-Chief of the postwar German army in 1926 and was considered the father of German army mechanization. Von Seeckt's message coincided with Patton's: A new weapon may give advantage to the offense, but in time the defense defeats it. Air war expands the battlefield but does not change it. The next war will start with an air exchange, followed by a struggle between small professional armies, followed by fighting between mass armies. The victor in the first phases has opportunity to prevent the enemy from using its masses. Essential to the professional army are great mobility from numerous and efficient cavalry, mechanized, and motorized units with rapid replacement of men and weapons.

During Christmas 1930, Patton read von Seeckt's *Thoughts of a Soldier*, published that year in English in Britain. As he had researched Erich von Ludendorff's memoirs in the early 1920s for the German method of organizing wartime staffs, he now mined von Seeckt's memoirs in the same way. (See inset on page 91.) When von Seeckt said on page 116 that the commander "must leave the wearisome daily routine to the Chief of Staff in order to keep his own mind fresh and free for the great decisions," Patton wrote *"Bull."* When von Seeckt wrote that the chief of staff must resign if he disagrees with his commander on an important decision, Patton registered his approval by underlining in red. (117) Patton finally expressed his exasperation with the German concept of a commander-chief of staff team by writing "Why is a Chief of Staff necessary?" In World War II, Patton would empower his two chiefs of staff, Generals Hobart Gay and Hugh Gaffey, to issue orders in his name, much in the German way. Both would keep diaries that illuminate Patton's masterful use of his staffs to accomplish military miracles on short notice.

Patton wrote in red pencil on the last page of von Seeckt's book, "One of the very best books on war I have ever read." Patton underlined much from this passage on page 123, as if it was written by a kindred soul: "The essential thing is action. Action has three stages: the

Patton Annotations: reactions to von Seeckt's *Thoughts of a Soldier*

74   THOUGHTS OF A SOLDIER

in discharge of duty, every man may be faced, outside his profession, with the necessity for the last great sacrifice, as an ethical duty ; but in no other profession do killing and its corollary, readiness to die, form the essence of professional duty. If the true art of war lies in destroying the enemy, then its exponent must also be prepared to be destroyed himself. This conception of the soldier's function justifies us in speaking of soldiering as something unique. It is the responsibility for life and death which gives the soldier his special character, his gravity, and self-consciousness—not only the responsibility for his own life, which may be sacrificed, not light-heartedly but from a feeling of duty, but the simultaneous responsibility for the lives of comrades and, in the end, for the life of the enemy, whose death is not an act of independent free will on the part of the killer, but an acknowledgment of professional duty. The feeling of responsibility for oneself and others is one of the most vital characteristics of the soldier's life. Responsibility towards oneself demands the most exacting inward and outward training for the military profession, so that the final sacrifice may not be made in vain. Responsibility for others leads us to the next and no less important demand made on the soldier.

The soldier's field of activity is man, who controls science, technics and material. The army is a combination of many men with the same serious aim. This gives the soldier's profession a quite peculiar bond of unity, a corporate sense which we call

[Patton margin annotation: "killing"]

THE CHIEF OF THE GENERAL STAFF   119

training of all, especially of the older officers, to the very limit of their capacity and therewith of their right to remain in their positions. Then we shall secure the correct mixture of the two great components of successful leadership : experience and youth.

[Patton handwritten annotation:] This seems to boil down to the pernicious doctrine that the C.G. is the front end the C of S the brains. I think that this is very bad. The staff system as practiced tends to dressing by committees and induces lack of force. Why is a Chief of Staff necessary? If used he should be chosen by not for the commander.

THE ESSENTIAL THING

THE essential thing is action. Action has three stages : the decision born of thought, the order or preparation for execution, and the execution itself. All three stages are governed by the will. The will is rooted in character, and for the man of action character is of more critical importance than intellect. Intellect without will is worthless, will without intellect is dangerous.

I shall endeavour to trace the evolution of action from its components in all three stages. Comparisons between the soldier, whom I select as the type of person whose business is action, and others on whom action is incumbent, will readily present themselves. The soldier, then, as a typical man of action, must be equipped with the knowledge and education necessary for the accomplishment of his task. It is good but not necessary that he should have had time in the course of his professional studies to prepare himself for the great moment of his life—the moment of action. The value of the knowledge acquired by study must not be over-estimated. The soldier faced with the necessity for independent decision must not mentally search the pages of his professional encyclopædia nor seek to remember how the great generals of history, from Alexander to

[Patton margin annotation: "Action ="]

[Patton handwritten annotation:] Knowledge to be of value must be spontaneous not the result of memory.

---

130   THOUGHTS OF A SOLDIER

be described here. One evening before a battle I was taking steps to discover whether our order had reached all the quarters concerned, and I received the brief answer in an honest Berlin accent, " Ick greife an."* He had understood, and that was the essential thing.

     * *Ick greife an*, I attack.

[Patton handwritten annotation:] One of the very best books on war I have ever read. x GSP Dec 28 '30

decision born of thought, the order or preparation for execution, and the execution itself. All three stages are governed by the will. The will is rooted in character, and for the man of action character is of more critical importance than intellect. Intellect without will is worthless, will without intellect is dangerous."

Patton's Christmas reading in 1930 also included Lieutenant Ernst Junger's stirring account of his combat action with the 73rd Hanoverian Fusilier Regiment in World War I, translated as *Storm of Steel* in 1929. Patton wrote at the end of the book, "A fine account of a fighting man with none of the usual moral bunk to detract from its stark manhood and grim virtue." That was a gibe at the introduction by Englishman R. H. Mottram, who found Junger childish, his violence rewarded by defeat. Mottram wrote, "He was nearly as good a specimen as ever worshiped Mars, and to what end did he come? To that inescapable doom that brings to meet violence precisely such resistance as shall cancel and annul it." (vii) "Bull," wrote Patton. "The men who won were just as violent else they would not have won—and more lucky." As with the Prussian generals, Patton felt a kinship with this lieutenant, particularly over his sense of duty. In the late 1930s Patton would require his son to read *Storm of Steel*.

Why was Patton so intent on reading anything in English by or about the Prussians, even during the busy times of his balancing act between the horse and the tank? His nephew Frederick Ayer, Jr., suggested two connections in *Before the Colors Fade*, published in 1964. He wrote that as a boy he received a photograph from Uncle George from Hawaii, with this note: "This is my war face which I have been practicing before a mirror all my life. I am going to use it again to scare hell out of the Germans." Ayer added that Uncle George felt strongly "that we had left things unbalanced by Versailles, that disarmament was dangerous and that certainly there would be another war. Sometimes he said it would be against the Japanese, sometimes against the Russians; but he was always sure it would come." (3)

Ayer reported a second connection between Patton and the German military philosophers of war. In September 1944, when Ayer was a lieutenant colonel in charge of Federal Bureau of Investigation personnel in the European theater in World War II, he visited Uncle George at Third Army headquarters in Nancy, France. He later reconstructed Patton's talk to staff members: "I have studied the German all my life. I have read the memoirs of his generals and political leaders. I have even read his philosophers and listened to his music. I have studied in detail the accounts of every damned one of his battles. I know exactly how he will react under any given set of circumstances. He hasn't the slightest idea what I'm going to do. Therefore, when the day comes, I'm going to whip hell out of him." (165)

CHAPTER EIGHT

Countdown to World War II 1931–1940

MAJOR PATTON'S new assignment in the summer of 1931 did not require him to give up his house at 3117 Woodland Drive in northwest Washington, D.C., because he was detailed as a student to the Army War College in the southeastern part of the city. For a year he would focus on strategy, national military policy, and the command of large military forces. The War College was also the Army's strategic planning center and maintained a library appropriate to that function. Patton's personal library continued to grow, and he mined all lectures, books, intelligence reports, and even foreign newspapers to fill his note cards and to write a series of papers that were distributed in the War Department.

While studying the first half of the course, Patton prepared a fifty-six-page paper entitled "The Probable Characteristics of the Next War and the Organization, Tactics, and Equipment Necessary to Meet Them." Although that had been a favorite theme of his in the past, much of the research was recent. For example, he started his historical background by differentiating armies based on quantity (masses of conscripted ill-trained men) from those based on quality (small forces of mobile, highly trained professionals). The idea was reflected in note cards on his reading of the 1923 edition of Charles Oman's *The Art of War in the Middle Ages*. (See Oman cards 3 and 4, inset on page 96.) Patton's preference for small, mobile, highly trained forces appeared in the extensive use of "professionals," "regulars," and "mobility."

His note cards of the 1931 period indicate he sought a better understanding of mass armies of the past. He returned to Friedrich von Bernhardi's *The War of the Future*—not the copy he had heavily annotated in 1921 but apparently a newer edition, perhaps from the War College library, with a different pagination and an updated text. (See two "Burnhardi" note cards inset on page 96.)

In his "Probable Characteristics" paper, Patton summarized why large conscript armies are occasionally advantageous: the sense of power and security they engender in the popular mind, the enthusiasm they arouse by having the entire population share the burden of war, the illusion of low costs of a truly national army, and the ability to fight on many fronts simultaneously.

On the other hand, he argued that small, professional forces could achieve quick and decisive victories, could better disperse in the face of coming air power, and could be armed with the latest complex weapons without bankrupting governments. Some of those ideas he derived from lecturers he heard at the War College and from his 1931 reading of Rear Admiral Bradley Fiske's *The Art of Fighting*. (See Patton note cards 4 and 5, inset on page 97, especially note 28 about Regular Army and Regular Navy.) He concluded that the next war would be fought by small, affordable professional armies, which would bring decisive results in a much shorter time than was required in the Great War. The commandant of the War College commended him for work of exceptional merit and forwarded the study to the War Department.

Patton had that paper in mind even before he entered the War College. His contacts with the intelligence community while he was serving in the War Department were cited in notes obviously used in the paper. Patton paraphrased an English translation from a German military gazette article on "The Next War" (see note card inset on page 97), and he reacted to writings by two French generals by writing that views on armies "oscillate between two poles: the nation in arms or the professional army." Patton's cards also included notes taken from his reading of R. M. Johnston's 1920 *First Reflections on the Campaign of 1918*, a short book of seventy-nine pages. The last chapter, "Our Army of the Future," called for a small army of professional soldiers of four to eight divisions, backed by a "million low power troops *immediately* available in an emergency." Johnston instructed Patton at Leavenworth, but his book was critical of the preparation of American officers for their work in France in the Great War.

Also affecting Patton's thinking about conscript versus professional armies was Brigadier General E. L. Spears' *Liaison, 1914: A Narrative of the Great Retreat*, which Patton dated "Christmas, 1931." On three note cards Patton cited quotations from Spears on the sources of the initial French defeats, such as: "faulty training of the troops and complete misapprehension on the part of the officers of the conditions of modern warfare. A CONSCRIPT ARMY WILL INVARIABLY BE INFERIOR IN THIS RESPECT TO A PROFESSIONAL ONE." Patton added, "(Our temporary officers [in World War I] were very defective due to lack of training and practice in command.) 298." Patton also heavily annotated portions of the book dealing with strategy; on page 36 he wrote, "In 1909 Col. Fiebeger taught at West Point that Germany would come through Belgium." Spears tracked British and French cavalry operations in the 1914 retreat, and on page 329 Patton wrote "Panic." He read about the German side of those operations in *The Advance From Mons, 1914* by Captain Walter Bloem of the 12th Brandenburg Grenadiers. He signed the book: "G.S.Patton Jr. Apr 11, 1932."

A paper filled with many of Patton's views on mechanized units circulated through the War Department in 1932. Produced by a student committee chaired by Patton, it defined mechanized forces as not only transported in vehicles but fighting from them, while motorized forces dismounted from their vehicles in order to fight separated from their vehicles; this became Army official usage a year later. The report reflected much of Patton's thinking at the time: mechanized forces should assist, not supplant, both infantry and cavalry; mechanized units should be developed by existing arms and be tested in combined arms maneuvers. In preparing that paper, Patton probably used his copy of the Leavenworth 1925 manual *Tactics and Technique of the Separate Branches*; its sections on the movement speeds of U.S. Army units were heavily annotated.

In the early thirties Patton distilled much of his thinking about war into eleven note cards entitled "Personal Ideas of G.S. Patton, Jr." Cards 1 and 2 reflected his devotion to maneuver, flank and rear attacks, and surprise. (See inset on page 97.) On card 6 his note 37 stated: " 'Prepare the pretext; the troops have marched.' Confessions of FtheG [Frederick the Great]. Masses make surprise impossible." Cards 10 and 11 cited new support for his beliefs in leaving initiative to subordinates, in using heavy punishments to maintain discipline, and in distrusting political leaders to do the right thing in military matters, whether they are revolutionaries or Woodrow Wilson. All those ideas would typify Patton's modus operandi during and after World War II.

Among the books Patton acquired in his War College years were Oliver Robinson's *Fundamentals of Military Strategy*, Henri Petain's *Verdun*, and Fred Shannon's two-volume *Organization and Administration of the Union Army*, which were barely annotated. But he lavished much attention on General John J. Pershing's two-volume *My Experiences in the World War*, in which Patton wrote extensive anecdotes of his arriving in London with Pershing from the *Baltic* in 1917, and then serving in the American Expeditionary Force headquarters in France. Patton noted how Pershing included him as aide-de-camp in his initial call on

Patton typed these note cards circa 1930 and 1931. The note cards on Charles Oman's *Art of War in the Middle Ages* show a preference for small professional armies over mass conscripted ones. "While war teaches fast, the best are always getting killed," wrote Patton on one of the note cards dealing with Friedrich von Bernhardi's *The War of the Future*, which Patton first read in 1921. Patton typed note cards on foreign military thought in 1931. "The Next War" offers a view that had appeared in a German military gazette. Its predictions did not all come true. Patton recorded his own views on eleven "Personal Ideas" note cards. Cards 1, 2, and 10 show his placing great importance on maneuverability, and his frequently repeated phrase that there can be "no Cannae without a Varro." The drawbacks to mass armies were reflected in Patton's note cards on Bradley Fiske's *The Art of Fighting*. (All cards come from the USMA Library.)

Oman 3.

14. VIKINGS 800-900 At beginning they were all volunteers ill armed. By 850 they were professionals and all armed and armored.To increase mobility they began ti steal horses for movement only.
   Their equipment and mobility made it hopeless to pursue them with general levies large, slow and ill armed

15. By 900 FEUDALISM began to evolve to meet the Vikings it consisted of small bands of professional mounted faiht whom the pesents supported in return for protection.

16. The local count with a few hundred men could easily defeat 10000 pes-nts.

17. CNUT established "HUSCARLS" 1054 A.D. they were a preminant professional group held in service when the men of the "BAN" were released after a war. 115.

18. 800-to 1000 Armor increased much in effectiveness and weight,qand cost.With its increase numbers decreased

Oman 4.

19. Last struggles of infantry marked by battles of HASTINGS-1066 and DYRRHACHIUM 1081.

20. Then cavalry became paramount but not numerous due to cost and complexity.

21. BYZANTINE ARMY- 580--1071. The old Roman type of arm finally disappeared in 580. The new army mostly professio cav which then came into being lasted with small change t till the end of the empite lo71.

22. This army was drilled ,disciplined equipped and trained to a high degree. P 172.

23. The professional soldier of the west was a good MAN AT ARMS. His counterpart in the east was just as good and in addition was a skilled tactician. 172.

24." STRATIGICON " The field service regulations of the time was compiled by MAURICE while he was a general under Emp. TIBERIUS II(I have it)

"THE WAR OF THE FUTURE" By Burnhardi. 1.

1. Cavalry was misunderstood it was wasted in being used as an offensive arm. 16.

2. In 1914 not enough men were called in Germany to merit the term nation in arms. 22.

3. The advent of huge masses incapable of rapid movement made it necessary to rest the flanks on natural obstacles length of front was also necessary to develop the combat strength of such masses. These circumsatnces induced the birth of "LINER STRATEGY"? 23.

4. Prior to 1914 the chief aim of a commander was to INVELOP . NOW lack of flanks make FRONTAL attacks necessary either to kill the enemy or else to make a hole and so develop artificial flanks.This has changed the aim of war. Now it consists in attempting to secretly mass a force capable of a surprise frontal attack to penetrate. 25

Burnhardi 3.

9. Masses not only affect tactics but still more vitally supply and hence Strategy.Till 1871 armies could live mostly off the country.Now they cant and the vast amount of rolling stock necessary to feed them demands a highly developed R and RR net and men to keep it up. 28.

10. The size of the theater needed by a mass makes it necessary to use RR and Trucks for all possible strategic moves.Thus alone can secrecy be maintained. 29.

11. Mass levies are bound to contain many men of inferior morals, war degenerates them still more and they are a focus of infection for average men. The training too is incomplete. Officers and NCO's are defective due to lack of the experience of command. 31

12. New officers only gradually reach the state of professionals for while war teaches fast the best are always getting killed.32

"THE NEXT WAR." Militar-Wochenblatt,25 July
1931-1

1. The war will start by surprise with out a declaration as Japan did in 1904. Chemicals from the air may be used.

2. War should be short and fast. War of movement is the ideal form.

3. Trench warfare may appear in some places.

4. Infantry will produce the decisions. The importance of artillery to pave the way for it grows.

5. Light artillery horse drawn, Medium tractor drawn.

6. The next war will demand not motorised but horse CAV.

7. Aviation has 3 missions, attack, reconnoissance, bombim

8. Inspite of treaties Gas will be used.

9. RR's still dominant transport, motors will increase.

PERSONAL IDEAS of G.S.PATTON,Jr.
(Probably most of them unintentional copies of forgotten books.)

1. Units are destroyed by attacking their flanks or rear. since masses cannot manuver they cannot make such attacks in a large theater they are susceptable to them.

2. Examples of flank attacks: CANNAE-ROOSBACH-LUTHEN-Chancerlorsville-Third Battle of GAZA.

3. Example of case where threat to flank weakened front so it could be pierced;CASTIGLIONE-BOUTZEN.

4. Lack of manuver fatal at:GETTYSBURG-FREDRICKSBURG-CAMBRAE-

5. WALL IS an inverted ditch. Wire an inverted mote.

6. No CANNAE with out a ~~VIRUS~~. Probably Gibbon.

VAUKO,

Patton-2.

7. Despite all the talk of surprise WE TO DAY seem bent on avaoding the use of it. We have identical armies, identical tactics, identical methods.
   The "AUDACITY about which Fredrick talked was possibly more useful due to surprise of its then novelty than to it other effects.

8. Cortez defeated a huge army of mexicans by the charge of 14 horsemen. WAS IT POWER OR SURPRISE.?? Surprise. Same is true with Tanks.

9. If we use same sort of armies . Same sort of Tactics Same sort of weapons,Where is surprise possible? The first nation to change restores surprise and will win.

10. Probably three types of armies. (1) Mob (2) Muscle and highly trained .(3) Mechanical. Small and of short duration.

Patton, 4.

18. Cost of pensions is so huge for large armies that it will destroy state.

19. Over-equipped armies loose mobility. Lecture Gen. Kallan, G-4.

20. The mechanization or motorization of large armies would strip industry of mechanics .(The cost would destroy the country) Sec. Payne.

21. Trucks and heavy busses useless save on special roads.

22. Too many weapons reduce mobility.

23. The initial use of large armies will be delayed due to lack of training and equipment. Gen. Macarthur.

24. Strategy can be modified to suit the intelligence and energy of the enemy. Fisk-Art of Fighting.

Patton 5.

Regular army used by THUTMOSE III 1450 B.C. Fisk.

26. If two untrained men fight there is not much skill shown. Fisk.

27. One trained man easily licks one untrained but is helpless against three. Apply same ideat to mass and professional armies.

28. Complexity of weapons amde the R.A. and the R.N. nece necessary. Fisk.

29. Those who speak of wars of material forget that the moral is to the physical as three is to one and also that MEN MAN MACHINES.

30. To get at the spiritual side of war we must go back the study of recent wars is still too gummed up with minute details and nomenclature.

Patton 10.

53. Automatic supply is inaplicabe beyond the regulating station in wars of movement.

54. Prior to 1914 FOCH rote that MOLTKE left complete initiative to his subbordinates.

55. Note the secrecy imposed in 600 A.D. by Maurice he did not let his units practice a complete manuver but only part at a time for fear the enemy would get onto it.

56. It is of interest to note that revolutions always undermine armies. In France in the revolution the Committee of Public Safety not only removed authority from offivers but also produced dishonesty in administration: "The administration of the army is overrun with brigands----They sell the rations of the horses-----. The 'Commisioners' of the army have become the worst of minopolisys." St.Just 1793.

the British king and in many subsequent conversations with Allied politicians and generals. Patton underlined or made sidelines at nearly every reference to Pershing's triumphant struggle with the Allies to have American troops committed to battle as an American army, not as fillers in the British and French armies. Patton seems merely to have scanned Volume II of the Pershing memoirs.

In July 1932, Patton returned to Fort Myer to assume the duties of executive officer of the 3rd Cavalry Regiment. Within weeks the regiment received orders to assist in dispersing some 20,000 Depression-ravaged war veterans who had marched to Washington to claim early payment on bonuses they were scheduled to receive in 1945. The 3rd Cavalry forces of some 200 troops and horses, along with those of the 16th Infantry, cleared Pennsylvania Avenue and the veterans' camps (flats in nearby Anacostia) by using tear gas and some rifle fire. The operation was successful from the standpoints of President Herbert Hoover, Secretary of War Patrick J. Hurley, and Army Chief of Staff Douglas MacArthur, all of whom, like Patton, believed that Communist agents had infiltrated the ranks of the bonus marchers and had threatened mob violence in the capital.

Later in 1932, Patton wrote "Federal Troops in Domestic Disturbances," a paper that drew heavily on S. C. Vestal's *The Maintenance of Peace*, a book he had begun reading in 1931. Patton started the paper with a history of domestic disturbances and then suggested proper soldier training for handling them. He cited the legions under Roman General Marius who put down the mobs unleashed by the Gracchus brothers—just as Vestal had cited them in his book. Patton wrote in the margins of the book: "the US Army is too small for foreign wars but is very useful at home," "good men must fight to maintain governments," and "might is right." (40, 92, 102.) "Domestic Disturbances" prescribed that tear gas should be backed up with vomiting gas and, should that fail, then to "open fire with one man per squad from a frontal attack while, at the same time, have men previously stationed in nearby buildings shoot into the rear ranks selecting apparent leaders. . . . If you must fire do a good job—a few casualties become martyrs, a large number an object lesson. . . ." (BPP I 900.)

Patton was equally bellicose in his Armistice Day speech in 1932 to the American Legion in Arlington, Virginia. "Disarmament is folly," he said. "Perpetual peace a futile dream. Yet . . . groups of internationally minded pacifists are constantly working to change Armistice Day into Disarmament Day. [They] are seeking to make us morally unworthy. . . . They hold to scorn the deeds of our fighting ancestors, of our dead comrades. They make a mock of courage, a joke of patriotism. This too we must combat or else contend with China for the prize as leading jellyfish of the world." (BPP I 904.)

While with the 3rd Cavalry, Patton kept abreast of reports on advances in military thinking in foreign armies. For example, he studied a May 1933 translation of Colonel Fabre de Faur's "Operative Reconnaissance in Future Wars," originally published in German in *Militar Wochenblatt*. In 1989, historian Steve E. Dietrich would link that study to Patton's World War II employment of "operational air reconnaissance up to 150 miles beyond the flanks of his own command and as far forward as practical, alerting him in advance of the danger of the German offensive of December, 1944." (Dietrich 409.)

Patton next read and heavily annotated what is probably the most celebrated book produced by Americans on tactics, *Infantry in Battle*, written at Fort Benning in the early 1930s under the direction of Deputy Commandant George C. Marshall. (See inset on page 100.) The book, a collection of vignettes from World War I, elicited comments from Patton, now a lieutenant colonel, such as "nothing is normal [in war]," "don't use complicated maneuvers," "don't move boundaries if you can help it," "don't criticize in front of men," and "execution is to plan as 5 is to 1." (1, 16, 20, 137, 146.) Patton's continuing interest in operational history would be demonstrated in 1936 by his purchasing G.J.R. Glunicke's *The Campaign in Bohemia, 1866* and Sisson Pratt's *Saarbruck to Paris, 1870*.

Military biography continued to be Patton's pleasure reading in the early 1930s. Beatrice gave him Arthur Weigall's *Alexander the Great*, and Patton agreed with the author that Alexander had a "fiery passion for personal glory and power." Nathan Ausubel offered him a new interpretation of *Superman: The Life of Frederick the Great*. He did not find Adolf Hitler's *My Battle* to his liking, for he stopped on page 38; he underlined, however, a reference to his hated politicians: "It is not the aim for our present-day Democracy to form an assemblage of wise men, but rather to collect together a crowd of subservient nonentities who can easily be led. . . . "

Patton dances with daughter Beatrice at her wedding to Lieutenant John K. Waters on June 27, 1934, in South Hamilton, Massachusetts. (Photo courtesy of the Patton Museum.)

Two biographies seized most of his reading attention in 1934—B. H. Liddell Hart's *Sherman* and Winston Churchill's four-volume *Marlborough*. He admired Sherman's army for its "living off the country." If 50,000 could do that in 1863, he asked, then why not in 1933? (200) In Volume III of *Marlborough* Churchill speaks against draining forces to regions where nothing decisive could be gained. Patton comments, "The above curious indeed in view of Churchill's action in the Dardanelles." (208)

Regardless of whether Patton's reading was in tactics, biography, or history, his annotations more often than not were framed in the ideas and vocabulary that today we associate with "leadership." Yet, he seemed strangely indifferent to books in his collection that were directed specifically toward that end. His copy of *Problems in Troop Leading*,

Patton Annotations: reactions to the U.S. Army Infantry School's *Infantry in Battle*

in the building where Division Headquarters was located before."

The advance guard and order of march were designated and a supplementary order was sent to the artillery.

The division commander marched with the advance guard. The maneuver was successful. Byzeziny was stormed and the staff of the VI Siberian Corps captured. The success of this action materially aided the remainder of the German forces in smashing through the hostile lines. The Russians becoming discouraged, withdrew, while the German units, taking along thousands of prisoners and much material, rejoined their main army.

From the German official account.

DISCUSSION

The Guards were in a situation as difficult and desperate as can be imagined. They had no information of the location of other German troops and no knowledge of the hostile dispositions, except that the enemy seemed to be everywhere in superior numbers. Their men were exhausted and their units depleted and intermingled. They were in a dense forest; it was bitterly cold, and night was falling.

Under such conditions a master effort could be made only by superior troops, commanded by determined leaders, working under a simple plan. The division commander took these considerations into account. His plan was based on the three essentials for a night operation: direction, control and surprise.

Troops became easily lost in a night march, particularly exhausted troops who are staggering forward in a daze. Things must be made as simple as possible for them. Accordingly the route that was prescribed facilitated the maintenance of direction. First, movement along the eastern edge of the wood to the north edge. From here Galkowek could be reached with little danger of the column getting lost. From Galkowek the march could continue straight to the north and be certain of intercepting the road which led directly to Byzeziny.

To insure the utmost control the division commander ordered that the advance be made in route column. It was no time for half measures. The men were completely exhausted, so much so that unless they were directly under the eyes of their leaders, they would

[32]

CHAPTER XI: COUNTERORDERS

Rapid changes in a situation necessitate changes in decisions. Counterorders will therefore be frequent and should be accepted as normal incidents of battle.

ONCE MADE, decisions should not be changed except for weighty reasons. Infantry commanders, however, are constantly confronted with changes in the situation that demand new schemes of maneuver and consequently new orders. With such kaleidoscopic suddenness does the situation veer and shift that it is not unusual for a subordinate unit to be ordered to initiate a certain line of action only to have the order countermanded before the action has gotten under way.

When counterorders do occur it becomes a paramount duty of all leaders to curb irritation and the instinctive tendency to criticize. Success in combat is certainly not rendered more likely by the muttered criticisms of junior officers—criticisms which rapidly and seriously affect the moral tone of the entire personnel.

Responsibility for changing a mission rests squarely with the commander. When the march of events has invalidated his original assignment he must of necessity take the new situation into account. Behind every counterorder there is usually a valid reason. If we are able to adopt the French proverb "To understand all is to forgive all" we shall meet changing orders with greater equanimity.

EXAMPLE I

The 2d Company 57th Infantry, part of the 14th Division, which in turn was part of the Second German Army, made a long march to the south on September 5, 1914, in pursuit of the retiring French. The 14th Division, on the right of the army, passed east of Montmirail.

The 2d Company crossed the Petit Morin and spent the night in a small village south of the river. At daylight, September 6, heavy cannonading was heard to the south. Instead of marching

[137]

CHAPTER XII: SUPERVISION

Leaders must verify the execution of their orders. The more untrained the troops, the more thorough and detailed this supervision should be.

A SUPERFICIAL reading of military text books is likely to convey the idea that the duties of a leader consist only of estimating the situation, reaching a decision, and issuing his order. It is evident, however, that, unless the orders of the commander are executed, even the most perfect plan will fail. On the other hand a poor plan, if loyally and energetically carried out by subordinate leaders, will often attain success.

A commander, then, must not only issue his order but see to its execution. It is the omission of this latter step that has caused many brilliant plans to go awry. Too often a leader assumes that once his plan is completed and his order issued, his responsibility for the action terminates. He seems to feel that he has discharged his obligation and that the execution remains entirely with his subordinates. Such an assumption is false even when dealing with veteran troops. Where poorly-trained troops are involved, the necessity for vigilance and supervision becomes even more imperative. Initiative must not be destroyed but the commander must nevertheless bear in mind the fact that the final credit or censure for the result of the action rests squarely with him. Consequently, he is not only justified, but is seriously delinquent, if he fails to carry out the supervision necessary to insure the proper execution.

The natural objection to the foregoing is that a leader cannot be everywhere at the same time. This is answered in that he must weigh the capabilities and limitations of his subordinates, determine the critical point, or time, of the action and lend the weight and authority of personal supervision where it is most needed.

EXAMPLE I

On the foggy morning of August 29, 1914, the 2d Guard Regiment of the German Army was just south of the Oise River. The

[146]

CONCLUSION

Until recently, armies fought in comparatively close order. Masses were held together by drill and by discipline. The enemy was in plain view. Now we usually struggle against an enemy whom we cannot see. We no longer fight in masses but in small groups—often as individuals. Therefore the psychological reaction of the individual becomes increasingly important.

In war, the soldier is the instrument with which leaders must work. They must learn to play on his emotions—his loyalty, his courage, his vanity, his sense of humor, his esprit de corps, his weakness, his strength, his confidence, his trust—. Although in the heat of battle there is no longer time to prepare soldiers for the impressions of war, there are, however, two simple means by which a leader may lessen tension:

He can do something himself that will give the men a feeling of security, or

He can require his men to do something that will necessitate activity and attention.

[192]

published at Leavenworth in 1918, was signed but not annotated. The same is true of his copies of G. Stanley Hall's *Morale* and Major Arthur Miller's *Leadership,* both published in 1920, and he did not even sign his 1924 Leavenworth manual *Psychology and Leadership.* Yet, in countless books he wrote "leadership" beside passages about heroic actions of commanders in action.

In the 1930s, two books on leadership fascinated him. Both were written by Germans: *A German Doctor at the Front* by Dr. Wilhelm His, translated and published in Washington in 1933; and *Battle Leadership,* consisting of lectures at Fort Benning in the early thirties by Captain Adolph von Schell of the German Army. Patton underscored in the von Schell book such words as "confidence," "pride," "attack," and "speed." He drew sidelines by: "If a leader awaits complete information before issuing an order, he will never issue one." (31) But what he marked in red is perhaps more important: "There is a certain danger in studying military history if we seek to obtain from it more than the eternal verities of leadership, morale, psychological effects, and the difficulty and confusion which battle entails." (66) In retrospect, it was those "eternal verities" that Patton had been seeking in his two decades of professional reading.

Nowhere is that seen more clearly than in his careful reading of the

Lieutenant Colonel Patton in Fort Myer, Virginia, in 1934. (Photo courtesy of the Patton Museum.)

first two volumes of Douglas Southall Freeman's *R. E. Lee: A Biography* as they came off Charles Scribner's press in 1935. He found much to commend in Lee when he repeatedly wrote "courage," "guts," and "personal reconnaissance" in the margins. But he thought Lee "lacked force," was "too weak" with subordinates, and "Too D____ Polite!" (II 419) He used those volumes to vent his rage against politicians by constantly writing "politics" and "politicians" in the margins, stating it was "an error" when Lee subordinated himself to civil authority (I 456), and finally asking: "Why should a soldier honor a politician?" (I 560) He occasionally noted that he and Lee were kindred spirits, writing "me too" when he read that Lee avoided fiction but enjoyed poetry. (I 454) Perhaps his greatest praise for Lee was in this comment: "This chapter is a good guide to organize disorder. It may be useful." (II 472) Patton's overall appraisal: "Lee seems to have been more an inspired leader than a great soldier." (II 250) To accompany his reading of *R. E. Lee*, Patton had *Lee's Dispatches* in which was written, "This book belonged to Papa. Taken by me in 1935. G.S.P., Jr."

In May 1935, Lieutenant Colonel Patton, nearly fifty years of age, was reassigned to Hawaii as G-2 of the Hawaiian Department at Fort Shafter. He arrived on the island in the fifty-two-foot schooner *Arcturus* after a month-long sail with Beatrice and three crew members. In preparation for the cruise he studied Captain Benjamin Dutton's *Navigation and Nautical Astronomy*; as navigator he made the landfall at Hawaii exactly and on time.

Asked to observe the June maneuvers, Patton replied with a five-page report that criticized commanders for "rigid adherence to methods of procedure current in the World War," staffs for remaining in their headquarters four miles behind the action, and transportation breakdowns that clogged roads vulnerable to enemy air and artillery attack. He deplored the command's philosophy, which he labeled "comfort first," for taking excess baggage to the field, illuminating camps, failing to post sentries, and not undertaking necessary reconnaissance and patrolling. He concluded that officers had not understood what little motorization they had achieved: "The army exists to kill men—not to groom vehicles." (BPP I 907.)

Patton's mind, perhaps influenced by his duties as an intelligence officer, shifted from tactical and operational considerations to the strategic level. His speech to the American Legion convention in August 1935 concluded that war is "the culmination of convergent commercial and political interests. Wars are fought by soldiers but they are produced by business men and politicians." (BPP I 909.) He wrote "The Causes of War," a November 1935 paper that reviewed the history of how wars start and concluded that we must "zealously prepare for the cataclysm which will inevitably occur when any pair of the several nations now

moving on lines of convergent political and commercial interests col-
lide."

In keeping with his intelligence duties in 1935, he read Nathaniel
Peffer's *Must We Fight in Asia?* and Upton Close's *Challenge: Behind the
Face of Japan.* In early 1936 he acquired John White's *Red Russia Arms,*
and in it he speculated if the training of a Soviet officer corps would
breed a new elite: "Messena, Napoleon's greatest general, was such a
product." (93) He then bought Tota Ishimaru's *Japan Must Fight Britain*
but did not comment on the words of that lieutenant commander of the
Imperial Japanese Navy.

On Armistice Day 1936, Beatrice gave her husband Duff Cooper's
Haig, later inscribed in the back, "An uninspired but instructive book.
G.S.P.Jr. 11-27-36." But Patton had his fun with it. On a picture of Henri
Petain, Marshal Haig, Marshal Foch, and General Pershing he wrote:
"After a heavy meal." Next to "[Marshal Joseph] Joffre was an engineer"

Lieutenant Colonel Patton
(second from left) and wife
Beatrice (second from right)
with friends aboard the
Arcturus during a sail in 1935
from San Pedro to Hawaii,
where Patton would assume
new duties with the General
Staff in Hawaii for two years.
(Photo courtesy of the
Patton Museum.)

he wrote, "Too bad." (103) Then he noted, "The power of the press is a bad thing. . . . The C.G. [commanding general] should write the release and make the assumptions." (109) That was followed by, "Civilians on Mil. Affairs—Bunk." (209) When the author wrote "The possibility of having to use troops in the suppression of civil disorder is always hateful to a soldier," Patton scribbled "I have done it and may again, and I hate it." (361) Finally, when Haig said "The government has a perfect right to send any one of us away at a moment's notice without giving us any reason," Patton responded "I doubt this right." (380)

Toward the end of 1936, Patton expanded his Napoleonic collection with three additions: *From Boulogne to Austerlitz: Napoleon's Campaign of 1805* and *Napoleon's Campaign in Italy: 1796–1797 and 1800,* both by R. G. Burton, and *The Leipzig Campaign: 1813* by F. N. Maude. None received annotation.

In 1936, Patton returned to a study of amphibious operations, which had first captured his attention on the Mexican border in April 1917 when he had received John Masefield's *Gallipoli.* (He subsequently bought a 1927 edition in Washington and annotated five pages.) In the 1920s he had acquired Sir Ian Hamilton's two-volume *Gallipoli Diary,* which Beatrice Patton would list as among Patton's favorites. In Hawaii in 1926 he had acquired Sir Gerald Ellison's *The Perils of Amateur Strategy as Exemplified by the Attack on the Dardanelles Fortress in 1915.* In 1929 Patton acquired a copy of Great Britain's *Final Report of the Dardanelles Commission, Part II, Conduct of Operations,* which he extensively annotated. Upon reading that Major General Hammersley at age fifty-seven was considered too old for division command, Patton commented pithily: "Lord Help Us!" (48) He was then a forty-four-year-old major.

In 1936, Patton studied John North's *Gallipoli: The Fading Vision* and *Military Operations: Gallipoli,* a volume of the British official history of the Great War by C. F. Aspinall-Oglander and A. F. Becke, in which Patton tabbed all the maps for quick reference. His study of those and other sources led to his writing a 128-page narrative and anlaysis of amphibious operations through history, ending with the Gallipoli operation; it contains his conclusions about why some landings succeeded while others failed.

In 1937, Patton played the role of commander of an invading force in maneuvers of the Hawaiian Division. He prophetically selected Pearl Harbor as his objective; his plan for putting enemy troops ashore assumed a large invasion fleet offshore, arriving in secrecy. A June 1937 warning letter from Patton to the chief of staff at Fort Shafter foretold the Pearl Harbor attack by the Japanese, which would occur four years later. (See inset on pages 105–107.) Patton's intense study of amphibious operations would help shape American doctrine in World War II and

This 1937 letter from Patton urged that steps be taken to prevent a surprise Japanese attack on the Hawaiian islands. Note the mention of Pearl Harbor in point 8a.

June 3, 1937.

Subject: Surprise.

To: Chief of Staff, Headquarters Hawaiian Department,
          Fort Shafter, T. H.

1. This study is based on the inescapable assumption that complete surprise offers the greatest opportunity for the successful capture of these islands.

2. It is reliably reported that during the last four years three or more Japanese division were embarked, moved to the coast of Asia and disembarked without any military attache, consular agent, foreign press correspondent, or any other foreigner living in Japan being aware of the fact until the troops were in action in Asia.

3. Some of the Mandated Islands, about which absolutely nothing is known, are only 2,500 miles distant, seven days' steaming over the loneliest sea lanes in the world. Who can say that an expeditionary force is not in these islands now?

4. At any time the political situation in Europe, or the demand by East Coast cities for participation in the Fleet's payroll may cause a part or the whole of the U.S. Fleet to leave the Pacific.

5. Since becoming modernized, Japan has never declared war.

6. A study of amphibious warfare taken in conjunction with the lessons of the concurrent exercises of this year clearly indicates that in order to attack Oahu an adjacent advance base must be secured, first as a landing field for carrier borne aviation, and later as a land base for ground troops.

7. To facilitate the capture and occupation of an advance base, the air and submarine forces on Oahu must be destroyed or neutralised.

8. A consideration of the foregoing impels the thought that when and if circumstances impel Japan to attempt the capture of these islands, the following method of procedure on her part is fraught with the gravest danger to us.

a. The unheralded arrival during a period of profound peace of a Japanese expeditionary force within 200 miles of Oahu during darkness; this force to be preceded by submarines who will be in the immediate vicinity of Pearl Harbor.

b. The disruption of all water, light, and telephone utilities by sabotage.

c. Incendiary fires in all army and navy hangars, wooden barracks and quarters, and in storehouses.

d. The assassination in their homes of the higher ranking officers.

e. Coincident with the above, an air attack by navy fighters and carrier borne bombers on air stations and the submarine base using either gas or incendiary bombs.

9. So far as information is available in this office, no ammunition or bombs, except in the case of seacoast forts, is actually in the hands of the troops.

10. Our estimates as to the length of time necessary to issue ammunition and bombs are based primarily on daylight operations or on the unrestricted use of electric lights.

a. During the concurrent exercises it took the Hawaiian Division working on a time schedule 13 ½ hours to draw and issue one day of fire of all types of ammunition. The 18th Wing states that one day of fire could be procured in about 5 hours. The 64th Coast Artillery estimates from 2 to 2½ hours for small arms ammunition and 3 hours for 3" ammunition. However, it should be noted that these estimates are based on a clear schedule and would be longer if all units attempted to draw at once.

b. While these time figures are commendably short, two points deserve consideration: First, in the case of a surprise attack all necessary damage could be inflicted on troops who were without means of resistance, and second, that a lack of electric lights and telephone communication occurring in conjunction with incendiary fires and the probable destruction of bridges would increase this time out of all reason.

c. Further, it is pertinent to remark that while the submarines are equipped on a war footing, all their officers and a large number of their men reside in Honolulu. Without telephones it would take some time to collect them.

-2-

11. While the guard or watchman system prevailing is fully adequate for peace conditions, it would be very simple for a determined alien to avoid detection and cause considerable damage by incendiary fires to storehouses, airplane hangars and their contents. Clearly a harmonical agreement must be struck between the fatigue which would be imposed upon the command by enlarging the guard system and the danger which a lack of its enlargement entails. In the event of the Fleet leaving the Pacific, it is believed that an enlargement of the present means of internal protection should be seriously considered.

12. In view of all the foregoing, attention is invited to the necessity of establishing certain precautionary measures:

a. The maintenance at all times in the hands of the troops of at least half a day's fire in the case if infantry and artillery, and of bombs and ammunition requisite for one mission in the case of the Air Corps.

b. The provision of lamps and candles with matches in all unit barracks and supply rooms.

c. The provision of acetylene or gas flares or floodlights in all depots and near all hangars.

d. The provision of assembly positions for all units to which on the receipt of an alarm they will proceed with their individual weapons and ammunition.

e. The provision on all posts of an alarm system, as for instance, three shots on the saluting cannon, at which signal all troops will immediately assemble at their prescribed positions as stated in paragraph d above.

f. The provision of a radio enunciation system with an instrument in the home and office of all post commanders in all post guard houses, in the home and office of the Department Commander and of his Chief of Staff.

13. It is realised that the events above enumerated are not likely of occurrence. On the other hand the vital necessity to Japan of a short war and of the possession at its termination of land areas for bargaining purposes may impel her to take drastic measures. It is the duty of the military to foresee and prepare against the worst possible eventuality.

S/ G. S. Patton, Jr.,
Lieut. Colonel, Cav.,
A. C. of S., War Plans.

-5-

Taken From - Military Bulletin 1505

probably would contribute to his selection as commander of the Western Task Force that invaded North Africa in 1942.

Patton's warning of an air strike on Pearl Harbor from Japanese carriers was undergirded by his study in April 1937 of *Air Power and Armies* by Britain's J. C. Slessor. Although the author wrote about establishing air superiority in the European environment in any coming war, Patton wrote "Hawaii" alongside Slessor's discussion of the importance of air bombardment of airdromes at the outset of any campaign. (60) Patton knew he was reading the thoughts of an air-power fanatic when he read: "It is, of course, agreed that the old-fashioned offensive on the ground is definitely a thing of the past; and as air forces increase in strength and efficiency, and if permanent fortifications, field defences, and anti-tank devices endow the defence on the ground with still greater strength relative to the attack, it is arguable that no belligerent will undertake offensive operations on the ground at all. Armies may become mere holding forces to garrison frontier defences, from the cover of which air forces will attempt to reduce the enemy to impotence and ultimate capitulation by attacks on his essential services, and war industries and transportation." Patton wrote in the margin, "Bull." (80) He showed the fragility of his own crystal ball, however, when he failed to foresee the great bombing raids to come in a few short years; he wrote on page 85, "I think that sure knowledge of retaliation will prevent bombing of civilian areas. No G.H.Q. was ever bombed in 1918— Why? Fear of retaliation." Patton's own reluctance to bomb civilian centers would not become apparent until he spared Palermo, Italy, in 1943.

Although Patton's marginal notes rejected Slessor's arguments for an air force separate from the ground commander's control, he seemed in general agreement with Slessor's priorities for employing air power: When battle is going on, priority should go to destroying enemy troops; in periods of comparative inactivity, priority should go to attacks on war production facilities; and in the transition from inactivity to battle, priority should go to cutting supply lines and destroying reserves. He paid particular attention to Slessor's suggestion that amphibious landings would be virtually impossible in the future unless the commander first obtained air superiority.

As his second tour in Hawaii came to an end, Patton tried and failed for the fourth time to be designated commandant of cadets at West Point. In the process he asked Pershing to help him, writing, "The best argument I have for my selection is based on . . . [my] having had close in battle service under you in both Mexico and France [which] would be a drawing card with the cadets. Since the World War none of the officers detailed as commandant have had such service. True it is not their fault but their misfortune but none the less I think that a little

Patton and Beatrice as sailors in June 1945. They're on a friend's boat in the waters off Boston.

blood and guts would be good for cadets." Thus, Patton coined the phrase that would become his monicker through World War II. (BPP I 911.) But the job went to Charles W. Ryder, who would command the 34th Division and be wounded in World War II.

Patton was told to report to the Cavalry Board at Fort Riley in the summer of 1937. He, Beatrice, son George, and three compatriots sailed the *Arcturus* back to California, where the schooner was sold. The family proceeded to Massachusetts for a long leave that grew into more than six months when Patton received a severely broken leg from the kick of a horse. He spent three months in the hospital and then convalesced at home until February 1938. There is little record of his reading during that period, when he could neither walk nor ride, but it is likely he read military biographies he had accumulated in the mid-1930s.

For example, he delighted in John Fortescue's 1925 *Wellington* and underlined a passage that said since Wellington had declined to admit all men are equal, democracy was an abomination to him. (303) Further, Patton wrote "true" beside Fortescue's observation: "It is indisputable that youths, born to a certain social position and to the unconscious exercise of command, obtain without effort as officers a readiness of obedience from their men that is beyond the power of their less fortunate brethren." (298) Patton also read Philip Guedalla's *Wellington,* a

1936 Christmas gift; when the author noted that all of Wellington's allies had been annihilated, Patton wrote "How luckey!" (193) Patton's notes on Wellington reflected his well-established beliefs on the military value of social classes and the fickle nature of allies.

General James G. Harbord's *The American Army in France, 1917–1919* arrived in the Patton household in 1936, inscribed by the author: "To George S. Patton III. Son of a very gallant and competent soldier. With best wishes from his godfather." Patton thoroughly annotated that book—a gift to his son from Pershing's wartime chief of staff—although many of the anecdotes mirrored those he had written into Pershing's memoirs in 1931. Patton noted, "I am the only officer of the *Baltic* party with no French medal. I was too frank." (197) He extensively underlined Harbord's discussion of policies regarding venereal disease among American personnel. He wrote, "Gen. P[ershing] with high courage faced this problem in Mexico by establishing a house under military guard. It worked. The rate fell from 16% to .01%. In Paris I personally saw every man treated each night at taps. We had no disease." (144) Patton wrote "true" next to a passage praising Pershing for his policy of not returning a soldier home until cured of venereal disease. (147) Patton's last entry was, "I saw Gen. Harbord in Paris on the 28th and he told me with tears in his eyes that he was leaving the front. He was and is a great soldier." (356)

Patton's professional reading in the late 1930s tended to look back in time. His copy of Oliver Spaulding's *Pen and Sword in Greece and Rome* was heavily annotated with comparisons between ancient cavalry and modern armor. The annotations also referred to his typescript copy of Spaulding's translation of Emperor Maurice's "Strategicon," written in 600 A.D. in the ancient city of Byzantium. For Christmas 1937 he received Sir Charles Oman's *A History of the Art of War in the Sixteenth Century*, in which he wrote on page 231, "Note decrease in size of units in an effort to secure mobility [in 1513]. Now our divisions are less than half World War size." Patton rounded out the decade by acquiring *Gustav Adolph the Great* by Nils Ahlund and both volumes of *Memoirs of the Confederate War for Independence* by Heros von Borcke, chief of staff to General J.E.B. Stuart.

When Patton arrived on February 8, 1938, at Fort Riley, he became executive officer of the 9th Cavalry and of the Academic Division—and therefore a member of the staff and faculty of the Cavalry School. Within months, he wrote a critique of the school's instruction, finding too little an emphasis on molding the personality and individuality of future combat leaders. His impact was not to be felt, however, because by the end of July he had been promoted once again, to colonel, and posted to Fort Clark, Texas, to assume command of the 5th Cavalry.

He wrote to Beatrice from Texas, "All one can do here is to Ride-

Read-Write & Swim." He wrote in a later letter: " . . . had dinner at El Moderno with Gen. Canones and the Mexican commander. You will like him and his wife and also the town. It is just as foreign as Saumur or more so. I am striking up numerous friendships with the ranchers who while crude are real people and have plenty of shooting and fishing to trade for a little politeness. . . . The sherrif and the County judge and the policeman are already my friends."

Patton participated in Third Army maneuvers and had a grand time outflanking the enemy with his cavalry and capturing command posts and an artillery colonel. (BPP I 929.) But his Texas idyll came to an end with orders to return to Fort Myer to command the Washington ceremonial 3rd Cavalry. An efficiency report on Patton by his commander, Brigadier General Kenyon A. Joyce, forecast the future: "Because of his innate dash and great physical courage and endurance he is a cavalry officer from whom extraordinary feats might be expected in war. A deep military student who is intensely interested in his profession. He is thoroughly qualified for the grade of brigadier general. Of outstanding value to the service in every way."

Patton arrived at Fort Myer in December 1938 just as the ten-week exhibition season for mounted drills began, giving him a reason to invite and receive distinguished military and civilian visitors. He started a series of dinners for Washington dignitaries. By July he had suc-

Christmas 1939 in Quarters 8 at Fort Myer, Virginia. Left to right: Colonel Patton, wife Beatrice, and daughter Beatrice Patton Waters. (Photo courtesy of the Patton Museum.)

ceeded in getting the new Army Chief of Staff, George C. Marshall, to make an extended stay at his quarters while the chief's quarters were undergoing repair. That proved fortuitous for Patton's future, because in September the Germans would march into Poland, and America would begin to repair its army of barely 200,000 men.

In the fall of 1939, General Leslie McNair began an army reorganization that reduced divisions from four regiments to three and trimmed regiments from four battalions to three. Those triangular divisions, which were given improved weapons and more vehicles, saved manpower while increasing maneuverability. The new concepts in structure, along with new concepts in mechanization, were tested in maneuvers the following spring. In the Third Army maneuvers in May, the 7th Mechanized Cavalry Brigade from Fort Knox was joined with the Provisional Motorized Tank Brigade from Fort Benning in an improvised armored division; together, that force was pitted against the men and horses of the 1st Cavalry Division. Patton participated as an

Colonel Patton, commander of the Washington ceremonial 3rd Cavalry, with members of his staff attending a review held in honor of Brigadier General Maxwell Murray. Photo was taken June 4, 1940, in Fort Myer, Virginia. (Photo courtesy of the Patton Museum.)

umpire. After he returned to Fort Myer he had two events to ponder. One was the striking defeat of the horse cavalry by the mechanized forces. The other was the dramatic defeat of France in May 1940 by the blitzkrieg tactics and equipment of Hitler's German army.

Patton decided to switch assignments from horse cavalry to mechanized forces. He therefore wrote to Brigadier General Adna Chaffee, who on July 15 would assume command of a newly formed I Armored Corps, to be composed of the 1st Armored Division at Fort Knox and the 2d Armored Division at Fort Benning. Chaffee replied, "I put you on my preferred list as a brigade commander for an armored brigade. I think it is a job which you could do to the queen's taste, and I need just such a man of your experience in command of an armored brigade. With two light armored regiments and a regiment of tanks employed in a mobile way, I think you could go to town." (BPP I 953.) Patton's good fortune continued with the July appointment of his old friend Henry L. Stimson as secretary of war. On the fifteenth of that month, while on leave in Massachusetts, Patton read in the morning paper that he was to command the 2d Armored Brigade at Fort Benning. In early August he wrote Pershing that his new command would have 350 officers, 5,500 men, 383 tanks, 202 armored cars, and twenty-four 105-mm howitzers.

Patton's lengthy marriage to the horse cavalry had ended, but the heady ideas fostered by that union were not left behind. Patton retained the cavalry's notions of speed, maneuver, flank and rear attack, firepower, shock action, leadership, and the exacting care of men and equipment; now he would apply them to men in machines.

CHAPTER NINE

Mastering Mobile Warfare 1940–1942

I N THE TWO YEARS that followed Patton's assumption of command of the 2d Armored Brigade, America would go to war with Japan, Germany, and Italy; enough mechanized materiel would start pouring out of American factories to equip sixteen American armored divisions. In those two years Patton would command the 2d Armored Division and then I Armored Corps, both under control of Lieutenant General Jacob L. Devers, who was picked by Army Chief of Staff Marshall to head the Armored Force after Chaffee retired because of illness. Devers was a West Point classmate of Patton's, a polo player, and an artilleryman who could be expected to stress firepower as much as Patton and his cavalrymen had stressed mobility.

In September 1940, Patton was promoted to brigadier general and acting commander of the 2d Armored Division, whose only fighting unit was the 2d Armored Brigade. In the following March the division was reorganized into two combat commands, CCA and CCB. In 1943 a third—CCR—would be added, and the division would be given enough combat battalions to provide three tank, three mechanized infantry, and three artillery, all to be assigned to the combat commands according to the mission. (See inset on pages 116 and 117.) Although "heavy" with 15,000 men, the 2d Armored Division was organizationally representative of the 12,000-man "light" armored divisions in Patton's 250,000-man Third Army as they fought from Normandy to Germany in 1944–1945.

Before Patton went to war in 1942, his mind had to include some

The typical tactical formation of the 2d Armored Division in 1945 shows the distribution of units in Division Headquarters, CCA, CCB, and CCR. This appeared in the USFETO report on the organization of the Armored Division, November 7, 1945. From the USMA Library.

COMBAT COMMAND "B"

CMDR:- CO of CC "B"
COMPOSITION:

Hq & Hq Co CC "B"   HQ ▭ CO

Armd Inf Bn (-1 Co)   ▭ (-)

Regt Recon Co   ▭

Armd Med Co   ▭

Inf Regt (-1 Bn) (Atchd)   ✕ (-)

TASK FORCE #1

CMDR:- CO Armd Regt
COMPOSITION:

Armd Regt (-1 Bn, Med Co,
   Rcn Co, Med Plat)   ▭ -)

Armd Inf Co   ▭

TD Co (-1 Plat)   TD -)

Armd Engr Plat   ▭

Armd FA Bn   ▭

TASK FORCE #2

CMDR:- CO Inf Bn
COMPOSITION:

Inf Bn   ✕

Med Tk Co   ▭

Med Tk Plat   ▭

Armd Engr Co (-1 Plat)   ▭ (-)

TD Plat   TD

Armd FA Bn   ▭

COMBAT COMMAND "B"

CMDR:- Armd Inf Regt
COMPOSITION:

Armd Inf Regt (-3 Bns)   ▭ (-)

Armd Inf Co   ▭

Med Tk Co   ▭

TD Plat   TD

Armd Engr Plat   ▭

Armd Med Det   ▭ DET

TASK FORCE #1

CMDR:- CC Tk Bn
COMPOSITION:

Tk Bn   ▭

Armd Inf Co   ▭

TD Plat   TD

Armd Engr Plat   ▭

TASK FORCE #2

CMDR:- CO Armd Inf Bn
COMPOSITION:

Armd Inf Bn (-2 Cos)   ▭ (-)

Tk Bn (-1 Med Co)   ▭ (-)

Armd Engr Co (-2 Plats)   ▭ (-)

TD Co (-2 Plats)   TD (-)

vision of the structure, training, and employment of mechanized forces, practically none of which had been seen before 1939. What was that vision and what were its sources?

We know that in the 1920s he had written of tanks, motorized infantry, and close-support aircraft penetrating deep behind enemy lines; but he had thought those were ideas too visionary, too expensive, and too technologically advanced for use in his lifetime. Through the 1930s he had thought the horse cavalry was the best means of getting to the enemy's flanks and rear. But he had never lost interest in the progress of mechanization. In 1931, for example, he bought Giffard Le Quesne Martel's *In the Wake of the Tank: The First Fifteen Years of Mechanization in the British Army*; on page 15 he wrote, "Tank army first mentioned in 1916."

The paper on mechanized units that Patton helped prepare at the Army War College not only circulated in the War Department in 1932 (see page 95), but it underpinned his lecture to officers at Fort Myer the next year. The lecture described how armored cars could be used effectively in reconnaissance and pursuit of the enemy and how tanks could deliver the decisive blow of an attack by being grouped in an offensive reserve and committed en masse at the right time. (Farago, *Ordeal and Triumph*, 121.)

In 1936, Patton bought Basil Liddell Hart's *The Future of Infantry* and thoroughly annotated his agreement. Liddell Hart called for a 500-man battalion that would fight from forty-eight "light cars" and forty-two "armored carriers," using stalk-and-skirmish tactics in an "expanding torrent," very unlike the linear trench warfare of the Great War. Patton drew a sideline by the author's recommendation that officers of that force should read military history, "especially the history of irregular wars, and even in military fiction. . . . Good infantry have always shown endurance; today they must also show agility. Light of foot, lightly equipped, and quick of thought, they are athletes engaged in a contest of skill." (69)

In contrast with Liddell Hart's vision was Lieutenant Colonel Walter R. Wheeler's *The Infantry Battalion in War*, which Patton annotated in 1937. While he did not complain about the book's failure to deal with mechanization, Patton did comment on passages having to do with fear in battle, physical conditioning of officers, and use of the bayonet.

In the late 1930s, Patton maintained two 3-ring notebooks of pamphlets on American military doctrine and tactics as they were published at the Command and General Staff College at Fort Leavenworth, Kansas. *Tactical Employment of Cavalry* had forty pages on mechanized cavalry, which Patton must have known well; but his copy, now in the West Point library, is not annotated. The pamphlet stated that mechanized cavalry units would be built around the combat car, described as "an armored vehicle of the fast tank type," possibly fully tracked. A brigade would contain two regiments, each of which would have two combat car squadrons. The organization provided for "powerful striking and holding elements; a system of command and communications, including a highly specialized radio system, simple and rapid, and capable of controlling highly mobile and dispersed elements; and a highly mobile system of supply and maintenance."

In 1937 the Cavalry School published *Cavalry Combat,* with much of its 500 pages devoted to World War I cavalry actions. Patton stopped annotating his copy on page 93, but he might have written the "General Discussion on Mechanization" at the end of the book, the preamble of which cited Cyrus' use of armored vehicles in the sixth century B.C. and Leonardo da Vinci's vision of covered chariots in 1482. (497) The eight-page discussion ended, "The light tank, and its cavalry counterpart, the combat car, as it stands today, *is one of the most redoubtable weapons of modern armies*; and must be recognized. Mechanized cavalry units, organized around the combat car are tactically self-contained and capable of independent employment . . . with all nations bending every effort to develop methods and produce weapons, which by their increased mobility, will tend to *prevent stabilization in modern war and create flanks.*"

Between February and July of 1938, Patton held the title of Director of Instruction at the Cavalry School at Fort Riley. That gave him reason to review the growing literature on mechanization, whether by J.F.C. Fuller, B. H. Liddell Hart, or the Germans. Decades later, Ladislas Farago would report in *Patton: Ordeal and Triumph* that the American military attaché in Berlin, Colonel Truman Smith, had kept Washington closely informed of military mechanization in Germany, and so had Major Albert C. Wedemeyer, a visiting student in the military school at Gatow, near Berlin. Farago would write, "When the writings of Guderian and Rommel were translated by G-2, Patton immediately sent for copies and devoured them, reading them again and again until he knew them by heart." (122) Heinz Guderian had set the pace in 1937 with an article in the journal of the Reich Federation of German Officers, and he had followed it in 1938 with *Achtung! Panzer!*, a description of German armored formations and their doctrine of employment. Erwin Rommel's *Infanterie Grieft An* had been published at the same time.

By late 1938, George C. Marshall, then chief of the U.S. Army War Plans Division, had been absorbing much of the same material. Farago later quoted Marshall: "Patton is by far the best tank man in the Army. . . . I want him nearer to Washington to be available when needed." Patton arrived to command Fort Myer shortly thereafter, presuming it would be his final assignment before retirement, but his tank expertise would soon take him to Fort Benning.

The G-2 translations continued to update Patton on mechanization. His reading might have included Fritz Heigl's *Taschenbuch der Tanks*, whose three volumes appeared in Munich in 1926, 1938, and 1939. After the German–Polish campaign in September 1939, Patton "reread Guderian's book and devoured a series of shrewd papers G-2 had prepared." In March 1941, G-2 issued "Evolution of Modern Battle Forces," a memorandum that concluded that the decisive factor in the Wehrmacht victory in Poland was the power of Germany's armored organizations. (Farago 136, 149.)

When Patton addressed the officers of the 2d Armored Division on September 3, 1940, the subject was "Armored Operations in Poland." He described how, one year earlier, fifty German divisions, including thirteen motorized and ten armored, had used air bombing and successive penetrating and flanking operations to destroy the Polish armed forces in a matter of days: "When the infantry had smashed a hole, the armored divisions either went through it or took advantage of the confusion of battle to get around the flank, and thereafter utilized exactly as Murat used his cavalry corps in the days of Napoleon." He noted that German casualties had been high, that much of the artillery was horse-drawn, that the Germans had committed only 2,500 of their 7,000 first-line airplanes, and that they had held 2,000 of their 6,000 tanks in reserve. He drew on a 1931 note card when he said, "There is an old latin saw to the effect that, 'To have a Cannae, you must have a Varro.' . . . to win a great victory, you must have a dumb enemy commander. From what we know at the moment, the Poles qualified with such a high command."

But he also observed that the organization of I Armored Corps was "so similar to the German that I shall not differentiate in describing how they operated." But how had the mechanized structures of the United States Army come to resemble those of the Germans? Patton suggested an answer by referring to Austrian General Ludwig Ritter von Eimannsberger's *Mechanized Warfare*, calling it "the first definite pronouncement on the German doctrine on armored warfare." The book, published originally in Munich in 1934 as *Der Kampfwagenkrieg*, was translated by Colonel Henry Hossfeld at the U.S. Army War College in 1935. Patton would have had access to it in the late 1930s when stationed at Fort Myer. Eimannsberger advocated retaining some tanks to support infantry but grouping most of them in new, highly mobile units capable of flank and rear attacks in the traditional cavalry role. (See inset on page 121 for Eimannsberger's vision of a mechanized division of three brigades of tracked battalions, with motorized artillery, anti-tank, and engineer units.) His vision was available to American mecha-

Patton called Ludwig Ritter von Eimannsberger's *Der Kampfwagenkrieg*, written in 1934, "the first definite pronouncement on the German doctrine on armored warfare." This diagram from an English translation shows Eimannsberger's vision of a mechanized division. From the USMA Library.

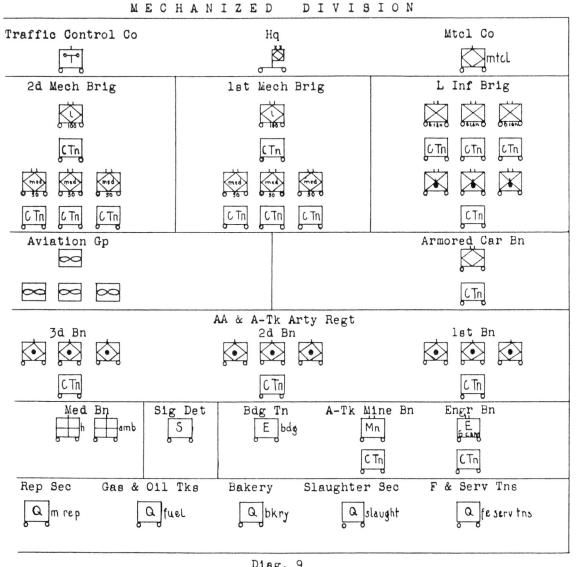

nization planners who crafted the organization and doctrine for Patton's World War II Third Army divisions and corps. There is a striking similarity between the structures of Eimannsberger's theoretical mechanized division and the 2d Armored Division commanded by Patton in 1941.

Patton was so committed to the methods and structure of mobile warfare, especially the parts that dealt with HABIT and fragmentary orders, that he finished his September 3 speech to division officers:

> In a former geological era when I was a boy studying latin, I had occasion to translate one of Caesars remarks which as nearly as I can remember read something like this.
>
> "IN THE WINTER TIME, CAESAR SO TRAINED HIS LEGIONS IN ALL THAT BECAME SOLDIERS AND SO HABITUATED THEM TO THE PROPER PERFORMANCE OF THEIR DUTIES, THAT WHEN IN THE SPRING HE COMMITTED THEM TO BATTLE AGAINST THE GAULS IT WAS NOT NECESSARY TO GIVE THEM ORDERS, FOR THEY KNEW WHAT TO DO AND HOW TO DO IT."
>
> This quotation expresses very exactly the goal we are seeking in this division. I know that we shall attain it and when we do may God have mercy on our enemies; they will need it.
>
> G. S. Patton, Jr.,
> Colonel, 2nd Armored Brigade

Patton's commitment to mobile warfare was so great that in 1944 tank leader Bruce C. Clark would tell the story of his asking General Patton for orders and being told, with a wave in the direction of Berlin, to "Go East! Just go East!"

As Patton molded the 2d Armored "Hell on Wheels" Division through the fall of 1940, he set about to educate his troops, the GHQ staff in Washington, and the general public on the methods of mobile warfare. He staged a highly successful road march from Fort Benning, Georgia, to Panama City, Florida; in the subsequent *Washington Star* article he stated that his division was modeled along the lines of the German panzer division—but with improvements. (BPP II 17.) He tried to change the rules for war games so that the loose control of flying columns deep in the enemy's rear would not result in penalized grading by the umpires. In May 1941, a newly promoted Major General Patton used football analogies when he addressed the entire division: "An armored division is the most powerful organization ever devised by the mind of men . . . that element of the team which carries out the running plays. We straight-arm and go around, and dodge, and go around. . . ."

Maneuvers in Tennessee in June 1941 demonstrated to the Washington brass the power, efficiency, and training of Patton's division. On the second day, they captured the enemy commander and his staff and terminated the maneuver hours ahead of schedule. In the next phase, they halted in nine hours an action that was to have taken two days. In the last phase, they swept around the defenders, cut lines of communication, and captured the objective town of Tullahoma in short order, with Secretary of War Henry Stimson looking on. On July 8, Patton assembled the entire division and explained to them on four giant maps what they had done, including the mistakes he had made. He had already appeared on the cover of the July issue of *Life* magazine, wearing a 2d Armored Division patch, a helmet with chin strap, and his war face.

Within two months, in maneuvers in Louisiana and Texas, Patton's

Brigadier General Patton (right) shakes hands with Brigadier General Courtney Hodges at Fort Benning, Georgia, in 1940. (USMA Library photo.)

Major General Patton, commanding officer of the 2d Armored Division, at Louisiana maneuvers in autumn 1941. (U.S. Army photo courtesy of the Patton Museum.)

division was paired with the 1st Armored Division under command of I Armored Corps. Third Army commander Lieutenant General Walter Krueger subsequently wrote to Patton, "I was impressed by the high morale, technical proficiency, and devotion to duty of the personnel of the 2d Armored Division. . . . Your leadership has produced a fighting organization."

The Patton team's performance in the Carolina maneuvers of November 1941 was summarized thirty years later by Martin Blumenson: "Patton and his men were a sensation. His control and coordination of his units were superb, and the division figuratively ran wild. What observers noted was a drive on the part of Patton that came close to obsession, the will to win. Everything was justified—even breaking the rules—if it led to victory." (BPP II 43.) Many thought Patton had broken the rules when he captured the enemy commander, Lieutenant General Hugh A. Drum, while Drum was being photographed by reporters at the outset of the maneuvers. Historian Christopher R. Gabel later wrote that Patton led "a spectacular raid against the rear of the opposing army during phase two of the Louisiana maneuvers, but little significance should be attached to this operation. Patton's raiding force was only a reinforced reconnaissance battalion, and it reached the enemy's rear only by playing fast and loose with the maneuver rules." (Gabel 6.) Thus, there are those who still do not agree with Patton on the nature of rules and who makes them, on the cavalry's doctrine of mobile warfare, or on the importance of how a commander instills the will to victory in his troops.

Not all armored unit commanders did as well as Patton in the maneuvers. He privately complained to Lieutenant General Jacob Devers that the armored forces should have controlled the infantry rather than having the reverse. "As it was, we were reduced to the speed, physical and mental, of the infantry," said Patton. He thought his own boss, Lieutenant General Charles L. Scott, had done a magnificent job under the circumstances, but Scott was criticized for losing control of his units and was reassigned from command of I Armored Corps. Scott wrote Patton, "When the enemy was pressing from all sides, when our own and the enemy's tactical dispositions were obscure, and when exacting and intricate night movements were ordered, I could always count on you and all the elements of your command being in the right place at the right time to meet effectively any hostile opposition." (BPP II 44.) Devers and the commanding generals of the regional armies who led the maneuvers, as well as Army Chief of Staff George Marshall, must have agreed that Patton's daring conduct was also very responsible conduct. He left the 2d Armored Division and took command of I Armored Corps on January 15, 1942.

After the Japanese bombing of Pearl Harbor, American strategists

Major General Patton and wife Beatrice at Fort Benning, Georgia, in 1942. (USMA Library photo.)

Enjoying themselves at Fort Benning, Georgia, in June 1942 are (left to right, foreground only): Brigadier General John S. "P." Wood, Major General Patton, and (probably) Major General Courtney H. Hodges, then Chief of Infantry in Washington. (USMA Library photo.)

reaffirmed an informal 1940 agreement with the British to give first priority to the defeat of Germany. In late January 1942, the effectiveness of General Erwin Rommel's forces in North Africa prompted the War Department to recommend that some American troops be prepared for desert warfare. By early March, Patton was on his way to California to find a site for a Desert Training Center where he could encamp and train some 20,000 soldiers of I Armored Corps. He determined the best location for his base camp would be twenty miles east of Indio, across a broad stretch of desert where the troops would be scattered in tents without electricity, heat, or hot water. By mid-April the troops were pouring in, to learn that within a month of arrival they would have to run a mile in ten minutes with full pack and rifle. Further, each man was limited to a small amount of water per day.

While the men learned how to adapt to the desert, Patton was in continual contact with higher command about the suitability of vehicles, equipment, and organizational structure. He argued forcefully and successfully for an armywide system of painting unit identification numbers on vehicles, a practice opposed by intelligence officers who wanted to keep the enemy uninformed, yet a practice that made for less confusion and fewer mistakes among friendly forces. He began to experiment with commanding units from the air by voice radio. He concluded that 200 vehicles was the maximum that could be handled in a single group insofar as movement, supply, and operations were concerned. (BPP II 64.)

During 1941 and the first half of 1942, Patton used maneuvers and the Desert Training Center to broaden his concept of mobile warfare and undergird it with the realities of weapons, equipment, maintenance, and supply. He was also operating a full-time school for officers, training them in command and staff procedures, and especially helping them shape their military values. Porter B. Williamson, who served Patton as a logistics officer during that period, took careful notes and later wrote *General Patton's Principles for Life and Leadership*. The book used anecdote and quotation to demonstrate many of the themes that were generic to the Patton mind. "Always do everything you ask of

Major General Patton (right) and his aide-de-camp, Captain Richard N. Jensen (who would be killed in North Africa), in April 1942. They are testing an experimental desert stove in Indio, California, near the Desert Training Center established by Patton to prepare soldiers for desert warfare. (USMA Library photo originally snapped by *Los Angeles Times* photographer George R. Watson.)

MRS. PATTON'S ANNOTATED LIST OF GENERAL PATTON'S FAVORITE BOOKS

Maxims of Frederick the Great.

Maxims of Napoleon, and all the authoritative military biographies of Napoleon, such as those by Bourienne and Sloane.

Commentaries, Julius Caesar.

Treatises by von Treitchke, von Clausewitz, von Schlieffen, von Seeckt, Jomini, and other Napoleonic writers.

Memoirs of Baron de Marbot, and de Fezansec, a colonel under Napoleon: We were translating the latter when he went to war in 1942.

Fifteen Decisive Battles of the World, Creasy.

Charles XII of Sweden, Klingspor.

Decline and Fall of the Roman Empire, Gibbon.

Strategicon, Marcus and Spaulding.

The Prince, Machiavelli.

The Crowd, Le Bon.

Art of War in the Middle Ages, Oman, and other books by him.

The Influence of Sea Power Upon History, Mahan, and other books by him. (*The Trilogy.*)

Stonewall Jackson, Henderson.

Memoirs of U. S. Grant, and those of McClellan.

Battles and Leaders of the Civil War. *R. E. Lee* and *Lee's Lieutenants,* Freeman.

Years of Victory and Years of Endurance, Arthur Bryant.

Gallipoli, Hamilton.

Thucydides' *Military History of Greece.*

Memoirs of Ludendorff, von Hindenburg, and Foch.

Ghengis Khan, Alexander and other biographies, Harold Lamb.

Alexander, Weigall.

The Home Book of Verse, in which he loved the heroic poems.

Anything by Winston Churchill.

Kipling, complete.

Anything by Liddell Hart, with whom he often loved to differ.

Anything by J. F. C. Fuller, especially *Generals, Their Diseases and Cures.* He was so delighted with this that he sent a copy to his superior, a major general. It was never acknowledged. Later he gave twelve copies to friends, colonels only, remarking that prevention is better than cure.

(Reprinted from "A Soldier's Reading," an article Beatrice Patton wrote for the November–December 1952 issue of *Armor* magazine.)

those you command," for example, was a theme transmitted to Patton's officers by their seeing him out in the field whenever his soldiers were out there, night and day, despite rain or boiling sun.

To underscore the idea that "punishment for mistakes must be immediate," Patton had a loudspeaker system through which soldiers sometimes heard a click followed by something such as: "This is General Patton. Colonel Blank you are removed from command immediately. You hear me? If you know what is good for you, you will stay away from me for a week." If an officer intervened to suggest a lesser punishment, Patton would lecture: "All that 'save the ego' nonsense is not for leadership in war. A dead man does not have any ego! How long after you touch a burning match does it take before you get burned? You get your punishment instantly by touching the match. That is the way Mother Nature works, and that's the way war works." (Williamson 39, 42.)

Under the general heading of "Any man who thinks he is indispensable, ain't," Patton advised: "We can expect that some of us will be killed. We do not want the loss of one man to stop our killing the enemy. Always have a man trained to take over your job in case you are killed. The test of your ability is whether you could be killed and nothing would be lost." Patton held frequent staff meetings so that information would be shared sufficiently and the impact of casualties would be lessened. (Williamson 60.)

During the busy time of preparing himself and his men for fighting, Patton continued to follow the War Department intelligence reports on the German army. "Description of Operations in Eastern Campaign," taken from the July 27, 1941, *Frankfurter Zeitung,* told Patton that "German armored forces may be over one hundred kilometers ahead of an action taking place between German infantry and enemy tanks."

He also continued to acquire books for his library. In March 1941 he bought Sir Archibald Wavell's *Allenby: A Study in Greatness* and T. H. Wintringham's *Mutiny: Being a Survey of Mutinies From Spartacus to Invergordon;* he left them unannotated. In the following January he ordered another copy of J.F.C. Fuller's 1936 *Generalship: Its Diseases and Their Cure;* it probably was for gift purposes, since the heavily annotated copy he had read in Hawaii (see Foreword) still remains in the Patton collection. When Beatrice Patton would list her husband's favorite books, she included, "Anything by J.F.C. Fuller, especially *Generals, Their Diseases and Cures* [sic]. He was so delighted with this that he sent a copy to his superior, a major general. It was never acknowledged. Later he gave twelve copies to friends, colonels only, remarking that prevention is better than cure." (See margin copy on this page for Beatrice Patton's complete list.)

When he was about to depart for the Desert Training Center he ordered Sir Archibald Wavell's *Generals and Generalship,* Thomas R.

Phillips' *Roots of Strategy,* William L. Shirer's *Berlin Diary*, and S.L.A. Marshall's *Blitzkrieg* and *Armies on Wheels.* Only Wavell is in the Patton collection today; Patton probably gave the others to fellow officers as he moved about during the war. Patton undoubtedly read *Blitzkrieg* upon its publication (1940) and used it in his lectures on the German operations in Poland, France, and Norway. *Armies on Wheels,* a 1941 sequel, described the mechanized campaigns as they had developed in North Africa, the mountains of Greece, and on the Russian steppes.

Central to Marshall's analysis was the thesis of J.F.C. Fuller's *Lectures on Field Service Regulations III,* published in Britain in 1932. Fuller gave a futuristic view of what the British Army's operations manual would look like if the army were motorized and mechanized. Marshall pointed out that 30,000 copies of Fuller's book were published for the German army in the 1930s and that it was circulated freely in the Soviet armed forces. It is highly probable that Patton had digested *Lectures on Field Service Regulations III* in the late 1930s. Marshall would publish an annotated version in 1943 under the title *Armored Warfare.*

By the time Patton went to fight in World War II he had without doubt read or heard of nearly every significant writing on mobile warfare that had been produced in English since the Great War, whether it had been written by advocates of cavalry, infantry, air power, or mechanization. He had followed with considerable intensity the intelligence community's interest in similar matters. Much of what he heard he discounted for practical reasons of economy, technology, and training. But he saw the German blitzkrieg example; he worked with newly created armored forces in maneuvers and on the desert; and when he went off to war he was America's most effective advocate of a daring armor doctrine.

Patton's strength of belief and will makes certain notes of B. H. Liddell Hart sound strange. Liddell Hart wrote of his discussions with Patton in England in 1944 concerning whether Patton would pursue the dash across Europe or revert to World War I tactics. Liddell Hart reconstructed those talks to make it appear as if he had to convince Patton to be bold. (See inset on page 130.) Patton was apparently up to an old trick of his—baiting his interrogator to see what the thinker's reaction would be. Patton wrote Beatrice that Liddell Hart "has developed a great love for me. He is very well read but badly balanced and has no personal knowledge of the facts of life so far as war is concerned. . . ." Beatrice's list of Patton's favorite books would include "Anything by Liddell Hart, with whom he often loved to differ." In 1948, Liddell Hart would also write about how he had influenced German General Heinz Guderian to adopt the concept of "the expanding torrent." But did he remember that Patton (and probably Guderian) had read Eimannsberger and that Patton had participated in writing all those papers and making all those lectures on mechanized warfare years before his country went to war?

In 1944, prior to D-day, B. H. Liddell Hart met with Patton in England and came away thinking he had convinced Patton to use bold tactics. Liddell Hart gave his impression of that discussion in this memorandum dated February 20, 1948. From the USMA Library.

NOTES ON TWO DISCUSSIONS WITH PATTON, 1944

Before the landing in Normandy, the prevailing opinion of most of the higher British and American generals had swung back to the view that independent armoured drives were no longer practicable, nor sound in principle. Towards the end of a two-months' tour of the American forces that I made in February and March 1944, I met General Wood, commanding the U.S. 4th Armored Division. We found ourselves in close agreement about armoured tactics, and equally in disagreement with the prevailing view that 1940 drives could no longer be attempted. Wood had just returned from a Conference where our C.I.G.S. Alan Brooke, had taken this line, and he was much disturbed about the impression it had made on most of the American generals present. Wood told me that Patton had just arrived in this country, saying that he was a keen reader of my books, and suggested that I should hasten to see him, and use any persuasion I could to counter the prevailing opinion— as he feared that Patton might be "got at" and induced to accept this.

So I got in touch with Patton and, hearing that he would like to see me, drove to his headquarters at Peover Hall, near Knutsford (Manchester), where he had recently arrived. I was impressed with his dynamic qualities, and the greater sense of drive that he gave one than most of the generals I had met. We had a very good talk, and found ourselves in the closest agreement about tank tactics. But I was rather disconcerted to find him saying he did not think that, when the Allied armies got to France, they would be able to repeat the kind of armoured drives the Germans had achieved in 1940. He felt that we should have to go back to 1918 methods. While questioning this, I felt it best to put the contrary arguments in the form of an "indirect approach." He had told me that before the war he had spent a long vacation studying Sherman's campaigns on the ground in Georgia and the Carolinas, with the aid of my book. So I talked of the possibilities of applying "Sherman methods" in modern warfare— moving stripped of impediments to quicken the pace, cutting loose from communications if necessary, and swerving past opposition, instead of getting hung up in trying to overcome it by direct attack. It seemed to me that by the development and exploitation of such Sherman methods, on a greater scale, it would be possible to reach the enemy's rear and unhinge his position—as the Germans had already done in 1940.

I think the indirect argument made some impression. At any rate, when I spent another evening with him in June, just before he went over to Normandy, he was no longer talking about 1918 methods, but on much bolder lines. The way that, after the break-through, he actually carried out his plans, in super-Sherman style, is a matter that all the world knows. I had a letter from Wood, just as the 4th Armored Division had reached the Seine, to tell me how successfully such methods had worked.

CHAPTER TEN

To War and Glory
1942–1945

M AJOR GENERAL PATTON was directed on July 30, 1942, to report to the War Department to participate in planning for the Allied invasion of North Africa. He flew to England to join Lieutenant General Dwight Eisenhower, who had been named Supreme Allied Commander for Operation Torch, which would send American and British forces into Morocco and Algeria on November 8. Patton commanded the Western Task Force, which made three successful landings and captured Casablanca, Morocco, from the Vichy French. (See map on page 169.)

Over the next three years Patton would achieve the childhood dream that had driven him all his life—to become a great war hero. But unlike Alexander or Napoleon, he did it in remarkably few days in combat. The Moroccan landing, which many (including Patton) considered risky, ended with a French surrender in three days. Patton then was kept out of combat for four months, until he took command of II Corps in Tunisia in March 1943. Patton, by now promoted to lieutenant general, gave his four divisions ten days of intensive training and then took them into combat against German and Italian forces. In thirty days he had accomplished his mission of linking up with British forces that were attacking across North Africa. Eisenhower then ordered him to turn II Corps over to Major General Omar Bradley, freeing Patton to direct U.S. planning for the invasion of Sicily, set for July 10, 1943.

Patton led the U.S. Seventh Army in landings on the southern

Lieutenant General Patton at the beachhead in Gela, Sicily, on July 11, 1943. (U.S. Army photo courtesy of the Patton Museum.)

shores of Sicily, and he captured Messina on August 17, ending the campaign after thirty-eight days of combat. He then sat in Palermo for five months while it was decided whether he would participate in fighting in Italy or southern France or in an invasion of the European continent across the English Channel.

The decision having been agreed upon at the highest levels, Patton moved to England where for another five months he prepared the U.S. Third Army—not for the June 1944 landings in France, but as the follow-on forces that would break out of the beachhead and aim for Paris. He arrived in France on July 6 and activated the Third Army for combat missions on August 1. There followed his most prolonged period of combat: the breakout and dash across France, the slugging match toward the Siegfried line at the German border, the Battle of the

Lieutenant General Patton (foreground) goes ashore at Licata, Sicily, in July 1943. (USMA Library photo from the U.S. Naval Institute Proceedings.)

Lieutenant General Patton in England in June 1944. On the back of the photo he wrote, "I don't know which Duke lives here, but had my picture taken in front to add class." (USMA Library photo.)

Lieutenant General Patton talks to wounded servicemen in Sicily in July 1943. Patton frequently visited his wounded troops. (U.S. Army photo courtesy of the Patton Museum.)

Bulge, and the advance into Germany. His combat period ended with German surrender on May 9, 1945. Adding those 319 days of combat to those experienced in Africa and Sicily, Patton had only 391 days, or barely thirteen months, to establish his reputation as a war hero. That he did so in such a short exposure has been amply demonstrated, both by the worldwide recognition of his reputation and by its duration into what is now approaching a half-century of the test of time.

The long periods of waiting during World War II were frustrating for Patton, but they were also times for reflection, for prethinking the next phase of operations, and for writing a vast compendium of diaries, letters, speeches, and studies. That body of literature reveals the Patton mind of the wartime leader and begins to explain why his reputation as the consummate warrior was so thoroughly established in a few months of decision-making and action in combat. Patton's wartime writings also show how much he drew on the lifetime of professional study that he took with him to the battlefield in 1942.

The habits of keeping diaries and writing letters to Beatrice were accelerated as he took on his war-fighting stance. He supplemented that record with random memoranda to himself: Notes on Arabs, Notes on Combat, Notes on the Sicilian Operation, Notes on France. Linkages to his prewar thinking were shown in his many letters of instruction to his commanders, particularly in a March 6, 1944, letter that first advised his new Third Army commanders on how to command. These phrases peppered that letter: lead in person; visit the front daily; observe, don't

Patton with staff and commanders in France in 1944. Left to right: an unidentified man; Major General Horace L. McBride; Brigadier General Paul D. Harkins; Patton; Brigadier General Hobart Gay; and Major General Walton Walker. The dog, an English bull terrier named Willie, was Patton's constant companion. (USMA Library photo from *Warrior: The Story of Gen. George S. Patton* by the editors of *The Army Times*.)

meddle; praise is more valuable than blame; make personal reconnaissance; issuing orders is 10 percent, execution is 90 percent; plans should be made by people who are going to execute them; tell the troops what they are going to do and what they have done; visit the wounded personally; if you do not enforce discipline, you are potential murderers; and DO NOT TAKE COUNSEL OF YOUR FEARS. In the next month, four additional letters of instruction conveyed more of his familiar phrases.

Through the years those phrases had been written in the margins and underlined repeatedly in his hundreds of professional books. Since 1921 he had written exhaustively on how to command. In a March 21, 1944, letter to "Darling B.," he stated "I have been working for two days with pad, stenographer, and glue pot on a new letter of instruction on the art of slaughter. It is most tedious as most of it is taken from former letters I have written, but one can only say a thing once and I have said most of them so often."

Much of what Patton wrote for his commanders during World War II was an explication of the Patton mind on the method of warfare that he had conceived in the prewar years. It could be capsulized in one word: ATTACK. In a June 5, 1943, letter of instruction to subordinate commanders before the Sicilian campaign, he employed these phrases: Use the means at hand to inflict the maximum amount of wounds, death, and destruction on the enemy in the minimum time; casualties vary directly with the time you are exposed to effective fire—rapidity of attack shortens the time of exposure; if you cannot see the enemy, shoot at the place he is most likely to be; when mortars and artillery are silent, they are junk—see that they fire; battles are won by frightening the enemy—fear is induced by inflicting death and wounds on him—death and wounds are produced by fire; having the bayonet fixed makes our men want to close—only the threat to close will defeat a determined enemy; never permit a unit to dig in until the final objective is reached; numerical superiority, while useful, is not vital to successful offensive action—the fact that you are attacking induces the enemy to believe that you are stronger than he is; a good solution applied with vigor now is better than a perfect solution ten minutes later; IN CASE OF DOUBT, ATTACK!; we can conquer only by attacking; continued ruthless pressure by day and by night is vital.

Major General Kenyon A. Joyce (left), one of Patton's mentors, listens to Patton in Sicily in 1943.

That he successfully imbued the Seventh Army with his spirit is indicated by this entry in his war diary on July 14, 1943, days after the Sicilian invasion. "I bet [British Vice Air Marshal] Wigglesworth a bottle of whiskey against a bottle of gin that we would take Palermo by midnight on the 23rd. He was very skeptical, but I believe without logical reason, that we can do so because I am sure that the enemy, German or Italian, cannot resist our continuous attacks. One Italian prisoner, an officer, is alleged to have said in a captured letter that the Americans were strange people; they attacked all day, marched all night, and fired all the time." That description might also have depicted the troops of Patton's childhood hero, Stonewall Jackson.

In a speech to the home front in July 1943, Beatrice Patton quoted from her husband's order for the landing in Morocco: "We shall attack and attack and attack until we are exhausted, and then we shall attack again. A pint of sweat will save a gallon of blood. . . ." Perhaps General Dwight Eisenhower put Patton's method of warfare in the best perspective when he wrote to General Marshall in Washington on August 24, 1943:

> He [Patton] has conducted a campaign where the brilliant successes scored must be attributed directly to his energy, determination, and unflagging aggressiveness. The operations of the Seventh Army in Sicily are going to be classed as a model of swift conquest by future classes in the War College in Leavenworth. The prodigious marches, the incessant attacks, the refusal to be halted by appalling difficulties in communications and terrain, are really something to enthuse about. This has stemmed mainly from Patton. He had fine division and corps commanders, but it is obvious that had he been willing to seize on an excuse for resting or refitting, these commanders could have done nothing. He never once chose a line on which he said "we will here rest and recuperate and bring up more strength." On the contrary, when he received an order from [General Harold] Alexander that made it look as if he was to remain rather quiescent in the Enna region, he immediately jumped into a plane, went to Alexander, got the matter cleared up, and kept on driving. [Hobbs 121.]

Lieutenant General Patton (center) speaks with Army Chief of Staff General George C. Marshall (right) in Nancy, France, in October 1944. (USMA Library photo.)

During the breakout from the Normandy landing, Patton had his corps driving west, south, and east. On August 6, 1944, he wrote his old cavalry commander, General Kenyon Joyce: "We are having one of the loveliest battles you ever saw. It is a typical cavalry action in which, to quote the words of an old story, 'The soldier went out and charged in all directions at the same time, with a pistol in each hand, and a sabre in the other.' " The next week, onetime Patton mentor General Harbord wrote him: "You have come through as I always knew you would, and are the greatest American cavalryman of your time or any other time that I know of." (BPP II 502, 513.) But was the Patton warfighting method of sustained attack consistent with the role of cavalry that Patton had memorized from the manuals between the wars? Or was that more the task of heavy infantry, with cavalry ready to exploit a breakthrough or outflank the enemy to get light forces into his rear?

Certainly the Patton mind revealed many of the cavalryman's ideas as he solved the daily problems of combat. In his diary entry of August 5, 1944, he mentioned talking with Generals Bradley and Hodges about boundaries within 12th Army Group: "I succeeded in getting the boundary I desire as it keeps me on the outside—on the running end." But he was also adjusting to the conditions of modern war with its weapons of greater lethality and mobility. After his campaigns in Morocco and Tunisia he wrote Senator Henry Cabot Lodge: "As a result of this war I have had three changes of heart. . . . I believe in heavy field artillery; and I am strong for telephone wires instead of radio." (The third change was his new belief in female nurses in the combat zone. BPP II 230.) Heavy artillery and wire were barely the tools of the attacking cavalryman, but they were essential to sustained attack in heavily defended positions.

Perhaps the greatest legacy that Patton derived from his two decades of reading the history, theory, and practice of cavalry operations was his conviction that battles are won by those who take risks, both in confronting personal danger and in committing units to battle. He believed that taking risks was the trademark of those who fought from horseback, and he reserved contempt for those who plodded along the safe paths of caution. On August 9, 1944, he wrote Beatrice from Normandy: "If I were on my own, I would take bigger chances than I am now permitted to take. Three times I have suggested risks and been turned down and each time the risk was warranted." Patton's reputation for taking tactical and operational risks, however, may have cost him the ultimate commands he sought. Could the most critical of operations be placed in the hands of a gambler? Bradley and Great Britain's Sir Bernard Law Montgomery, both more cautious than Patton, were given the senior commands in the Normandy invasion; Patton was never moved from Army to Army Group command, which went to so-called steadier men of less seniority and experience.

Patton's concepts of fear and the warrior soul were firmly entrenched, and throughout the war no one seemed successful in warning him away from taking great personal risks. As early as March 6, 1943, Eisenhower wrote him about his "personal recklessness," telling him he did not need to prove his personal courage, that he was needed "as a corps commander—not as a casualty." (BPP II 182.) Patton must have recalled those years of reading about the great warriors when he wrote in a June 9 letter to nephew Frederick Ayer, "In any of these fights, a general officer who does his duty has got to expose himself. Otherwise, he cannot look himself in the face and order men to do things he is afraid to do himself. I am sure that whatever success I have had resulted from my adherence to this belief. . . ." (BPP II 264.)

British General Bernard Law Montgomery (left) and General Patton en route to the airport at Palermo, Sicily, on August 2, 1943. (Photo courtesy of the Patton Museum.)

The risk-taking cavalryman was never more in evidence than in the great breakout and pursuit across France during August 1944—from Brest to Verdun, a distance of 500 miles, in barely thirty days. All the cavalryman's tricks of speed in outflanking the enemy and firing up his rear areas came into play. But novel conceptions also were introduced, such as employing the XIX Tactical Air Command to safeguard the Third Army's south flank. When XII Corps Commander Manton Eddy asked how concerned he should be about his exposed right flank, Patton replied, "That depends upon how nervous you are by nature."

Patton's dramatic pursuit allowed not only for the early liberation of Paris, but for the advance of all Allied armies in the wake of confused and retreating Germans. It was universally conceded that only Patton could have done what he did. Patton agreed. He wrote Beatrice on September 1, 1944, "Really I am amazed at the amount of ground the Third Army has taken, and it is chiefly due to me alone. . . . "

Within a month of the breakout, Patton abandoned the cavalryman's version of attack and reverted to a slugging match with his armored and infantry divisions in eastern France. This began with strictures on gasoline and ammunition and instructions to remain static while offensive operations were given priority in the northern sectors of the Allied line. But Patton's version of "static" was constant small-scale attacks to "rectify" the line, kill Germans, and keep the aggressive spirit alive in his troops. By November he was crossing the Moselle River—at its highest flood stage since 1919—and investing the great fortress at Metz. The Patton method of warfare continued under all conditions of mission, terrain, weather, and enemy capability. It had been gleaned from the minds of military chieftains through the centuries.

Visitors to Patton's forces—senior military and civilian officials, journalists, Allies—came away praising his soldiers for their aggressiveness, superb performance of duties, and high morale. But how could that be when he called for continuous attack even in the most adverse conditions of weather and enemy tenacity? The answer is a leadership

Left to right: Averell Harriman, U.S. ambassador to Russia; Colonel James Galt; and Lieutenant General Patton, in France in November 1944. (USMA Library photo.)

Lieutenant General Patton (seated, with cigar in mouth) in France in 1944. He labeled this photo ''Me and the Correspondents.'' (USMA Library photo.)

style based on a lifetime study of history's great military commanders—Alexander, Frederick, Napoleon, Jackson. From them he learned that the successful commander causes his soldiers to believe that he cares about them, that under him they have the best chance to survive and achieve the glory they crave. They must understand the necessity for strict discipline and tough training and accept it as being in their own best interests.

That Patton cared for his soldiers was demonstrated by his constant presence in the front lines, facing the dangers they faced. But they felt it, too, in his making sure they had the best food, equipment, and weapons available. According to Robert S. Allen in his *Lucky Forward*, Patton told the Third Army staff, "In battle, troops get temperamental and often ask for things which they really do not need. However, when humanly possible, their requests should be met no matter how unreasonable." (34) It became widely known among medics that Patton's soldiers had the fastest and most efficient medical care throughout the European theater, partly because of his frequent visits to the hospitals that cared for the wounded.

While visiting hospitals, he slapped two soldiers for skulking, and the incidents were so widely celebrated in the press that he was forced to make public apologies throughout the Third Army. But as it became known that Patton was taking care of the good soldiers who had to make up for the inadequacies of a few, his popularity grew even more.

What was not known was his prewar study of malingering in earlier armies, for which the punishment was often a firing squad. Nor did they realize the depth of his zealousness, as seen in his diary entry for August 9, 1943: "Bradley . . . reports that . . . three Seventh Army soldiers have deserted and were caught in civilian clothes with the natives. I shall try to have them shot. Desertion in face of the enemy—the bastards."

To tell soldiers what he stood for, Patton perfected a short speech—really a drama or morality play—which he acted out before vast audiences of troops as they came under his command and prepared for battle. A version that was purified of its shocking profanity became the opening scene of the 1970 movie *Patton,* and a less-purged version was reprinted in Blumenson's *Patton Papers* in 1974. His phrases echoed the battle exhortations of all great commanders: Americans love to fight; America loves a winner; Americans despise a coward; Americans play to win; you are not all going to die—only 2 percent; death must not be feared; death in time comes to all of us; every man is scared in his first action; some men get over their fright in a minute, others take an hour, for some it takes days; but a real man will never let the fear of death overpower his honor, his sense of duty to his country, and his manhood.

Patton went on to extol constant alertness, teamwork, each man doing his job, inevitable victory, and pride in being a part of that victory—repeating the story he first used in the early twenties about not having to tell your grandchildren that you spent the war shoveling manure in Louisiana. He told them what they wanted to believe, that everything had a purpose, that they were doing the right thing—and all in a vernacular that was naughty and manly.

In his correspondence Patton was as brutal about killing Germans as he was in his speeches. In his 1943 Memorial Day message to the troops he wrote: "To conquer, we must destroy our enemies. We must not only die gallantly; we must kill devastatingly. The faster and more effectively you kill, the longer you will live to enjoy the priceless fame of conquerors." (BPP II 257.) A month earlier he had written in his diary, "Men, even so-called great men, are wonderfully weak and timid. They are too damned polite. War is very simple, direct, and ruthless. It takes a simple, direct, and ruthless man to wage war. Some times I wonder if I will have to laugh at myself for writing things like the above. But I think not." Thus the public Patton was a reflection of the inner Patton, reflecting in turn his nearly forty years of reading and thinking about war. He wrote Beatrice: "We are fighting fanatics with non fanatics. Cromwell was faced with the same thing and in answer to it produced the 'New Model Army.' He used religious intolerance. That won't work now." Patton's order to kill Germans was an attempt to make his troops more "fanatical."

It was inevitable that he would have to defend himself against charges of abetting atrocities in the handling of prisoners. The investigations produced some adverse publicity, but Patton showed that he had taken proper action against American personnel who shot German prisoners. (BPP II 431.)

What the public did not see, however, was his quiet commentary opposing the bombing of populated centers. In his "Account of Capture of Palermo" he wrote, "I called off the air bombardment and naval bombardment which we had arranged, because I felt enough people had been killed, and felt that with the drive of the 2d Armored Division we could take the place without inflicting unproductive losses on the enemy." In his diary he wrote of Messina, "The town is horribly destroyed—the worst I have seen. . . . I do not believe that this indiscriminate bombing of towns is worth the ammunition, and it is unnecessarily cruel to civilians." Patton could have read similar views in the several biographies of Wellington in his library. On August 8, 1944, Patton wrote Beatrice that he had had to order the destruction of St. Malo in Brittany: "I hate to do it, but war is war. Usually I have not bombed cities." (BPP II 299, 323, 504.)

In early April 1945, Patton accompanied Assistant Secretary of War John McCloy on a drive through Frankfurt, Germany, a city in ruins. He wrote in his diary that he had "called Mr. McCloy's attention to the wanton and unnecessary bombing of civilian cities. He agreed with me and later stated that he had mentioned this to Generals Devers and [Alexander] Patch, who had the same opinion. We all feel that indiscriminate bombing has no military value and is cruel and wasteful, and that all such efforts should always be on purely military targets and on selected commodities which are scarce. In the case of Germany it would be oil." He added on April 9, "McCloy . . . said he intended to make a public statement to the effect that I am not only a great military commander but probably the best instructor general in the army. He said that there had been efforts to make it appear that I could do nothing but attack in a heedless manner." Patton's zealous pursuit of continuous attack and destruction of enemy forces obscured his belief in the proper limits of military power—a belief that had its roots in the moral precepts of the prewar officer corps.

That Patton was not alone in his reluctance to bomb civilian populations if there was no military target was recounted by Ronald Schaffer in his 1985 book *Wings of Judgment: American Bombing in World War II.* He told of how Army Air Corps enthusiasts in the spirit of military theorist Giulio Douhet had argued since the 1920s that armies would become useless as air power bombed the enemy into submission. Patton and his colleagues had always dismissed that argument.

But as the strength of the American Army Air Force grew in Europe after 1943, America's policy to pinpoint-bomb military targets and critical resources such as oil facilities was challenged by Douhet thinkers, who argued that the German people could be forced into early surrender by the "terror bombing" of cities such as Berlin, Leipzig, and Dresden. President Franklin Roosevelt added the argument that the German people must be taught a lesson they would remember for generations, thus avoiding a return to Nazism. The British had advocated those theories since Nazi bombings early in the war, even though their own resistance had been hardened by the attacks.

Many American air generals demurred, remembering the history of the American army and fearing for the public image of the future Air Force. Those objectors included General James Doolittle, who, ironically, had led the first raid on Tokyo in 1942 and had commanded the Eighth Air Force, which made the early raids on Berlin.

The advocates of terror bombing prevailed, however, and the dénouement came with the destruction of Dresden, without significant military targets, by British and American bombers on February 13–14, 1945. Two months later, Patton had his conversation with Secretary McCloy. Throughout the decades, Patton consistently believed that bombing defenseless populations created more resistance rather than less, generated retaliation, wasted crews and equipment, and was probably not moral—or, as he put it, was "cruel." Regardless, the ruins would still have to be fought for and occupied by ground soldiers.

Toward the end of the war, Patton received more assurances that he had succeeded in his appeal to the fighting instincts of his soldiers and that the soldiers believed he cared for their well-being. Herbert Lehman, director general of the United Nations Relief and Rehabilitation Agency, wrote him in January 1945, reporting having been on a troopship with many wounded American soldiers. Lehman said a large proportion had volunteered the information that they wished they were serving under Patton. (BPP II 622.) At about the same time, General Everett Hughes wrote Beatrice that some people previously had wondered whether soldiers would serve under Patton, but now everyone wanted to be in his Army. (BPP II 622, 624.)

But Patton knew the limits of his appeal. He wrote in his diary on January 13, 1945, about how confidence had changed the attitude of his soldiers: "They all feel that they are on the winning side, pursuing a beaten enemy; while yesterday . . . they were dubious as to whether we could stop the German attack. . . . Now that they all feel the enemy is licked, they are sure of themselves. Until today I was the only one sure of victory."

Patton's confidence in victory, just like his confidence in his method of warfare and his leadership style, was rooted in a personal philosophy that sustained him throughout the war. What were the elements of that

Left to right: Generals Bradley, Eisenhower, and Patton. Time and place unknown.

philosophy, and what were their sources?

Beginning with the Morocco landing, his diary and letters were filled with comments on his belief in destiny. On the ship *Augusta* in early November 1942 he wrote: "I can't decide logically if I am a man of destiny or a lucky fool, but I think I am destined. Five more days will show. I really do very little, and have done very little about this show. I feel my claim to greatness hangs on my ability to lead and inspire. . . . I have no personal fear of death or failure. This may sound like junk, or prophecy, within a week. We had a CPX [command post exercise] this morning which was very dull. I can't see how people can be so dull and lacking imagination. Compared to them I am a genius—I think I am." Later, on November 9, he wrote: "I have been doing some extra praying. I hope that whatever comes up, I shall be able to do my full duty. If I can do that, I have nothing more to ask. Fate will determine whatever success I shall attain. . . ."

Writing in his diary on May 23, 1943, during the planning for the Sicily campaign, he fulminated against his British bosses in the Allied command structure and then said, "The thing I must do is to retain my SELF-CONFIDENCE. I have greater ability than these other people and it comes from, for lack of a better word, what must be called greatness of soul based on a belief—an unshakable belief—in my destiny. The U.S. must win—not as an ally, but as a conqueror. If I find my duty, I can do it. I must." On June 26 he wrote Beatrice, "I don't expect to get killed, but if I am, I hope it is a nice clean job. But I have the feeling of being a chip on the river of destiny going to a predestined place of whose location I am ignorant. My chief concern is to do my full duty, retain my self-confidence, and follow my star."

If his belief in his destiny ever flagged, it was only when crises, such as the publicity about slapping the soldiers, threatened his holding command positions. His diary entry on December 25, 1943, reaffirmed his faith: "My men are crazy about me, and this is what makes me most angry about [columnist] Drew Pearson. . . . My destiny is sure and I am a fool and a coward ever to have doubted it. I don't any more. Some people are needed to do things, and I have to be tempered by adversity as well as thrilled by success. I have had both. Now for some success."

Occasionally, Patton indicated that his destiny was personally directed by God. His diary entry for June 19, 1943: "I pray daily to do my duty, retain my self-confidence, and accomplish my destiny. No one can live under the awful responsibility I have without Divine help. Frequently I feel that I don't rate it." To Beatrice in January 1944 after surviving an artillery shelling: "Mathematically I should be dead as none of the four craters was more than 30 feet from me, but I am not dead or even hurt. It gave me great self confidence. The Lord had a perfect cut for me and pulled his punch. . . . You have no idea how much that near miss cheered me up. I know I am needed!" (See margin copy on this page for "God of Battles," a prayer-poem Patton wrote in 1943.)

It might not be misplaced to speculate that Patton's surest anchor in the stronger winds of World War II was the abiding sense of history that forever welled up in his mind. He wrote to his son on June 6, 1944, about the influence of his sense of history on his wartime decision-making: "To be a successful soldier, you must know history. Read it objectively. . . . You must read biography and especially autobiography. . . . In Sicily I decided as a result of my information, observations, and a sixth sense that I have that the enemy did not have another large scale attack in his system. I bet my shirt on that and I was right. . . . What success I have had results from the fact that I have always been certain that my military reactions were correct. Many people do not agree with me; they are wrong. The unerring jury of history written long after both of us are dead will prove me correct."

Historical parallels were constantly on Patton's mind. When he observed the situation in Normandy on July 2, 1944, he immediately wrote Eisenhower that the German Schlieffen Plan of 1914 could be applied. "All we have to do is to change the pivot from Alsace to Caen, and you have it." A month later an operation such as he had described brought about the German defeat in Normandy. Patton's subordinates also received frequent history lessons, as when corps commander Manton Eddy questioned whether he should be fighting with a river at his back, and Patton reminded him that Hernando Cortés purposely burned his ships behind him in his invasion of Mexico in 1518. The press received history lessons, too; when they asked Patton in September 1944 if lack of supplies would prevent his attacking, he answered, "At Chancellorsville, Lee was asked why he attacked when he was outnumbered three to one. Lee said he was too weak to defend." (BPP II 470, 558, 555.)

Patton never missed an opportunity to visit an historical site. On January 5, 1943, he recorded in his Moroccan diary, "Went to Volubilis. This was a Roman city founded in 42 B.C. and was the capital city of the Roman province of West Africa. . . . The ruins are very impressive. . . . [General Ernest N.] Harmon and I could not but think we, the modern equivalent of a Legate, were walking the very streets where our predecessors had walked in shining brass 2,000 years ago." In the spring he noted the great Minerva temple at Thelepte in Tunisia, and flew over the barren ground that had once been ancient Carthage. In Sicily he wrote Beatrice that a temple column at his command post near Gela had been cited by Roman historian Pliny; and he described to her in detail his palace in Palermo, with its chapel built by the Normans in 1040. On a January stint with the British in the Middle East, he traced Edmund Allenby's advance in 1918, entered Jerusalem through the gate

God of Battles

From pride and foolish
  confidence
From every weakening creed
From the dread fear of
  fearing
Protect us, Lord and lead.
Great God, who through the
  ages
Hast braced the bloodstained
  hand.
As Saturn, Jove or Woden
Hast led our warrior band,
Again we seek thy counsel,
But not in cringing guise.
We whine not for thy
  mercy —
to slay: God make us wise.
For slaves who shun the
  issue
We do not ask thy aid.
To Thee we trust our spirits
Our bodies unafraid.
From doubt and fearsome
  boding,
Still Thou our spirits guard,
Make strong our souls to
  conquer,
Give us the victory, Lord.

—George S. Patton, Jr.

that "Tancredi had stormed," found the pyramids near Cairo not as great as those in Mexico, and wrote that the Egyptian monuments at Karnak surpassed any ruins in the world. After a Patton trip to Malta, Beatrice was informed that "The forts used by the knights in the great siege of 1528 are different from any I have ever seen. They are pre-Vauban [before the Marquis de Vauban, a French military engineer who died in 1707] but are artillery forts with walls up to 16 feet thick and very high."

In his "Notes on France," 1944, Patton wrote that he was traversing the route that William the Conqueror had taken in Brittany, passing "through Coutances where even yet the most striking cathedral I have ever seen in France stands as evidence of the uneasy conscience of William's successors." Patton carried with him one of the interwar French tourist "blue guides," Findlay Muirhead's *North-Western France*. In March 1945, during the advance into Germany, he wrote in his diary, "Visited Trier. . . . So did Caesar . . . whose Gallic wars I am now reading. It is interesting to view in imagination the Roman legions marching down the same road." He felt he could "smell the sweat of the legions."

Patton's untutored reading of history through the twenties and thirties empowered him to be a great tactician, a master of the operational art, a superb logistician, and an extraordinary leader. But it did nothing to correct a Patton flaw—his inability to work with Allies and civilian politicians, that element of high command that is essential to the success of coalition warfare. (See Chapter 8.) His marginal notes that went unanswered in his library appeared again in his wartime notes. A conference with the British was "war by committee." After several months

Lieutenant General Patton at Fougeres, France, in August 1944. On the back of this snapshot Patton wrote, "The 2d conqueror of Fougeres. The other one did it in 1200?" (USMA Library photo.)

in North Africa he wrote, "No State Department people should be permitted in a theater of war, nor at the peace treaty." During the planning for the Sicily operation, he wrote in his diary, "As usual the Navy and the Air are not lined up. Of course, being connected with the British is bad. So far, this war is being fought for the benefit of the British Empire and for post-war considerations. No one gives a damn about winning it for itself now." In August 1943, when Patton was reporting to Eisenhower through British General Harold Alexander, Patton recorded in his diary that Alexander came to see him "to see what he could steal" for the invasion of the Italian mainland. "If I suggest to Ike that this is the case, he will tell me I don't see 'the big picture.' I wish to God he was an American." Patton left dangling whether "he" referred to Alexander or Ike. (BPP II 237, 263, 229, 339.)

Publicly, Patton was more reserved in his commentary. Before the Sicily landing he told American soldiers that they would be fighting alongside their Allies: "For years we had competed with them in tennis, in sailing, on the track, in shooting, and in polo. Once more we were in a competition—a competition to see who would first defeat our common foe. It would be the grandest tournament of all." Patton won that tournament at Messina. (BPP II 265.)

As the war moved into France, Patton became more vitriolic in his private criticism of the British, but he maintained his public facade, even when Bradley, Montgomery, Eisenhower, and Churchill were voicing their heated disagreements over strategy and related issues. Patton's restraint was due partially to Eisenhower's warnings that he would relieve Patton of command if he spoke out against the British; however, his reading of German generals on the importance of obedience and unity of command had made a singular impression upon him, so much so that he was unwilling to take action on behalf of the ideas recorded in his diaries and letters. (See Chapters 5 and 7 for Patton's reading of the Germans.)

Exercising restraint and bowing to the unity of command, Patton praised the Russians in public statements, even though his May 14, 1945, diary entry referred to them as savages and "recently civilized Mongolian bandits." Five days earlier he had urged Under Secretary of War Robert P. Patterson to keep the American armies in Europe intact and to turn them on the weakened Soviet armies if Joseph Stalin did not restore self-government to the European peoples under Soviet control. Patterson cautioned that Patton was underestimating the strength of the Russians. Patton replied that they were so primitive that their supply system would not last more than five days; after that, "if you wanted Moscow, I could give it to you." (BPP II 698.) Although Patton's prewar library contained little on the Soviet Union and communism, he had read extensively on balance-of-power diplomacy and strategy, and he

Lieutenant General Patton in May 1945 at a place called Valhalla, near Regensburg, Germany. (USMA Library photo.)

sensed correctly that the Soviets were filling a power vacuum in Eastern Europe and would challenge the West for hegemony throughout the Continent. Four years would pass before America and its allies would begin to constitute a Soviet containment force, under the umbrella of the North Atlantic Treaty Organization.

Patton's misreading of postwar realities was more than just a problem of being ahead of his time. For all of his study of the American nation's reactions to war, especially to the Civil War and World War I, he did not fathom the war weariness of the American public in 1945

General Patton (right) with wife Beatrice Patton (left) and sister Anne ''Nita'' Wilson Patton in California in the summer of 1945.

and their demand to bring the armies home, demobilize them, and get on with normal peacetime pursuits. During a June triumphal tour throughout the United States, however, he began to sense the anti-military mood, and he gladly returned to his Third Army soldiers.

His difficulty in accepting the Allied policies for occupying defeated Germany was rooted in an historically based conception of how wars should end. His favorite model was Appomattox, where Ulysses Grant treated Robert E. Lee and his officers with courtesy and directed the Confederate soldiers to take their sidearms and horses and go back to their farms peaceably. His study in the 1920s of the Versailles Treaty and its spiteful treatment of Germany had convinced him the Germans again would become a menace. After he defeated the Vichy French in Morocco in 1942, he did not impose the harsh settlement crafted by the State Department, but left the government in the hands of French officers who would take their guidance from him—a verbal pact sealed with a glass of champagne.

Regardless of his wartime rhetoric about killing Germans and "hating the Hun," Patton believed peace should be waged without retribution. He approached his duties as occupation commander in eastern Bavaria by looking upon German soldiers as defeated warriors who deserved respect. He was appalled at an Allied policy that required him to ship German "disarmed enemy forces" to France for labor details; he thought it violated not only the Geneva Convention on prisoners of war but also the spirit of the American Constitution's Bill of Rights. In addition to caring for the 1,589,000 German prisoners of war under his control, he showed great concern for the welfare of the 7,295,000 German civilians in his zone, all of whom were faced with lack of food, fuel, and security in a ravaged land. (Third Army Report, November 1, 1945.)

Between May and October 1945, he conscientiously carried out the Allied policy of denazification by removing from office 61,611 former Nazis and denying them governmental employment. But in September, he began to suggest publicly that this denial of experience and skills in critical governmental positions threatened the Germans with starving and freezing in the coming winter. He was misquoted in the American press as equating the views of low-level Nazis with beliefs no more harmful than those of American Democrats or Republicans. That unleashed a torrent of public criticism that demonstrated the demand for retribution against Germans by an American populace who had been on a crusade against Nazism, totalitarianism, and militarism. Patton's vision of a forgiving peace could not prevail, and he agreed with Eisenhower that he should be reassigned from occupation duty to directing the writing of the war's historical record.

After April 1945, peacetime reorganization put Patton in command of the largest field army in the history of the United States: the Third

Lieutenant General Patton in front of his namesake bridge at the Saar River crossing in November 1944. Building the bridge are "The Mighty Midgets." (USMA Library photo.)

Army had more than 500,000 officers and men, assigned to thirty-two divisions and to Third Army corps and army units. As peace was restored they were put to work rebuilding bridges, reopening mines, and operating camps for 1,800,000 displaced persons, even while their own numbers dwindled as they were repatriated to the United States. That Patton could control, maintain, and supply such vast forces is a testimony to his consummate skills in managing disparate organizations and complex staffs and his careful attention to teaching others how to do the same. Those skills and that careful focus stemmed directly from his years of studying how military commanders in the past had solved many of the same kinds of problems. He had penciled words such as "staff" or "overcontrol" or "use of chief of staff" countless times in the margins of his library's books, and he revived their significance in the war's later years.

Patton's most brilliant World War II success, in the Battle of the Bulge, was made possible by his having trained his Third Army staff and subordinate commanders to respond miraculously to his wishes. The success started when he and they redirected six divisions into the southern flank of the German attack into the Ardennes that had begun on December 16, 1944. Although most historians have since written that no Allied commander anticipated that attack, Patton had been warned as early as December 9 by his intelligence officer, Colonel Oscar W. Koch, that German divisions were massing to the north of the Third Army zone, and Patton had ordered limited outline planning to meet that threat. Patton, who had served in intelligence assignments and had forecast the Japanese attack on Pearl Harbor, always had his staff reconnoitering far beyond his area of responsibility. On December 12, when Koch warned of many German divisions massing near Trier, Patton ordered his staff to study a possible Third Army counterattack to the north, even though his forces were programmed to launch a major offensive to the east. By the time Eisenhower could call a meeting—held December 19 in Verdun—to discuss the crisis caused by a deep German penetration, Patton was able to say that he could attack the vulnerable southern flank with three divisions on December 22 and follow with three more divisions.

In three days, Patton's divisions extricated themselves from combat and traversed up to 100 miles on icy roads, often under night blackout conditions, to arrive on time to launch the offensive. After four days of fighting on the new front, the 4th Armored Division fought its way into the encircled American garrison in Bastogne. For the next three weeks fighting continued in Patton's meat grinder. On January 16, 1945, Patton's troops met American First Army troops attacking south into the Bulge.

Patton then published "Notes on Bastogne Operation," which stated the 17 divisions of the Third Army had suffered 24,598 casualties and suggested that estimates of nearly 104,000 German casualties were probably low. Patton's vow to "kill Krauts" had resulted in a blow from which the Germans could not recover. The map he included with his "Notes" was a tribute to the staff and commanders he had trained since 1942. It shows how six divisions successfully moved from the attack on one front to the attack on a distant front. (See inset on page 155.) According to "Patton Before the Bulge" by Steve E. Dietrich, all Patton told his staff and commanders on the morning of December 19 was: "We pride ourselves on our ability to move quickly. But we're going to have to do it faster now than we've ever done before." (16)

Later that same day, when he told Eisenhower and the gathering at Verdun that he could attack toward Bastogne three days later, not a per-

Map from Patton's "Notes on Bastogne Operation" shows how six divisions moved from the attack on one front to the attack on a distant front in December 1944. From the USMA Library.

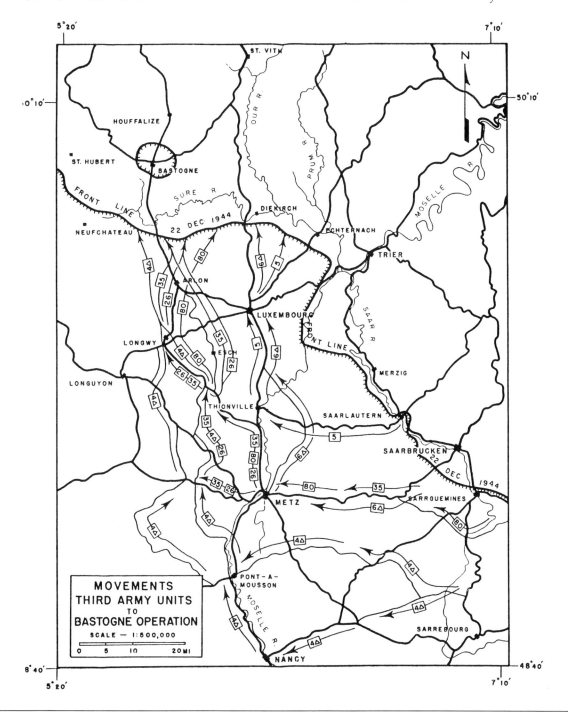

son in the room at first believed him. He spent nearly an hour convincing them, until Eisenhower finally ordered what Patton advocated. It was as if Patton had spent a lifetime of professional study for that one moment. He had taught himself again and again that the battlefield would always be unclear to the commander, who must make decisions without perfect information. He had also learned from his study of the past that the future would present largely unforeseeable and unpredictable situations and that the commander who responds quickly with creative solutions is the one who prevails. This was perhaps his greatest lesson for future commanders: prepare for the unknown by studying how others in the past have coped with the unforeseeable and the unpredictable.

In the midst of World War II, Patton kept up his study of the past, with fare as varied as Julius Caesar in ancient Gaul, the Normans in Sicily, Napoleon in Spain, the Americans in the Philippines, and the Germans in Italy in World War I. (See inset beginning on page 157.) Those were histories of bellicose men in bellicose times. Patton became increasingly bellicose in letter and spirit as the war went on. In March 1943, he wrote Beatrice: "I wish we had more of the killer instinct in our men. They are too damned complacent—willing to die but not anxious to kill. I tell them that it is fine to be willing to die for their country but a damned sight better to make the German die for his. No one has ever told them that. . . . The B[ritish] have suffered and are mad, but our men are not. . . . Roman civilization fell due to the loss of the will to conquer. . . . The cycle is returning. . . ." The same bellicosity about fighting appeared in his April 1944 reply to former West Point classmate Robert H. Fletcher, who had asked what effect education has in producing successful generals. Patton cited their Professor Fiebeger as having taught them that good generalship requires "a desire to fight," good health, historical knowledge, and intelligence. (BPP II 692. For a fuller and more accurate version of what Fiebeger said, see Patton's cadet notes on pages 20 and 21.)

Patton's bellicose stance appeared often in his statements about the inevitability of war, a theme that he carried from his writing between the wars. He wrote Frederick Ayer just before departing Sicily, "I have already met several quite intelligent men who say 'Now we will have no more wars.' . . . The avowed purpose of the Treaty of Vienna in 1814 was to see that that was the last war. About 1700 B.C. the Hittites, Cretans, and Egyptians had a tri-party treaty to avert wars, and we learned about it in 1914. Some explorers discovered the bricks with the treaty on them—yet before the mud had dried, the Egyptians and Cretans had ganged up and destroyed the Hittites. If we again think that wars are over, we will surely have another and damned quick." (See his "The End of War," page 49.)

Patton's Reading During World War II

Throughout the war Patton carried with him *Rudyard Kipling's Verse,* one volume published in 1940. He wrote in the front: "G S Patton Jr. Feb 1942. Ft. Benning Ga." His son would carry that same volume in the Vietnam War.

As he sailed in October 1942 for the North African landing, Patton made this terse entry in his diary: "I finished the Koran —a good book and interesting." Within weeks he would initiate talks with the sultan of Morocco by stating that he would require American troops to show respect for Mohammedan institutions. (BPP II 97, 121.) Patton also reported reading several novels while on shipboard, such as *Three Harbors, The Raft,* and *The Cairo Garter Murders;* he found Ernest Hemingway's *The Sun Also Rises* "pretty sticky." Once off the *Augusta* he reverted to his more traditional literary interests and on April 23, 1943, reported to Beatrice that he had seen "the swellest old book in a jewelry store to day. It was open at the picture of Montgomery spearing the King in the eye. It is a sort of a pictorial history of France with maps of each epoch. I am trying to buy it but no one is interested to find out what the owner wants."

In the months following the Sicilian campaign, Patton read deeply into the history of Sicily and its many occupying armies. His copy of Henry Knight's 1838 *The Normans in Sicily* contains his signature followed by "Palermo, 1943." On November 28, 1943, he wrote Eisenhower that he had been reading James Osborne's *The Greatest Norman Conquest,* which described how twelve brothers from Normandy conquered southern Italy and Sicily in the late eleventh century. He told Ike: "There are many points in common with our operations. The Normans were very careful and meticulous planners. They always attacked. They were masters of landing operations, and they pursued a ruthless offensive in which the armored knights played practically the role of tanks." He wrote Beatrice, "I feel I may be either William Fer-a-Bas or Roger of Sicily, probably the former, as he fought his last battle at 71. . . . Anyhow, they are great company and inspiring fighters." Patton also acquired in Palermo all five volumes of Edward A. Freeman's *The History of the Norman Conquest of England,* published in the 1870s; he left no annotations.

After a trip to Malta, he wrote Beatrice on January 7, 1944: "I saw a cortex of 1420 on velum which was an illustrated life of St. Anthony. . . . [An illustration] showed an armorers shop with suits of armor, helmuts, etc. displayed on sorts of coat hangers. The interesting thing is that armor of all types from 1000 to 1400 was on sale [in the illustration]. This shows that we are wrong in attributing definite dates to certain sorts of harness. The librarian did not know this and was much impressed by my wisdome. . . . I kept thinking how you would have enjoyed it. You are one of the few people sufficiently educated to appreciate it."

To his son George he wrote on June 17, 1944, "Your letter found me reading about the Philippine War 1899–1903 instead of fighting in this one." Earlier that month, on the day of the invasion at Normandy, he wrote Beatrice that it was "Hell to be on the sidelines" and thus "I guess I will read the Bible." In March 1944, "Sir E. Ramsden, Brit." had given him Arthur Bryant's *Years of Endurance,* about the Napoleonic Wars. Four months later, as Patton observed the stalemate in Normandy, he underlined "Instead of pushing boldly and snatching victory, they consolidated minor gains while the odds against them hardened" (356) and wrote beside it, "Now too, July '44."

On November 8, 1944, when his units were plagued by high water, he wrote in his diary: "Woke up at 0300 and it was raining like hell. I actually got nervous and got up and read Rommel's book *Infantry Attacks.* It was most helpful, as he described all the rains he had in September, 1914, and also the fact that, in spite of the heavy rains, the Germans got along. Went to bed and to sleep at 0345." On March 14, 1945, when he noted in his diary that he was reading *Caesar's Gallic War,* he was using a copy given him by General Frank McCoy at "Xmas 1943." On page 153 he underlined "Caesar had now to trust to speed and speed alone." The diary entry of that day also noted, "Called [XX Corps commander Walton] Walker and told him to turn on the heat as I feel we are not going fast enough."

During the long periods of waiting for new assignments, Patton tried to improve his foreign language skills. His reports to Beatrice include, "I still work on my phonograph daily" and "I started my German lessons this morning. My machine has the identical conversations in both French and German so I do them both and am about to go mad." Many of the books given to him and Beatrice were in French, such as *Du Débarquement Africain au Meurtre de Darlan,* written by Albert Kammerer, and *Histoire Militaire de la Chaouia depuis 1884,* published in Casablanca and signed by its author, H. G. Conjeaud. After the war, Victor Joly's *Les Ardennes* was presented to him in Brussels; and Karel Plicka's *Praha* was given to him in Czechoslovakia by a man who signed his name "Benes." A 1945 history of the French 2nd Armored Division, *Le 2e DB,* had a long dedication page written by the book's author, French General Jacques Leclerc.

Perhaps the last book Patton acquired for his professional reading was a Thomas R. Phillips distillation of military classics called *Roots of Strategy;* he wrote in the front, for the last time, "G.S. Patton, Jr. Nov 45." By then he had already drafted most of the sections of his memoirs, to be published in 1947 by Beatrice under the title *War As I Knew It,* a best seller for generations to come.

Patton was at his most bellicose when he extolled man's participation in war as an edifying experience that brought out the best in man's nature: sacrifice, loyalty, a hope for immortality. In a speech to Seventh Army troops before the invasion of Sicily he said, "Battle is the most magnificent competition in which a human being can engage. . . . It brings out all that is best; it removes all that is base." (Army Times, 113. See Ruskin, page 29.)

When he said he had a love for war he knew he was reciting the words of past warriors, including Robert E. Lee, who had said it was fortunate that war was so terrible, lest we become too fond of it. Patton sensed the awe of the spectacle, the wonder at being present at world-shaking events, and the binding camaraderie that had been the wartime experience of countless soldiers through the centuries; and he knew those emotions were felt by the soldiers of World War II, as described after that war by J. Glenn Gray in *The Warriors.*

Patton was thus a bellicose man who trained himself to meet the needs of the bellicose times in which he lived. Those who later interpreted him as a medieval knight, hopelessly out of place in the twentieth century, should pause at his effectiveness in the century of total warfare. And they should investigate the sources of his popularity in the middle and late twentieth century among vast populations just as bellicose as he.

Patton's funeral, December 22, 1945, in a Protestant church in Heidelberg, Germany.
(USMA Library photo originally taken by Acme Newspictures Inc. of New York.)

Conclusion

G EORGE S. PATTON, JR., DIED of injuries sustained in an automobile accident on December 21, 1945, and was buried alongside many of his soldiers at Hamm, Luxembourg. For sixty years, he had prepared for his profession of arms and had lived the life of a military gentleman. In thirteen months of wartime combat, he had achieved his childhood dream of becoming a famed battle hero.

Forty-six years after his death, a tribute to Patton's military genius was emblazoned on a large sign in a Gulf War allied headquarters in Saudi Arabia. It read: "Hold 'em by the nose and kick 'em in the ass—General George S. Patton, Jr." Under the sign, scores of desert warriors were translating this dictum into military operations that limited the war to one hundred days and held allied casualties to a minimum.

Some of these soldiers knew how Patton had taught himself this fundamental military principle, starting when he was barely twenty years old as he scribbled "rear attack" and "flank attack" in the margins of his books. The source of his genius was in his library and in on-the-job learning, rather than in the army schooling system; his less creative contemporaries averaged more than ten years in student and faculty time while Patton served little more than four years studying in army schools.

Patton's military genius was grounded in his reading lists, note cards, and voluminous writings on the organization, tactics, and technology of future warfare. The "sacred truths" that he uncovered in the schools he often characterized as promoting a warfare that was too cautious, too defensive, too inefficient, and too controlled by staff procedures.

The Patton mind that emerged from this crucible of private study was capable of creating a kind of warfare that was so fast and so destructive of the enemy that the battle could be won with a minimum of friendly casualties and expenditure of materiel. The Patton mind also envisioned a warfare that placed limits on the amount of violence to be visited on innocent bystanders, and anticipated peace treaties without vengeance or retribution.

Patton's reading of military history may have rendered him unsuited for the leadership of allies in coalition warfare, in contrast to, say, the equally creative Eisenhower, who had read some of the same history. Nor did Patton's extensive study of American history seem to sensitize him to the strains of isolationism and war weariness of the American populace.

But regardless of these handicaps, Patton's military genius was indelible when it flowered in his bold actions in Sicily, in the drive across France, and in the Battle of the Bulge.

Patton's public image as a bellicose man suited the equally bellicose societies that dominated the nearly half-century following his death. Today these societies are beset by violence, whether in the streets, in the arts, or in their international confrontations. Despite the nuclear umbrella, war rages constantly among countless factions across the Earth's surface. Questions about the nature of military leadership regularly resurface.

One pauses if asked to name the world leaders of the past century who are recognized for having Patton's military knowledge, skills, insights, and values. Those who see him as an anachronistic medieval knight in the modern world should also recall how effectively he brought the trained, cultured mind to the scene of human catastrophe—the reign of total warfare in World War II.

That dual image of Patton was best captured in a brief story told in 1990 by General John R. Galvin, who held the post of Supreme Allied Commander Europe. In another role, a few years earlier, he had paused in a medieval church in Bad Wimpfen, Germany—a church that had apparently survived well the World War II destruction. A very senior cleric came to him and remarked that, as a young priest, he had found General Patton standing in the same place in 1945. Then the cleric added that Patton was doing a most unusual thing for a man of such reputation. The warrior, with notebook and pencil in hand, was sketching the stained-glass windows.

Appendices

Patton as a Collector of Rare Books

S OME FORTY BOOKS in the Patton Library at West Point indicate that he constantly approached the best booksellers of Europe and America in search of eighteenth- and nineteenth-century military volumes. He did not mar those collectors' items with his signature or date of purchase, and we know little of the history of those books or his acquisition of them. But most were and are classics.

In the field of military fortifications, for example, is Marshal Sebastien de Vauban's *De l'Attaque et de la Défense des Places* (short title), published in 1743, and all four volumes of Giuseppe Parisi's *Elementi di Architettura Militaire*, printed in Naples in 1771–1787.

The work of greatest value in this trove for collectors was never even published. *Military Architecture*, made up of hand-drawn plates, would have become a history of military building but for the death of its author, John Charnock of London, in 1807. Tinted in watercolors, the vast collection of outsized drawings was mounted into two great volumes.

Patton also acquired a copy of the Comte de Saxe's *Rêveries ou Mémoirs sur l'Arte de Guerre*, published in 1755, and two outsized volumes of French military drawings of that period: *Ecole de Cavalerie* by François Robichon de la Guerinière and *Marches et Évolutions de Cavalerie* by John Drummond Melfort. The Prussian Major General of Hussars, Charles Warnery, was represented in the collection by his *Remarks on Cavalry*, printed in London with twenty-four plates in 1798. In one of the unusual instances in which Patton signed a rare book, he wrote his name and "Feb. 22, '45" into a copy of *The History of Francis-Eugene, Prince of Savoy*, which had been written by "an English Officer" and printed in 1754. Patton's copy of Prince Eugene's *Memoirs* was published in 1811.

The eighteenth-century British Army was featured in four of the books: *A Treatise of Military Discipline* written in 1759 by Lieutenant General Humphrey Bland; *Rules and Regulations for the Sword Exercise of the Cavalry*, published originally by Great Britain's War Office in 1796 and reprinted in Philadelphia in 1808 (Patton had a copy of each); *Military Antiquities*, published by Francis Grose in 1812; and a quaint tome by Joseph Strutt, *The Sports and Pastimes of the People of England*, published in London in 1831.

Patton collected many volumes on the general history of European wars, the oldest being Henry Lloyd's *A Political and Military Rhapsody on the Invasion and Defence of Great Britain and Ireland*. The Spanish were represented by William Prescott's three-volume *History of the Conquest of Mexico*; Prescott's three-volume *History of the Reign of Philip the Second, King of Spain*; and a volume of William Napier's five-volume *History of the War in the Peninsula*. To study the French, Patton acquired all four volumes of the *Dictionnaire Historique des Batailles, Sièges, et Combats de Terre et Mer, Pendant La Revolution Française*, published in Paris in 1818 by the Société de Militaire et de Marins.

The oldest book in the collection about the wars of the Germans is Lloyd's 1781 *History of the Late War Between the King of Prussia and the Empress of Austria and Her Allies*; Volume II, published in 1790, is one of the few rare books that Patton had rebound in Hawaii after the 1925 fire. Not so rare, but of interest to researchers, is Theodore Rehtwisch's three-volume *Geschichte der Freiheitskriege in den Jahren 1812–1815*, published in the early 1900s. And one wonders how Patton came across Le Duc de Montesquiou-Frezensac's *Souvenirs Militaires 1804 à 1814*, published in Paris in 1869, for its bookplate says, "Belongs to the library of Headquarters, Department of Dakota."

The older American military books in the Patton collection include William Duane's *A Handbook for Infantry*, printed in Philadelphia in 1814; it was signed "G. S. Patton from A. D. Smiles, July 7, 1939." His copy of *The American Trooper's Pocket Companion: Being a Concise and Comprehensive System of Discipline for the Cavalry in the United States* was written by Nicholas Pariset and published in Trenton, New Jersey, in 1818. *The Pictorial Field-Book of the War of 1812* by Benson Lossing was published by Harper & Brothers in 1869.

Patton's American Civil War manuals included George McClellan's 1861 *Regulations and Instructions for the Field Service of the U.S. Cavalry in Time of War*; McClellan's 1862 *Bayonet Exercise for the Army*; and the U.S. War Department's printing of Poinsett's *Cavalry Tactics*. The books he read about Civil War generals included *Sherman and His Campaigns: A Military Biography*, written by S. M. Bowman and Richard Irwin in 1865; and Joel Headley's *Grant and Sherman*, R. R. Dabney's *Life and Campaigns of Lieutenant General Thomas J. Jackson*, and James McCabe's *Life and Campaigns of General Robert E. Lee*, all published the following year.

Patton's Napoleonic collection also contained these rare books: *The Battle of Waterloo* by "A Near Observer," 1815; *Manuscript Transmitted From St. Helena by an Unknown Channel* by Napoleon, published in 1817; two volumes of *Napoleon in Exile* by Barry O'Meara in 1822; two volumes of the *Journal of the Private Life and Conversations by the Emperor Napoleon at St. Helena* by Count De Las Cases in 1823; *Napoleon and the Grand Army in Russia* by General Gaspard Gourgaud in 1825; and two volumes of the 1827 *History of the Expedition to Russia Undertaken by the Emperor Napoleon in the Year 1812* by General Philip de Segur.

Patton's long-standing interest in body armor and military uniforms is borne out in his acquiring all three volumes of Samuel Rush Meyrick's *A Critical Inquiry Into Antient Armor,* published in London in 1824. He supplemented that with the five-volume *A Record of European Armour and Arms Through Seven Centuries* by Sir Guy Laking, the "Late Keeper of the King's Armoury," published in London in the early 1920s. He rebound that set in Hawaii in 1926, then bought an additional set and added to it Francis Cripps-Day's *A Record of Armour Sales, 1881–1924.*

Patton's interest in Vauban and the other great architects of military fortifications was seen again in the late 1930s when he acquired E. Viollet-le-Duc's *Annals of a Fortress*. Writing in the 1870s, the author selected a piece of ground at a junction of the Saone River in upper Burgundy and described how it had been fortified, first in 400 B.C., next in Caesar's time, then in the Dark Ages, the Middle Ages, the Renaissance, and finally in 1680 by Vauban. By 1813 it had undergone seven sieges, each of which is described in great detail. Patton signed the book in three places and penned his "R" on the binding to indicate he had read it.

How and when Patton acquired his significant collection of rare books on military subjects has yet to be explored. He did not travel in Europe between the wars, although Aunt Nannie did and often sent him the treasures she found. Why Patton acquired such a rare library is more easily pondered. It matched his conception of the learning and accouterments of the professional military gentleman.

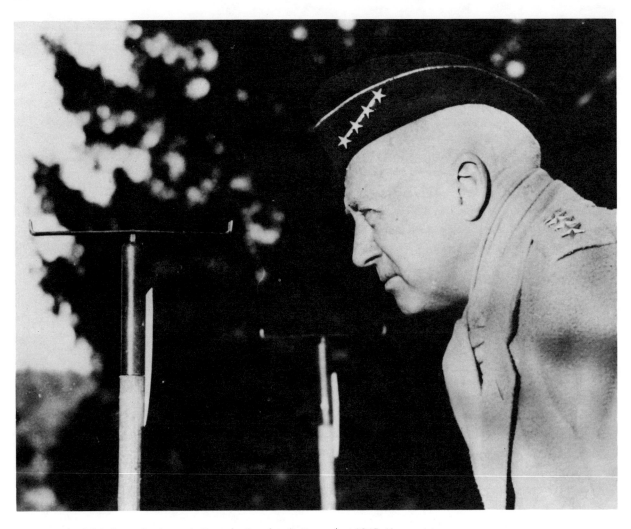

Patton at the 8th Infantry Regiment in Uppsala, Sweden, in November 1945. He went to Sweden for a reunion of participants from the 1912 Olympics. (USMA Library photo.)

Maps of
Patton Campaigns

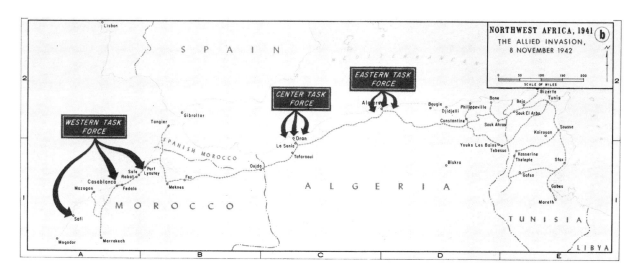

Map 1. Northwest Africa, 1942. From: Griess, *The Second World War Campaign Atlas*, Avery.

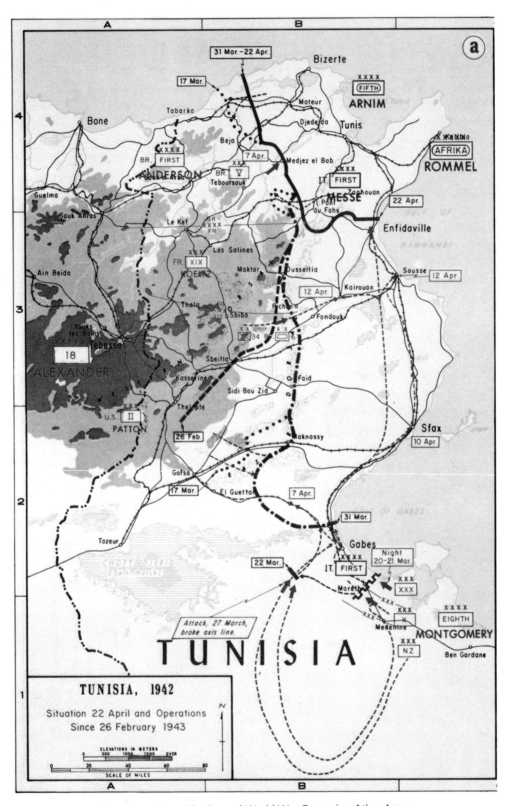

Map 2. Tunisia, 1943. From: Griess, *The Second World War Campaign Atlas*, Avery.

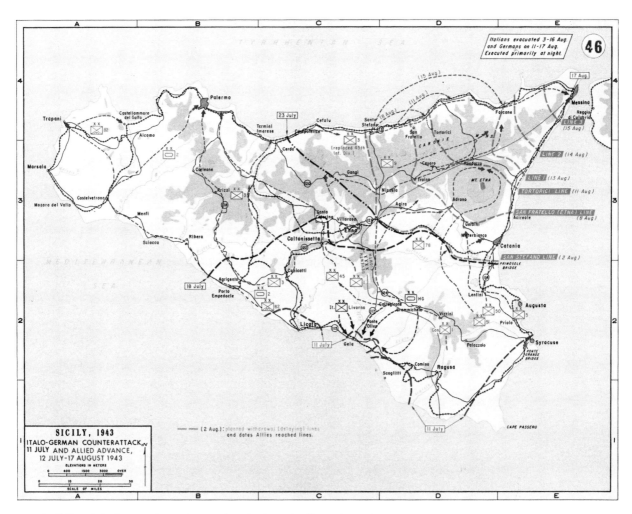

Map 3. Sicily, 1943. From: USMA, *Summaries of Selected Military Campaigns.*

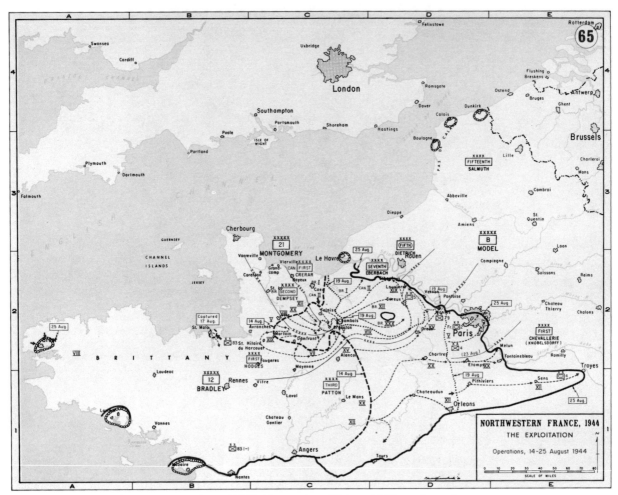

Map 4. Normandy to the Seine, 1944. From: USMA, *Summaries of Selected Military Campaigns*.

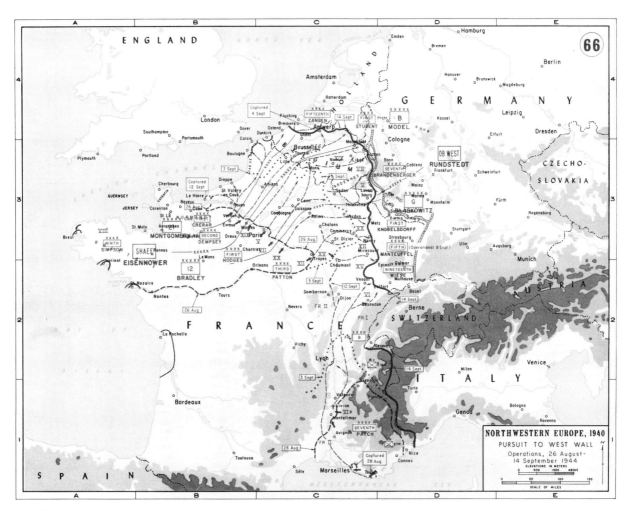

Map 5. Pursuit to the West Wall,1944. From: USMA, *Summaries of Selected Military Campaigns*.

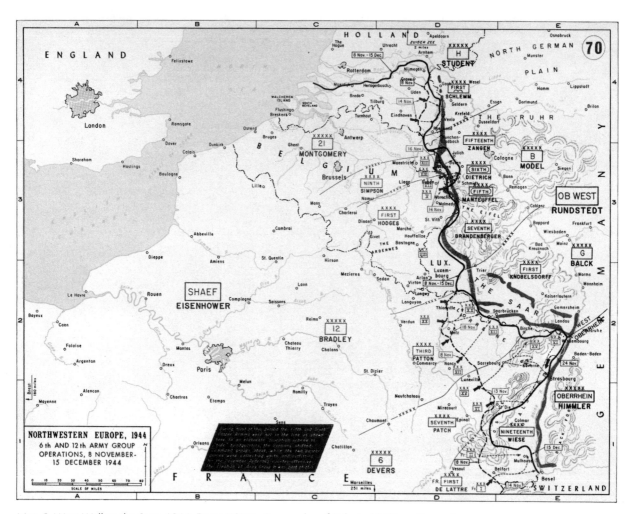

Map 6. West Wall to the Saar, 1944. From: USMA, *Summaries of Selected Military Campaigns*.

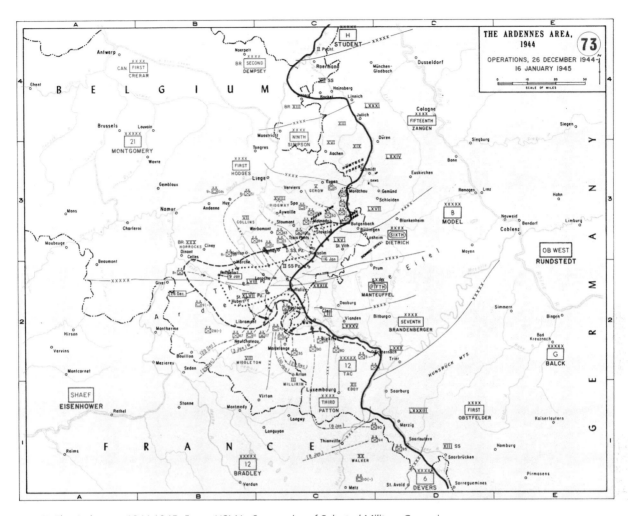

Map 7. The Ardennes, 1944-1945. From: USMA, *Summaries of Selected Military Campaigns*.

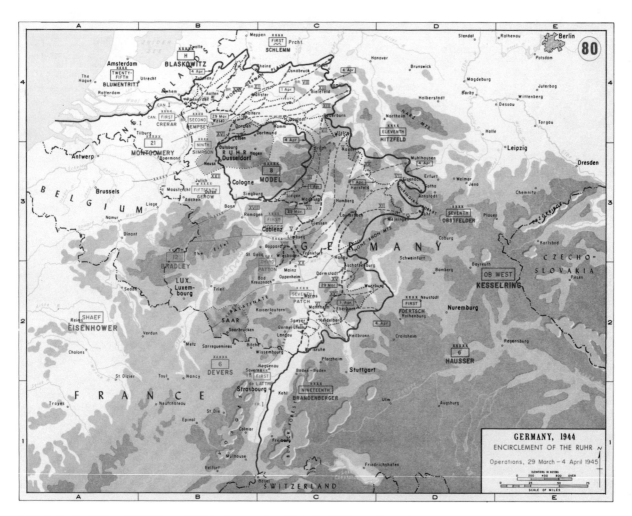

Map 8. To the Rhine, 1945. From: USMA, *Summaries of Selected Military Campaigns*.

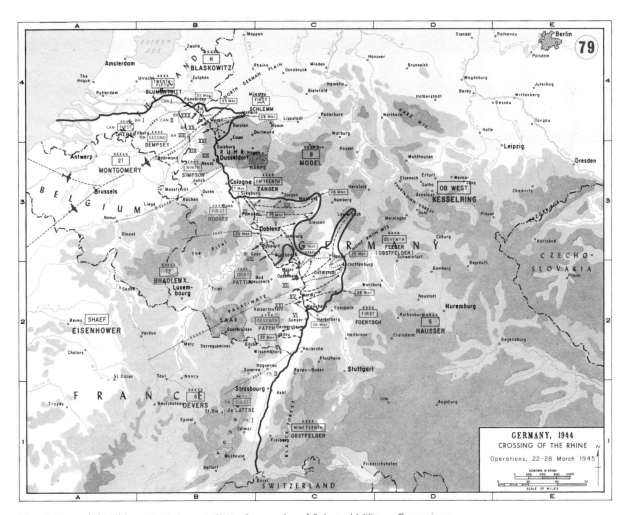

Map 9. Beyond the Rhine, 1945. From: USMA, *Summaries of Selected Military Campaigns.*

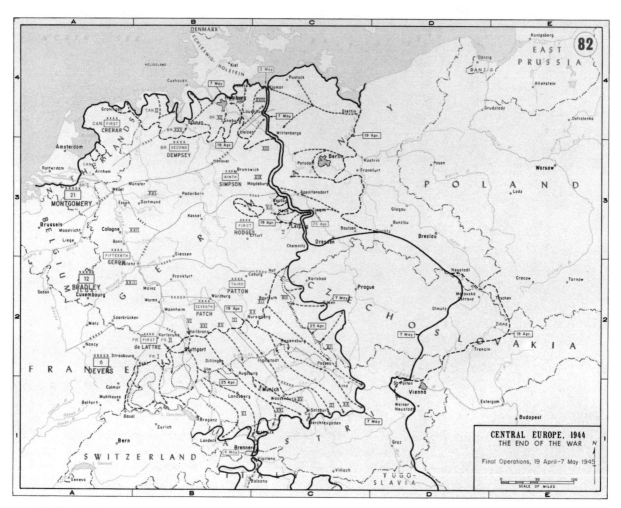

Map 10. The Final Pursuit, 1945. From: USMA, *Summaries of Selected Military Campaigns*.

Bibliography

THIS BIBLIOGRAPHY is an integration of two lists: (1) selected contents of the Patton Library as it was in the late 1940s in the Patton home in South Hamilton, Massachusetts, and (2) the contents of the Patton Collection in the United States Military Academy Library at West Point, New York, in the early 1990s. Also included are materials cited by the author in the text, most of which were referred to by Patton in his reading notes and writings, or by his family and associates, but which are not available in the Patton holdings. The USMA Library can provide many of these materials from its Special Collections and Circulation holdings. "WP" at the end of bibliographical entries indicates the item is in the Patton Collection at West Point. Entries also state which books Patton inscribed.

La 2e DB, General Leclerc, Combattants et Combats en France. Paris: Arts et Metiers Graphiques, 1945. Note: Inscribed to Gen. Patton by Leclerc, 25 Jul 1945. WP.

Ahlund, Nils; Roberts, Michael, tr. *Gustav Adolph the Great.* New York: Princeton University Press, 1940. Note: Inscribed "G. S. Patton from 13 July 1940."

Allen, Colonel Robert S. *Lucky Forward: The History of Patton's Third Army.* New York: The Vanguard Press, Inc., 1947.

Allen, Major General Henry T. *My Rhineland Journal.* Boston: Houghton Mifflin Company, 1923.

Alten, Georg Karl Friedrich Victor von; Barth, Charles Henry, tr. *Studies in Applied Tactics.* Authorized translation (with substitution of American Army organization). Kansas City, Mo.: F. Hudson, 1908. WP.

Army Times. *Warrior: The Story of General George S. Patton.* New York: G. P. Putnam's Sons, 1967.

Arthur, George Compton Archibald. *Life of Lord Kitchener.* New York: The Macmillan Company, 1920. 3 vols.

Aspinall-Oglander, C. F. *Military Operations, Gallipoli.* Becke, A. F., comp. London: Heinemann, 1935. (History of the Great War.) Note: Inscribed "G. S. Patton, Jr. Jan. 1936." Vol. 1. *Inception of the Campaign to May 1915.* WP.

Atkinson, Christopher Thomas. *Marlborough and the Rise of the British Army.* New York: G. P. Putnam's Sons, 1924. WP.

Aubry, Paul. *La ruee sur Saint-Malo.* Rennes: Les nouvelles, 1947. WP.

Ausubel, Nathan. *Superman, the Life of Frederick the Great.* New York: I. Washburn, 1931. Note: Inscribed "G. S. Patton, Jr. Sept 24 1932, Fort Myer, Va." WP.

Ayer, Fred Jr. *Before the Colors Fade: Portrait of a Soldier George S. Patton, Jr.* Boston: Houghton Mifflin Company, 1964.

Azan, Paul of the French Army; Coolidge, Julian L., tr. *The Warfare of Today.* Boston: Houghton Mifflin Company, 1918. (Eight lectures delivered before the Lowell Institute, Boston, October–November 1917.)

Baene, Antoine L. de. *Glory and Honor to the Armies of the United States of America, Liberators of Belgium, 1944–1945.* Bruxelles: J. Rozez, 1948. WP.

Balck, William; Bell, Harry, tr. *Development of Tactics– World War.* Fort Leavenworth, Kans.: The General Service Schools Press, 1922. 2 vols. Note: Inscribed "G. S. Patton, Jr." Annotated. WP.

Balck, William; Krueger, Walter, tr. *Cavalry, Field and Heavy Artillery in Field Warfare.* 4th enl. and completely rev. ed. Fort Leavenworth, Kans.: U.S. Cavalry Assoc., 1914. (Tactics: v. 2.) Note: Inscribed "G.S. Patton, Jr. Apr. 9, 1915, M.S.S." WP.

Balck, William; Krueger, Walter, tr. *Introduction and Formal Tactics of Infantry.* 4th completely rev. ed. Fort Leavenworth, Kans.: U.S. Cavalry Assoc., 1911. (Tactics: v. 1.) Note: Inscribed "G. S. Patton, Jr. Apr. 9, 1915, M.M.S." WP.

Baldock, Thomas Stanford. *Cromwell as a Soldier.* London: K. Paul, Trench, Trubner, 1899. WP.

Barrès, Maurice; Miall, Bernard, tr. *Memoirs of a Napoleonic Officer: Jean-Baptiste Barrès.* New York: The Dial Press, 1925. Note: Inscribed "G. S. Patton, Jr. 1928."

Begbie, Harold. *The Windows of Westminster.* New York, London: G. P. Putnam, 1924. WP.

Belloc, Hilaire. *Wolsey.* Philadelphia: J. B. Lippincott, 1930. WP.

Bergvall, Erik. *Vid Malsnoret.* Stockholm: Steinsviks, 1945. Note: Presented by the author to Gen. Patton in memory of the 1912 Olympics. WP.

Bernhardi, Friedrich Adam Julius von. *Germany and the Next War.* London: E. Arnold, 1912.

Bernhardi, Friedrich von. *How Germany Makes War.* New York: George H. Doran Company, 1914. Note: Patton "R" on binding.

Bernhardi, Friedrich Adam Julius von; Holt, F. A., tr. *The War of the Future, in the Light of the Lessons of the World War.* New York: D. Appleton, 1921. Note: Inscribed "G.S. Patton, Jr. Feb. 9, 1921." WP.

Bird, W. D. *The Direction of War: A Study of Strategy.* Cambridge (Eng.): At the University Press, 1920. (Cambridge military and naval series.) Note: Inscribed "G.S. Patton, Jr. June 25, 1926." WP.

Bjornstad, Alfred William. *Training Management.* 2nd ed. Omaha: Ralph Pub. Co., 1926. WP.

Bland, Humphrey. *Treatise of Military Discipline.* 8th rev. London: Printed for R. Baldwin [and others], 1759. WP.

Bloem, Walter; Wynne, Graeme Chamley, tr. *The Advance From Mons, 1914.* London: P. Davies, 1930.

Blum, Andre. *Histoire du costume en France.* Paris: Hachette, [c1924]. WP.

Blumenson, Martin. *The Many Faces of George S. Patton, Jr.* Colorado Springs: United States Air Force Academy, 1972.

Blumenson, Martin. *The Patton Papers.* Boston: Houghton Mifflin, 1972–74. 2 vols. Contents: vol. 1, 1885–1940; vol. 2, 1940–1945. WP.

Blumenson, Martin. *Patton: The Man Behind the Legend, 1885–1945.* New York: Berkley Books, 1985. WP.

Borcke, Heros von, Chief of Staff to General J.E.B. Stuart. *Memoirs of the Confederate War for Independence.* 2 vols. New York: Peter Smith, 1938 [1866]. Note: Inscribed "G.S. Patton, Jr. Ft. Myer. July 1939."

Bourrienne, Louis Antoine Fauvelet de. *Memoirs of Napoleon Bonaparte.* Boston: Dana Estes; n.d. 4 vols. Note: Inscribed "George S. Patton, Jr. from E.B.A. [Ellen Benning Ayer] Dec 27, 1910." WP.

Bowman, S. M.; Irwin, Richard Biddle. *Sherman and His Campaigns: A Military Biography.* New York, Cincinnati: C. B. Richardson, C. F. Vent, 1865. WP.

Brack, Antoine Fortune de; Carr, Camillo C.C., tr. *Avant Postes de Cavalerie Légère, Cavalry Outpost Duties.* 1st ed. New York: Wiley, 1893. WP.

Brady, Cyrus Townsend. *Indian Fights and Fighters.* Garden City, N.Y.: Doubleday, Page & Company, 1923. Note: One annotation, p. 188 "3 cav."

Brasted, Evelyn. *Soldier of God.* New York: Carlton Press, c1971. Note: Inscribed by author. WP.

Breasted, James Henry. *The Conquest of Civilization*. New York: Harper & Bros., 1926. Note: Inscribed "G.S. Patton, Jr. Jan. 31, 1928." WP.

Brinn'Gaubast, Louis Pilato de; Barthelemy, Edmond. *La tetralogie de l'anneau du Nibelung*. Paris: E. Dentu, 1894. WP.

The British-Boer War, 1899–1902. n.l.: n.p., n.d. Note: Inscribed "G.S. Patton, Jr. May 28, 1909." WP.

Bryant, Arthur. *Years of Endurance, 1793–1802*. London: Collins, 1942. Note: Inscribed "Presented to G.S. Patton, Jr. by Sir E. Ramsden, Brit. Mar 44."

Bryant, Arthur. *Years of Victory, 1802–1812*. London: Collins, 1945.

Bryce, James. *The American Commonwealth*. 2 vols. New York: The Macmillan Company, 1920. Note: Inscribed "G.S. Patton, Jr. Ft. Myer, Christmas 1920." (Vol. 2 only.)

Bryce, James. *The Holy Roman Empire*. New York: The Macmillan Company, 1913. Note: Inscribed "George S. Patton, Jr. Mar 29, 1915. M.S.S."

Buchan, John. *A History of the Great War*. Standard library ed. 2 vols. Boston, New York: Houghton Mifflin, 1923. WP.

Buchanan, George, Sir. *My Mission to Russia and Other Diplomatic Memories*. 2 vols. Boston: Little, Brown, 1923. WP.

Buddecke, Albert. *Tactical Decisions and Orders*. 3rd revised, 1906, ed. Kansas City, Mo.: Franklin Hudson Publ, 1908. Note: Signed "George S. Patton, Jr., 2nd Lieut. 15th Cav., Jan. 22, 1910." WP.

Burnod, General; D'Aguilar, G. C., tr. *Napoleon's Maxims of War*. Kansas City, Mo.: Hudson-Kimberly Publishing Co, n.d. Note: Inscribed "G.S. Patton, Jr., Maj GSC June 1, 1926."

Burton, R. G. *Napoleon's Campaigns in Italy: 1796–1797 and 1800*. London: George Allen & Unwin, Ltd, 1931. Note: Inscribed "G.S. Patton, Jr. Dec 1936."

Burton, R. G. (Indian Army). *From Boulogne to Austerlitz: Napoleon's Campaign of 1805*. Special Campaign Series no. 17. New York: The Macmillan Company, 1912. Note: "Patton" on cover.

Bywater, Hector C. *Navies and Nations*. Boston: Houghton Mifflin Company, 1927. Note: Inscribed "G.S. Patton, Jr. from Gen. Fox Conner, Christmas 1927."

Caesar, Julius. *The Commentaries of Julius Caesar*. New York: Bangs, 1852.

Caesar, Julius; Long, Frederick Percy, tr. *Caesar's Gallic War*. Oxford: The Clarendon Press, 1911. Note: Inscribed "G.S. Patton, Jr. from Gen. Frank McCoy. Xmas, 1943."

Calahan, Harold Augustin. *Gadgets and Wrinkles, A Compendium of Man's Ingenuity at Sea*. New York: Macmillan, 1938.

Calahan, Harold Augustin. *Learning to Sail*. New ed. New York: Macmillan, 1947. WP.

Calahan, Harold Augustin. *Learning to Cruise*. New York: Macmillan, 1948. c1936. WP.

Calahan, Harold Augustin. *Learning to Race*. New York: Macmillan, 1948. c1934. WP.

Callwell, Charles Edward. *The Life of Sir Stanley Maude, Lieutenant General*. Boston: Houghton Mifflin, 1920. Note: Inscribed "G.S. Patton, Jr." WP.

The Cavalry Journal. *Basic Cavalry Manual: A Textbook of Basic Cavalry Training for General Cavalry Training and for the Reserve Officers Training Corps*. Washington, D.C.: National Service Publishing Company, 1930. WP.

The Cavalry Journal, Horsed and Mechanized. London: Royal United Service Institution, 1906–1942. Note: Holdings: Vol. 30, nos. 115–117; vol. 31, nos. 120, 122–123. WP.

Cerezo, Saturnino Martin; Dodds, F. L., tr. and ed. *Under the Red and Gold: Being Notes and Recollections of the Siege of Baler*. 2nd ed. Kansas City, Mo.: Franklin Hudson Publishing Co., 1909. Note: Inscribed "G.S. Patton, Jr. 1916." WP.

Champney, Elizabeth Williams; Champney, Frere. *Romance of Old Belgium, From Csar to Kaiser*. New York: G. P. Putnam, [1915?] WP.

Chanal, Francois Victor Adolphe de; O'Brien, Michael James, tr. *The American Army in the War of Secession*. Leavenworth, Kans.: G. A. Spooner, 1894. Note: Inscribed "G.S. Patton, Jr., Maj GSC, June 1, 1920." At end: "Finished Sept 15, 1926. A good account."

Charnock, John. *Military Architecture*, [1800?] Note: Manuscript copy in 2 folio volumes with hand-colored plates. Work was never published. WP.

Churchill, Frank Gordon. *Horseshoeing*. Fort Riley, Kans.: The Cavalry School, 1933. WP.

Churchill, Frank Gordon. *Practical and Scientific Horseshoeing*. Kansas City, Mo.: Franklin Hudson Publ. Co., 1912. Note: Inscribed "GS Patton, Jr. Maj 3 Cav, Fort Myer, Va., 1921." WP.

Churchill, Lady Randolph Spencer (Mrs. George Cornwallis-West). *The Anglo-Saxon Review, A Quarterly Miscellany.* London: Mrs. George Cornwallis-West, 1900. Note: Vol. 7. December 1900. WP.

Churchill, Winston. *Marlborough, His Life and Times.* 6 vols. New York: C. Scribner's Sons, 1933–38. Vols. 1–4. Note: Inscribed "G.S. Patton, Jr. from Mrs. E.K. Merrill, Jan. 1934."

Clausewitz, Carl von. *General Carl von Clausewitz On War.* London: W. Clowes, 1909. Note: Inscribed "Finished August 15, 1910, George S. Patton, Jr." WP.

Clausewitz, Carl von. *On War.* New and rev. ed. Maude, F.N. (Col.), Intro. and notes. 3 vols. London: Kegan, Paul, Trench, Trubner, 1918 (3rd impr.). Note: Inscribed "G.S. Patton, Jr. May 29, 1926." WP.

Close, Upton. *Challenge: Behind the Face of Japan.* New York: Farrar & Rinehart, Inc., 1934. Note: Inscribed "G.S. Patton, Jr. Nov 1935."

Codman, Charles R. *Drive.* Boston: Little, Brown and Company, 1957.

Cohen, Louis. *Napoleon Anecdotes.* 2 vols. London: Robert Holden & Co., Ltd, 1925.

Colin, Jean Lambert Alphonse; Pope-Hennessy, L.H.R., tr. *The Transformation of War.* London: H. Rees, 1912. Note: Inscribed "G.S. Patton, Jr., Maj GSC. Schofield Bks, Jan 27, 1927."

Collier, William F.; Schmitz, Leonhard. *International Atlas,* consisting of 75 maps. New York: Putnam, n.d. WP.

Conjeaud, H. G. *Histoire militaire de la Chaouia depuis 1894.* Casablanca: Editions du Moghreb, [between 1938 and 1948]. Note: Inscribed by author. WP.

Cooper, Duff, Viscount Norwich. *Haig.* Garden City, N.Y.: Doubleday, Doran, 1936. Note: Inscribed "G.S. Patton, Jr., November 11, 1936 from B."

Cowper, Henry Swainson. *The Art of Attack.* Ulverston: W. Holmes, 1906. WP.

Cox, Jacob Dolson. *Atlanta.* New York: C. Scribner's Sons, 1909. c1882. (Campaigns of the Civil War, v. 9.) WP.

Cox, Jacob Dolson. *The March to the Sea: Franklin and Nashville.* New York: Charles Scribner's Sons, 1913. Note: Inscribed "G.S. Patton, Jr. May 30, 1926."

Creasy, Edward Shepherd. *The Fifteen Decisive Battles of the World From Marathon to Waterloo.* London: Macmillan, 1914. Note: Inscribed "G.S. Patton, Jr., Maj GSC, June 30, 1926."

Cripps-Day, Francis Henry. *A Record of Armour Sales, 1881–1924.* London: G. Bell and Sons, 1925. WP.

Cunliffe, John W. and Thornton, Ashley H., eds. *The World's Best Literature.* Volume 2 of The Warner Library. New York: The Knickerbocker Press, 1917. WP.

Cunninghame Graham, Robert Bontine. *Pedro de Valdivia, Conqueror of Chile.* London: W. Heinemann, 1926. WP.

Cutchins, John Abram. *A Famous Command, the Richmond Light Infantry Blues.* Richmond, Va.: Garret and Massie, 1934. WP.

Cuyás, Arturo. *Appleton's New Spanish-English and English-Spanish Dictionary.* New York: D. Appleton and Company, 1906. Note: Inscribed "George Patton, Jr. Dec 30 1906."

Dabney, R. R. *Life and Campaigns of Lieutenant General Thomas J. Jackson.* New York: Blelock and Company, 1866. Note: Inscribed "This book belonged to Papa. Taken by me in 1935. G.S.P., Jr."

Davis, William Stearns. *Europe Since Waterloo.* New York, London: The Century Co, [c1926]. Note: Inscribed "G.S. Patton, Jr., Maj GSC, Jan 1927."

De Las Cases, Count. *Journal of the Private Life and Conversations by the Emperor Napoleon at St. Helena.* 2 vols. London: Printed for Henry Colburn and Company, 1823.

DeGaulle, Charles. *The Army of the Future.* London: Hutchinson and Co, [1940].

Dening, Basil Cranmer. *The Future of the British Army: The Problem of its Duties, and Cost and Composition.* London: H.F. & G. Witherby, 1928.

Denison, George Taylor. *A History of Cavalry From the Earliest Times, With Lessons for the Future.* London: Macmillan and Co., Ltd., 1913.

Deslys, Charles. *l'héritage de Charlemagne.* 2 vols. Paris: L. Hachette, 1864. WP.

DeWet, Christiaan Rudolf. *Three Years War (October 1899–June 1902).* Popular ed. Westminster [London]: A. Constable, 1903.

Dietrich, Steve E. "Patton Before the Bulge: In a Position to Meet Whatever Happens." n.l.: n.p., November 1988. Note: Typescript. WP.

Dietrich, Steve E. "The Professional Reading of General George S. Patton, Jr." *The Journal of Military History.* 53 (October 1989): 387–418.

Dmitri, Ivan. *Flight to Everywhere.* 1st ed. New York: Whittlesey House, 1944. Note: Inscribed by author. WP.

Dodd, William E. *Lincoln or Lee.* New York: The Century Co, 1928. Note: Inscribed "G.S. Patton, Jr. June 1928."

Doyle, Arthur Conan. *The Adventures of Gerard.* New York: McClure, Phillips and Co., 1903.

Doyle, Arthur Conan. *The Great Boer War.* New York: McClure, Phillips and Co., 1902.

Doyle, Arthur Conan. *Sir Nigel.* New York: McClure, Phillips and Co., 1906.

Doyle, Arthur Conan. *The White Company.* New York: Cosmopolitan Book Corp, 1922.

Draper, Lyman Copeland; Allaire, Anthony; Shelby, Isaac. *King's Mountain and Its Heroes. History of the Battle of King's Mountain, October 7th, 1780, and the Events Which Led to It.* Cincinnati: P. G. Thomson, 1881.

Duane, William; United States Adjutant General's Office. *A Handbook for Infantry.* 8th ed. Philadelphia: Printed for the author, 1814. WP.

Durand de Dauphiné. *Un Français en Virginie, voyages d'un Français exile pour la religion, avec une description de la Virgine & Marilan dans l'Amerique* d'apres l'edition originale de 1687. Paris: E. Droz, 1932. WP.

Dutton, Benjamin. *Navigation and Nautical Astronomy.* 5th ed. Annapolis, Md.: United States Naval Institute, 1934. WP.

Edmonds, James Edward. *Military Operations, France and Belgium, 1914.* London: Macmillan, 1922. 2 vols. plus atlas. Note: Official History of the Great War. WP.

Edmonds, James Edward. *Military Operations, France and Belgium, 1918.* London: Macmillan, 1935. Note: Official History of the Great War. WP.

Eimannsberger, Ludwig Ritter von. *Der Kampfwagenkrieg.* Munich: J. F. Lehmanns Verlag, 1934. Note: Translated by Colonel Henry Hossfeld, *Mechanized Warfare,* Army War College, March–April 1935. WP.

Ellison, Gerald. *The Perils of Amateur Strategy: As Exemplified by the Attack on the Dardanelles Fortress in 1915.* London (etc.): Lomgmans, Green, 1926. Note: Inscribed "G.S. Patton, Jr. May 10, 1931." WP.

Encyclopaedia Britannica. London: Encyclopaedia Britannica Company, Ltd., 1922.

"An English Officer," *The History of Francis-Eugene, Prince of Savoy.* n.l.: n.p., 1754. Note: Inscribed "G.S. Patton, Jr. Feb. 22, 1945." WP.

Eugene, Prince of Savoy, Shoberl, F., tr. *Memoirs.* London: Henry Colburn, 1811.

Falkenhayn, Erich von. *The German General Staff and Its Decisions, 1914–1916.* New York: Dodd, Mead, 1920.

Falls, Cyril. *War Books, A Critical Guide.* London: Peter Davies, 1930. Note: Inscribed "G.S. Patton Jr., Apr. 11, 1932." WP.

Farago, Ladislas. *The Last Days of Patton.* New York: McGraw-Hill, 1981.

Farago, Ladislas. *Patton: Ordeal and Triumph.* New York: Ivan Obolensky, Inc., 1963.

Faur, Fabre de. "Operational Reconnaissance in Future War (German)." U.S. War Department Military Intelligence. Supplement from *Militar Wochenblatt.* n.l.: n.p., [1933]. Patton Collection, Library of Congress. WP.

[Feyel, Paul]. *Jeanne d'Arc.* [Paris]: Hachette, [c1925] (Encyclopedie par l'image.) Note: Signed by author. WP.

Fiebeger, G. J. *The Campaign and Battle of Gettysburg.* n.l.: n.p., 19—?. Note: Signed: "George Patton, Cadet U.S.M.A., April 19, 1909." Inserted: *Visit of First Class to Gettysburg Battlefield.* West Point, N.Y.: Military Academy Press, 1909. WP.

Fiebeger, G. J. *Campaigns of the American Civil War.* West Point, N.Y.: Academy Printing Office, 1910. Note: Annotated, "Finished April 17, 1909." WP.

Fiebeger, G. J. *Elements of Strategy.* n.l.: n.p., n.d. Note: Inscribed "George Patton, Cadet U.S.M.A."

Fiske, Bradley A. *The Art of Fighting: Its Evolution and Progress.* New York: The Century Co, 1920.

Foch, Ferdinand; Belloc, Hilaire, tr. *The Principles of War.* New York: H. Holt, 1920.

Foch, Marshal; Belloc, Hilaire, tr. *Precepts and Judgments.* London: Chapman and Hall, Ltd., 1919.

Fortescue, John William. *Wellington.* New York: Dodd, Mead and Company, 1925.

Fournier, August; Adams, Annie Elizabeth, tr. *Napoleon I.* 2 vols. New York: Henry Holt and Company, 1911. Vol. 1 only. Note: Inscribed "George S. Patton, Jr. from Aunt Nannie. 11 November 1911."

France. Ministere de la Guerre; Chaffee, Adna Romanza, tr. *Manual of Equitation of the French Army for 1912.* Washington, D.C.: G.P.O., 1913. (War Dept. document no. 437.) Note: At head of title: War Dept. Office of the Chief of Staff. War College Division. General Staff. WP.

Freeman, Douglas Southall. *R.E. Lee, A Biography.* 4 vols. New York, London: C. Scribner's Sons, 1935–36. Note: Vol. 2 annotated "G.S. Patton, Jr. from Katherine Merrill [sister-in-law], April 15, 1935."

Freeman, Edward Augustus. *The History of the Norman Conquest of England: Its Causes and Results.* Rev., 2nd ed. 5 vols. plus index. Oxford: The Clarendon Press, 1869–1879. Note: All volumes inscribed "G.S. Patton, Jr. Palermo, 1943."

French, Viscount, of Ypres. *1914.* Boston: Houghton Mifflin Company, 1919. Note: Inscribed "G.S. Patton, Jr. June 7, 1920."

Freytag-Loringhoven, Baron Hugo von. *Deductions From the World War.* London: Constable and Company, Ltd., 1918.

Fries, Amos Alfred; West, Clarence J. *Chemical Warfare.* 1st ed. New York: McGraw-Hill Book Co., 1921. WP.

Froissart, John Thomas, tr. *Chronicles of England, France, Spain and the Adjoining Countries: From the Latter Part of the Reign of Edward II to the Coronation of Henry IV.* Rev. ed. 2 vols. New York: The Colonial Press, [c1901]. WP. Note: Vol. 2 inscribed "George S. Patton, Jr. from His Father, May 20, 1921. Fort Myer." WP.

Fuller, J.F.C. *Armored Warfare. An Annotated Edition of Lectures on Field Service of Regulations III.* Harrisburg, Pa.: Military Service Publishing Company, 1943.

Fuller, J.F.C. *The Foundations of the Science of War.* London: Hutchinson & Co, [1926].

Fuller, J.F.C. *The Generalship of Ulysses S. Grant.* New York: Dodd, Mead and Company, 1929. Inscribed "G.S. Patton, Feb 4, 1930."

Fuller, J.F.C. *Generalship, Its Diseases and Their Cure: A Study of the Personal Factor in Command.* Harrisburg, Pa.: Military Service Publishing Co, [c1936]. Note: Inscribed "G.S. Patton, Jr. Apr 18, '36."

Fuller, J.F.C. *Tanks in the Great War, 1914–1918.* New York: E. P. Dutton, 1920.

Gabel, Christopher R. "The 1941 Maneuvers: What Did They Really Accomplish?" *Army History* 14 (April 1990): 5.

Gade, John Allyne. *Charles the Twelfth. King of Sweden.* Boston, New York: Houghton Mifflin, 1916.

Gaffey, Hugh G.; Gay, Hobart R. *Diary of Chief of Staff of General George S. Patton, Jr.: Thursday, July 8, 1943 to Tuesday, May 8, 1945.* Note: Photocopy of typescript. WP.

Ganoe, William Addleman. *The History of the United States Army.* New York: D. Appleton, 1924.

Garber, Max Bruce. *A Modern Military Dictionary.* 1st ed. Washington, D.C.: M. B. Garber, c1936. WP.

Gauthiez, Pierre. *Paris.* Grenoble: J. Rey, B. Arthaud, [1928]. WP.

General Staff, Berlin, Great; Historical Section; Lane, Colonel Herbert du, tr. *The War in South Africa.* London: John Murray, 1906. Vol. 2 only.

Gibbon, Edward. *The History of the Decline and Fall of the Roman Empire.* Vol. 1. Deluxe ed. New York: The Nottingham Society, [n.d.] Note: Inscribed "G.S. Patton, Jr. November 18, 1909."

Glunicke, G.J.R. *The Campaign in Bohemia, 1866.* London: George Allen & Unwin; New York: The Macmillan Co, 1907. Special campaign series, no. 6. Note: Inscribed "G.S. Patton, Jr. Dec. 1936." WP.

Goltz, Colmar von der, Freiherr; Ashworth, Philip A., tr. *The Nation in Arms.* London: Hugh Rees, Limited, 1906. Note: Inscribed "G.S. Patton, Jr. 2d 5 15th Cav. Jun 17, 1910."

Goltz, Colmar von der, Freiherr; Dickman, Joseph Theodore, tr. *The Conduct of War: A Brief Study of Its Most Important Principles and Forms.* Kansas City, Mo.: The Franklin Hudson, 1896. WP.

Gordon, John Brown. *Reminiscences of the Civil War.* New York: C. Scribner's Sons, 1903. Note: Inscribed "George S. Patton, 1922, Lake Vineyard."

Gourgaud, Gaspard. *Napoleon and the Grand Army in Russia.* London: Martin Bossange and G. B. Whittaker, 1825.

Gray, J. Glenn. *The Warriors.* New York: Harper and Row, Publishers, 1967.

Great Britain. Dardanelles Commission. *The Final Report of the Dardanelles Commission.* London: H.M.S.O., [1919]. Pt. 2. Conduct of operations, with appendix of documents and maps. WP.

Great Britain. Egyptian Expeditionary Force. *A Brief Record of the Advance of the Egyptian Expeditionary Force Under the Command of General Sir Edmund H. H. Allenby. July 1917 to October 1918.* London: H.M.S.O., 1919. WP.

Great Britain. War Office. *Cavalry Training. Volume II, War, 1929.* London: H.M.S.O., 1929. WP.

Great Britain. War Office. *Rules and Regulations for the Sword Exercise of the Cavalry.* London: Printed for the War Office, and sold by T. Egerton, Military Library, Whitehall, 1796. WP.

Great Britain. War Office. *Rules and Regulations for the Sword Exercise of the Cavalry.* Philadelphia: J. Humphreys, 1808. Note: Reprint of 1796 ed. WP.

Griess, Thomas E., ed. *Campaign Atlas to the Second World War.* Wayne, N.J.: Avery Publishing Group, Inc., 1989.

Grose, Francis. *Military Antiquities Respecting a History of the English Army From the Conquest to the Present Time.* London: Stockdale, 1812. 2 vols.

Grosser Bilderatlas des Weltkrieges. 3 vols. Munchen: F. Bruckmann a.g., 1915–19. Note: Only 2 vols. WP.

Grow, Robert W. "The Ten Lean Years: From the Mechanized Force (1930) to the Armored Force (1940)." *Armor* XCVI 1–4 (January, March, May, July 1987): 22, 25, 21, 34.

"G.S.O." *G.H.Q. (Montreuil-sur-Mer).* London: Philip Allan, 1920. WP.

Guderian, Heinz. *Achtung! Panzer!* Stuttgart: Union Deutsche Verlagsgesellschaft, 1937.

Guderian, Heinz. *Armored Forces and Their Cooperation With Other Armies.* Fort Humphreys, D.C.: Army War College, 1937. Note: Typewritten. 39 p. Translation of: Guderian, Heinz. *Die Panzertrup-*

pen und ihr Zusammenwirken mit den Anderen Waffen. Berlin: E. S. Mittler, 1937. 35 p.

Guedalla, Philip. *Wellington.* New York, London: Harper & Brothers, 1931.

Guizot, M. *The History of France.* New York: Nottingham Society, 1869? 8 vols. Note: Inscribed "George S. Patton Jr. 15 Cav Nov. 18, 1909." WP.

Gullett, Henry Somer. *The Australian Imperial Force in Sinai and Palestine, 1914–1918.* Sydney: Angus & Robertson, 1923. WP.

Hagemeyer, Hans, ed. *Deutsche Grosse.* Otto, Hans George, text; Schneider, Otto, illus. Munchen: F. Eher Nachf. G.m.b.H., 1944. (Schriftenreihe der Buckerkunde: v. 9.) WP.

Hagood, Johnson. *The Services of Supply: A Memoir of the Great War.* Boston: Houghton Mifflin Company, 1927. Note: Inscribed "G.S. Patton, Jr. Nov 1928."

Haig, Douglas. *Cavalry Studies, Strategical and Tactical.* London: H. Rees, 1907. Note: Inscribed "G.S. Patton, Jr." WP.

Haig, Douglas. *Features of the War.* Document no. 952, Office of Adjutant General. Washington, D.C.: Government Printing Office, 1919.

Hall, G. Stanley. *Morale: The Supreme Standard of Life and Conduct.* New York: D. Appleton and Company, 1920. Note: Inscribed "G.S. Patton, Jr. May 30, 1926."

Hamilton, Ian. *Gallipoli Diary.* New York: G. H. Doran, 1920. 2 vols.

Hamley, Edward Bruce. *The Operations of War Explained and Illustrated.* 5th ed. Edinburgh: W. Blackwood, 1889.

Hamley, Edward Bruce. *The War in the Crimea.* New York: C. Scribner's Sons, 1891.

Harbord, James Guthrie. *The American Army in France, 1917–1919.* Boston: Little, Brown, 1936. Note: Signed by author.

Hatch, Alden. *George Patton: General in Spurs.* New York: Julian Messner, Inc., 1950. WP.

Hawkins, Desmond. *War Report.* London: G. Cumberlege, Oxford Univ. Press, 1946. WP.

Headley, Joel Tyler. *Grant and Sherman: Their Campaigns and Generals.* New York: E. B. Treat & Co, 1866. Note: Later edition published under title: *Our Army in the Great Rebellion.* WP.

Heigl, Fritz. *Taschenbuch der Tanks*. 3 vols. Munchen: J. F. Lehmann, 1926, 1938, 1939.

Hemingway, Ernest. *The Sun Also Rises*. New York: Scribner's, 1926.

Henderson, David. *The Art of Reconnaissance*. London: John Murray, Albermarle Street, 1916. Note: Inscribed "G.S. Patton, Jr. Oct 16, '23." Patton's 1908 edition at WP.

Henderson, George Francis Robert; *Stonewall Jackson and the American Civil War*. 2 vols. New York: Longman, Green, 1919. 1st ed. 1898. Note: Vol. 2 inscribed "G.S. Patton, Jr., 1899." Vol. 1, p. 337, "Papa read me this book first when I was about 12."

Henderson, George Francis Robert; Malcolm, N., ed. *The Science of War: A Collection of Essays and Lectures, 1891–1903*. New York: Longman's, Green and Co., 1919. Note: Inscribed "G.S. Patton, Jr."

Henry, Professor Lucien E. *Napoleon's War Maxims: With His Social and Political Thoughts*. Aldershot: Gale & Polden, Ltd, 1899. Note: Signature and date probably removed in 1925 rebinding.

Hindenburg, Paul von. *Out of My Life*. New York: Cassell and Company, Ltd, 1920.

His, Wilhelm; Blech, Gustavus Maximillan; Kean, Jefferson Randolph, tr. *A German Doctor at the Front (Die Front der Arzte)*. American ed. Washington, D.C.: The National Service Publ. Co., c1933.

Hitler, Adolf; Dugdale, Edgar Trevelyan Stratford, ed. and tr. *My Battle*. Boston, New York: Houghton Mifflin, [1933]. Note: Inscribed "G.S. Patton, Jr. March 15, 1934."

Hobbs, Joseph Patrick. *Dear General: Eisenhower's Wartime Letters to Marshall*. Baltimore: The Johns Hopkins Press, 1971.

Hoffman, Chief of the German General Staff, General von. *The War of Lost Opportunities*. New York: International Publishers, 1925. Note: Inscribed "G.S. Patton, Jr. August 2, 1926."

Hohenlohe-Ingelfingen, Kraft Karl August Eduard Friedrich, Prinz zu; James, Walter H., ed. *Letters on Strategy*. London: K. Paul, Trench, Trubner, 1918. 2 vols. Note: Inscribed "G.S. Patton, Jr., Maj GSC, May 29, 1926."

Hohenlohe-Ingelfingen, Kraft Karl August Eduard Friedrich, Prinz zu; Walford, N.L., tr. *Letters on Cavalry*. New impression, 2nd ed. London: Stanford, 1911. Note: Inscribed "G.S. Patton, Jr. 1926."

Holmes, T. Rice. *Caesar's Conquest of Gaul*. 2nd ed. Oxford: Clarendon Press, 1911. Note: Inscribed "G.S. Patton, Jr., Maj. GSC June 30, 1926."

Humphreys, Andrew A. *The Virginia Campaign of '64 and '65*. New York: Charles Scribner's Sons, 1916. Note: Inscribed "G.S. Patton, Jr. Maj GSC, Jan 29, 1925."

India. Army. First Indian Corps. *Notes of the First Indian Army Corps, From October, 1917 to November, 1918*. Fort Leavenworth, Kans.: General Service Schools Press, 1928. WP.

Ishimaru, Tota; Rayment, Guy Varley, tr. *Japan Must Fight Britain*. New York: The Telegraph Press, [1936]. Note: Inscribed "G.S. Patton, Jr. April 1936."

Jacks, Leo Vincent. *Xenophon: Soldier of Fortune*. New York, London: C. Scribner's Sons, 1930. Note: Inscribed "G.S. Patton, Jr. Apr. 23, 1930."

Johnson, Douglas Wilson. *Battlefields of the World War*. American Geo-graphic Soc., n.d. 11 folded plates in slipcase. WP.

Johnson, Robert Underwood. *Battles and Leaders of the Civil War*. Buel, Clarence Clough, ed. 8 vols. New York: The Century Co., 1884–1888. Note: Vol. 2, Part 1 inscribed "G.S. Patton, Jr. Bought in 1909 and 1910 at W.S. Lindon."

Johnston, Robert Matteson. *First Reflections on the Campaign of 1918*. New York: H. Holt and Company, 1920.

Johnstone, Henry Melvill. *A History of Tactics*. London: Hugh Rees, 1906. WP.

Joly, Victor. *Les Ardennes*. Bruxelles: A. N. Lebegue, n.d. WP.

Jones, Ralph Ernest; Rarey, George Howard; Icks, Robert Joseph. *The Fighting Tanks Since 1916*. 1st ed. Washington, D.C.: The National Service Publ. Co., 1933. WP.

Junger, Ernst; Creighton, Basil, tr. *Storm of Steel: From the Diary of a German Storm-Troop Officer on the Western Front*. Garden City, N.Y.: Doubleday, Doran, 1929. Note: Inscribed "G.S. Patton, Nov 27, 1930."

Kammerer, Albert. *Du débarquement africain au meurtre de Darlan*. Paris: Flammarion, c1949. Note: Inscribed to Mrs. George S. Patton, Jr.

Keith, Alexander. *The Signs of the Times, as Denoted by the Fulfilment of Historical Predictions, Traced Down From the Babylonish Captivity to the Present Time.* 2nd ed. 2 vols. Edinburgh: William Whyte, 1832. Note: Vol. 2 only. WP.

Keynes, John Maynard. *The Economic Consequences of the Peace.* New York: Harcourt, Brace and Howe, 1920.

Keyser, Charles Shearer. *The Liberty Bell, Independence Hall, Philadelphia.* Philadelphia: Allen, 1893. WP.

Kiesland, Alexander L.; McCabe, Joseph, tr. *Napoleon's Men and Methods.* London: A. Owen and Company, 1907.

Kipling, Rudyard. *Rudyard Kipling's Verse.* New York: Doubleday, Doran and Co., Inc., 1940. Note: Inscribed "G.S. Patton, Jr. Feb 1942, Ft. Benning, Ga." and "Carried by G.S. Patton, Jr. in World War II from Morocco to Bod Tolz." Rebound 1988.

Klarwill, Victor von, ed. *The Fugger News-Letters.* Chary, Pauline de, tr. New York: Putnam, 1925. WP.

Kluck, Alexander von. *The March on Paris and The Battle of the Marne, 1914.* London: E. Arnold, 1920.

Knight, Henry Gally. *The Normans in Sicily: Being a Sequel to "An Architectural Tour in Normandy."* London: J. Murray, 1838. Note: Inscribed "G.S. Patton, Jr. Palermo, 1943."

Koch, Oscar W. with Hays, Robert G. *G-2: Intelligence for Patton.* Philadelphia: Whitmore Publishing Co., 1971.

L'Armee Française. [Paris]: Hachette, c1932. (Encyclopedie par l'Image, Histoire.) WP.

Laking, Guy Francis; Cosson, Charles Alexander, Baron de; Cripps-Day, Francis Henry, ed. *A Record of European Armour and Arms Through Seven Centuries.* London: G. Bell and Sons, 1920–22. 5 vols. WP.

Lamb, Harold. *Ghengis Khan, The Emperor of All Men.* Garden City, N.Y.: Garden City Publishing Co., Inc., [1927].

Lambie, Margaret. *Verdun Experiences.* Washington, D.C.: Courant Press, 1945. As written in the *Vassar Quarterly* on November 1919. WP.

Lea, Homer. *The Day of the Saxon.* New York, London: Harper & Brothers, 1912. Note: Inscribed "George S. Patton, Jr. Jan. 31, 1913 from B.A.P."

Le Bon, Gustave. *The Crowd: A Study of the Popular Mind.* London: T. Fisher Unwin, 1914. Note: Inscribed "George S. Patton, Jr. July, 1915."

Lee, Robert E.; Freeman, Douglas Southall; De Renne, Wymberley Jones, ed. *Lee's Dispatches: Unpublished Letters of General Robert E. Lee, C.S.A., to Jefferson Davis and the War Department of the Confederate States of America, 1862–65.* New York, London: G.P. Putnam's Sons, 1915. Note: Inscribed "This book belonged to Papa. Taken by me in 1935. G.S.P. Jr."

Lehmann, Rudolf; Olcott, Nick, tr. *The Leibstandarte.* Winnipeg, Manitoba, Can: J. J. Fedorowicz, c1887. 1 vol. plus mapbook. Note: Vol. 1 only published. WP.

Lewis, D. B. Wyndham; Belloc, Hilaire, preface. *Francois Villon, A Documented Survey.* New York: The Literary Guild of America, 1928. WP.

Liddell Hart, Basil Henry. *The Future of Infantry.* Harrisburg, Pa.: Military Service Publishing Co., 1936. WP.

Liddell Hart, Basil Henry. *Great Captains Unveiled.* Boston: Little, Brown, 1928.

Liddell Hart, Basil Henry. *A Greater Than Napoleon, Scipio Africanus.* Boston: Little, Brown, 1928.

Liddell Hart, Basil Henry. *Sherman: Soldier, Realist, American.* New York: Dodd, Mead, 1929.

Liggett, Hunter. *Commanding an American Army: Recollections of the World War.* Boston: Houghton Mifflin Company, 1925. Note: Inscribed "G.S. Patton, Jr. Oct 1925."

Linenthal, Edward Tabor. "Part III: George S. Patton: The Archaic Warrior in the Twentieth Century." *The Changing Images of the Warrior Hero in America; A History of Popular Symbolism.* Volume 6 in Studies in American Religion. Lewiston, N.Y.: The Edwing Mellen Press, 1982.

Livermore, Thomas Leonard. *Days and Events, 1860–1866.* Boston, New York: Houghton Mifflin, 1920. WP.

Lloyd, Ernest March. *A Review of the History of Infantry.* New York: Longman's, Green, and Co., 1908. Note: Inscribed "G.S. Patton, Jr. July 4, 1925."

Lloyd, Henry. *The History of the Late War in Germany; Between the King of Prussia, and the Empress of Germany and Her Allies.* 2 vols. London: Printed for S. Hooper, 1781 and 1790. Note: Inscribed by father, "Cadet George S. Patton, U.S. Military Academy, West Point, N.Y. Oct. 20 1908." WP.

Lloyd, Henry. *A Political and Military Rhapsody on the Invasion and Defence of Great Britain and Ireland.* n.l.: Sold by T. and J. Egerton, 1792. WP.

Loliee, Frederic Auguste. *Du prince de Benevent au duc de Morny*. Paris: Emile-Paul, 1928. (Talleyrand et la Societe française, v. 1.) WP.

Longman, Frederick William. *Frederick the Great and the Seven Years' War*. London: Longmans, Green, 1917. WP.

Longstreet, James. *From Manassas to Appomattox: Memoirs of the Civil War in America*. 2 vols. Philadelphia: J. B. Lippincott, 1895.

Lossing, Benson John. *The Pictorial Field-Book of the War of 1812; or, Illustrations, by Pen and Pencil, of the History, Biography, Scenery, Relics, and Traditions of the Last War for American Independence*. New York: Harper & Brothers, 1869.

Ludendorff, Erich. *Ludendorff's Own Story, August 1914–November 1918: the Great War From the Siege of Liege to the Signing of the Armistice*. 2 vols. New York: Harper, [1919]. Note: Inscribed "G.S. Patton, Jr. Feb 20, 1920."

Ludwig, Emil. *Wilhelm Hohenzollern, the Last of the Kaisers*. New York: G. P. Putnam's, 1928, c1927. Note: Inscribed "G.S. Patton, Jr., Nov. 1928."

Ludwig, Emil; Paul, Eden; Paul, Cedar, tr. *Napoleon*. New York: Boni & Liveright, 1926.

Machiavelli, Niccolo; Thomson, Ninian Hill, tr. *The Prince*. 2nd, rev. and corr. ed. Oxford: The Clarendon Press, 1897.

Mackenzie, Frederick. *Diary of Frederick Mackenzie*. Vol. 1. Cambridge, Mass.: Harvard University Press, 1930. Note: Inscribed "G.S. Patton, Jr., Green Meadows, Sept 1930."

Mahan, Alfred Thayer. *The Influence of Sea Power Upon the French Revolution and Empire*. Boston: Little, Brown, 1892.

Mahan, Alfred Thayer. *The Influence of Sea Power Upon History, 1660–1783*. 12th ed. Boston: Little, Brown, [c1918]. Note: Inscribed "G.S. Patton, Jr., Maj G.S.C., Feb 13, 1925."

Malleson, George Bruce. *Ambushes and Surprises*. London: W. H. Allen, 1885. Note: Inscribed "G.S. Patton, Jr. May 1932." WP.

Mandle, William D.; Whittier, David H., comps. *The Devils in Baggy Pants*. Paris: Draeger Freres, [1945?] WP.

Marbot, Jean-Baptiste-Antoine-Marcelin, Baron de; Butler, Arthur John, tr. *The Memoirs of Baron de Marbot, Late Lieutenant-General in the French Army*. 2 vols. London, New York: Longmans, Green, 1892.

Marcus Aurelius, Emperor of Rome; Collier, Jeremy; Zimmern, Alice. *The Meditations of Marcus Aurelius*. London: W. Scott, [1892?] Note: Inscribed "George S. Patton, Jr., from His Father. May 20, 1921. Fort Myer."

Le Maquis de Lorris. Heitersheim/Bade: Joseph Hartmann, [1945?] WP.

Marshall, Charles; Maurice, Frederick Barton, ed. *An Aide-de-Camp of Lee, Being the Papers of Colonel Charles Marshall, Sometime Aide-de-Camp, Military Secretary and Assistant Adjutant General on the Staff of Robert E. Lee, 1862–1865*. Boston: Little, Brown, 1927.

Marshall, S.L.A. *Armies on Wheels*. New York: Morrow and Company, 1941.

Marshall, S.L.A. *Blitzkrieg*. Washington, D.C.: Infantry Journal, 1940.

Martel, Giffard Le Quesne. *In the Wake of the Tank: The First Fifteen Years of Mechanization in the British Army*. London: Sifton, Praed, 1931. Note: Inscribed "G.S. Patton, Jr. May 25, 1931."

Masefield, John. *Gallipoli*. New York: The Macmillan Co., 1917. Note: Inscribed "G.S. Patton, Jr. Apr. 27, 1917." WP.

Masefield, John. *Gallipoli*. New York: The Macmillan Company, 1927. Note: Inscribed "G.S. Patton, Jr. Nov 1928."

Massey, William Thomas. *The Desert Campaigns*. McBey, James, illus. London: Constable and Co. Ltd., 1918. Note: Inscribed on cover "G.S. Patton, Jr." WP.

Massey, William Thomas. *How Jerusalem Was Won, Being the Record of Allenby's Campaign in Palestine*. London: Constable, 1919. WP.

Maude, Frederick Natusch. *The Leipzig Campaign: 1813*. New York: The Macmillan Company, 1936. Note: Inscribed "G.S. Patton, Jr. Dec 1936."

Maude, Frederick Natusch. *The Evolution of Modern Strategy From the XVIIIth Century to the Present Time*. London: W. Clowes, 1905. WP.

Maude, Frederick Natusch. *War and the World's Life.* London: J. Murray, 1907. Note: Inscribed "G.S. Patton, Jr. Read in 1911. Reread in 1925."

Maurice, Emperor of Byzantium. Spaulding, Oliver, tr. "Strategicon." n.l. n.p. n.d. Note: Typescript of preface and book one. Patton Collection. Library of Congress and USMA Library. Annotations by George S. Patton, Jr.

Maurice, Frederick Barton. *The Last Four Months: How the War Was Won.* Boston: Little, Brown, 1919. WP.

Maurice, Frederick Barton. *Soldier, Artist, Sportsman: The Life of General Lord Rawlinson of Trent . . . From His Journals and Letters.* Boston: Houghton Mifflin, 1928. Note: Inscribed "G.S. Patton, Jr. October, 1928."

Maurice, Frederick Barton. *Forty Days in 1914.* New York: G. H. Doran Co., [1919].

Maycock, F.W.O. *The Invasion of France, 1814.* London: George Allen and Unwin, 1914. Note: Inscribed "G.S. Patton, Jr. Dec. 1936."

Mazure, Felix; Mazure, Hubert. *Deux lycéens chez les fantomes de Patton.* Paris: Fasquelle, c1946. Note: Inscribed by the authors to Mrs. George S. Patton, Paris, November 4, 1966.

McCabe, James D., Jr. *Life and Campaigns of General Robert E. Lee.* New York: Bleock & Company, 1866. Note: Inscribed "This book belonged to Papa. Taken by me in 1935. G.S.P., Jr."

McClellan, George Brinton. *Manual of Bayonet Exercise.* Philadelphia: J. B. Lippincott, 1862, c1852. Note: "Printed by order of the War Department." WP.

McClellan, George Brinton. *Regulations and Instructions for the Field Service of the U.S. Cavalry in Time of War; to Which is Added, The Basis of Instruction for the U.S. Cavalry, From the Authorized Tactics.* Philadelphia: Lippincott, 1861. WP.

McClellan, George Brinton; Prime, William Cowper. *McClellan's Own Story.* New York: C. L. Webster, 1887.

McCoy, Joseph G. *Historic Sketches of the Cattle Trade of the West and Southwest.* Glendale, Calif.: Arthur H. Clark Co., 1940. (The Southwest historical series, v. 8.) WP.

McTaggart, Maxwell Fielding. *From Colonel to Subaltern: Some Keys for Horseowners.* London, New York: Country Life, C. Scribner's Sons, 1928. WP.

Melfort, John Drummond, 1st Earl of. *Marches et Évolutions de Cavalerie.* Paris: Chez Nyon and Chez Firmin Didot, 1776? WP.

Menéval, Baron Claude-Francois de, ed. *Memoirs Illustrating the History of Napoleon From 1802 to 1815.* 2 vols. New York: D. Appleton and Company, 1894.

Meyrick, Samuel Rush. *A Critical Inquiry Into Antient Armour.* London: Printed for R. Jennings, sold by J. Gale, 1824. In 3 vols. with 80 plates. WP.

Miller, Arthur Harrison. *Leadership: A Study and Discussion of the Qualities Most to Be Desired in an Officer.* New York, London: G. P. Putnam's Sons, 1920. Note: Inscribed "GS Patton, Jr., May 30, 1926."

Mitchell, William A. *Outlines of the World's Military History.* Harrisburg, Pa.: Military Service Publishing Company, 1940.

Moberly, F. J. *The Campaign in Mesopotamia, 1914–1918.* London: H.M.S.O., 1924. Note: Inscribed "G.S. Patton, Jr. Oct. 13, 1926." WP.

Moltke, Helmuth, Graf von; Bell, Clara Courtenay (Poynter); Fischer, Henry W., tr. *The Franco-German War of 1870–71.* London: Harper & Brothers, 1914.

Montesquiou-Fezensac, Raymond Aymery Philippe Joseph, Duc de. *Souvenirs Militaires de 1804 a 1814.* 3 ed. Paris: J. Dumaine, 1869. WP.

Montgomery-Massingberd, Archibald, Armar. *The Story of the Fourth Army in the Battles of the Hundred Days, August 8th to November 11th, 1918.* 2 vols. London: Hodder and Stoughton, c1920. WP.

Morrison, John Frank. *Seventy Problems, Infantry Tactics, Battalion, Brigade and Division.* Fort Leavenworth, Kans.: U.S. Cavalry Assoc., 1914. WP.

Mottiston, John Edward Bernard Seely, Baron. *Adventure.* Orpen, William; Munnings, A. J., illus. New York: Frederick A. Stokes, 1930. Note: Inscribed "G.S. Patton, Jr. May 9, 1930." WP.

Muir, William; Weir, T. H., ed. *The Life of Mohammed.* A new and rev. ed. Edinburgh: J. Grant, 1923. Note: Inscribed "G.S. Patton, Jr. Dec. 1926."

Muirhead, Findlay. *Belgium and the Western Front, British and America.* London: Macmillan, 1920. (The Blue Guides.) WP.

Muirhead, Findlay; Monmarche, Marcel. *North-Western France*. London: Macmillan, 1926. (The Blue Guides.) WP.

Muirhead, Findlay; Monmarche, Marcel. *Southern France*. London: Macmillan, 1926. (The Blue Guides.) WP.

Munson, Edward Lyman. *The Principles of Sanitary Tactics*. A Handbook on the Use of Medical Department Detachments and Organizations on Campaign. Menasha, Wis.: George Banta Publishing Company, 1917. Note: Inscribed "G.S. Patton, Jr. Maj GSC, June 9, 1926."

Napier, William Francis Patrick. *History of the War in the Peninsula and in the South of France, From A.D. 1807 to A.D. 1814*. New standard ed. 5 vols. New York: A. C. Armstrong & Son, [1856?] WP.

Napoleon Bonaparte. *Manuscript Transmitted From St. Helena by an Unknown Channel*. London: John Murray, Albemarle Street, 1817.

National Geographic Society (U.S.). *Insignia and Decorations of the U.S. Armed Forces*. Rev. ed. Washington, D.C.: The Society, 1944. WP.

Naylor, William K. *Principles of Strategy, With Historical Illustrations*. Fort Leavenworth, Kans.: General Service Schools Press, 1921.

Neame, Philip. *German Strategy in the Great War*. London: E. Arnold, 1923. WP.

"A Near Observer." *The Battle of Waterloo*. London: J. Booth and T. Egerton, Military Library, Whitehall, 1815.

Newnes, George, Ltd. *Newnes Motorists Touring Maps and Gazetteer*. London: George Newnes, [1940?] WP.

Nicolas, René; Babbitt, Katharine. *Campaign Diary of a French Officer*. Boston, New York: Houghton Mifflin, 1917. Note: Inscribed "G.S. Patton, Jr., Apr. 25, 1917. Prides, Mass."

Nogales Mendez, Rafael de. *Four Years Beneath the Crescent*. New York: C. Scribner's, 1926. Note: Inscribed "G.S. Patton, Jr. Nov. 5, 1926." WP.

North, John. *Gallipoli: The Fading Vision*. London: Faber and Faber Limited, 1936. Note: Inscribed "G.S. Patton, Jr. Oct 24 '36."

Nye, Roger H. Album of Note Cards about Patton Library books not at West Point. Provides information on Patton annotations and signatures. USMA Library. WP.

Nye, Roger H. "The Patton Library Comes to West Point." *Assembly* XLVI 4 (February 1988): 18.

Obpacher, Josef. *Das k.b.2. Chevaulegers-Regiment Taxis*. Munchen: Bayerisches Kriegsarchiv, 1926. (Grinnerungsblatter Deutsche Regimenter, heft 26.)

Okakura, Kakuzo. *The Awakening of Japan*. New York: Century Co., 1905. WP.

Oman, Charles William Chadwick. *England Before the Norman Conquest: Being a History of the Celtic, Roman and Anglo-Saxon Periods Down to the Year A.D. 1066*. New York, London: G. P. Putnam's Sons, Methuen, 1910. Note: Inscribed "G.S. Patton, Jr. Nov 11, 1913, Lake Vineyard" and "Dec 31, 1926."

Oman, Charles William Chadwick. *A History of the Art of War in the Middle Ages*. 2nd., rev. and enl. ed. 2 vols. Boston: Houghton Mifflin, [1923?] Note: Vol. 1 only. Inscribed "G.S. Patton, Jr."

Oman, Charles. *A History of the Art of War in the Sixteenth Century*. New York: E. P. Dutton and Company, Inc., 1937. Note: Inscribed "G.S. Patton, Jr., Christmas 1937 from B."

Oman, Charles. *Studies in the Napoleonic Wars*. New York: Charles Scribner's Sons, 1930. Note: In-scribed "G.S. Patton, Jr. Apr 23, '30."

O'Meara, Barry E. *Napoleon in Exile*. 2 vols. London: W. Simpkin and R. Marshall, 1822. Note: Inscribed "G.S. Patton, Jr. May 1930."

Osborne, James van Wyck. *The Greatest Norman Conquest*. New York: E. P. Dutton and Company, Inc., 1937.

Overland Routes to the Gold Fields, 1859, From Contemporary Diaries. Glendale, Calif.: Arthur H. Clark Co., 1942. (The Southwest historical series, v. 11.) WP.

Palermo. ed. Inglese. *Palermo: ente nazionale industrie turistiche*, 1937. WP.

Pardieu, Marie Felix de; Martin, Charles Fletcher, tr. *A Critical Study of German Tactics and of the New German Regulations*. Fort Leavenworth, Kans.: United States Cavalry Association, 1912. WP.

Pariset, Nicholas. *The American Trooper's Pocket Companion*. Trenton: Day & Hopkins, 1793. Note: Photocopy, bound. WP.

Parisi, Giuseppe. *Elementi di architettura militare*. 4 vols. Napoli: Giuseppe Campo, 1780–1787. WP.

Patton, Beatrice Ayer. "A Soldier's Reading." *Armor* 61 (November–December 1952): 10. Note: Photocopy. WP.

Patton, George S., Jr. *Cadet Notebooks, 1907–1909 and 1908–1909.* Library of Congress: Washington, D.C.

Patton, George S., Jr. *Diary: August 5, 1942 to December 3, 1945.* 8 vols. (looseleaf) Note: Typescript. Library of Congress, Washington, D.C. Photocopy. WP.

Patton, George S., Jr. "The Form and Use of the Saber." *Journal of the United States Cavalry Association* 23 (March 1913), 95. Note: Photocopy. WP.

Patton, George S., Jr. Lectures, speeches, articles in Patton Collection manuscript boxes. WP.

Patton, George S., Jr. *Letters: October 23, 1942 to July 30, 1943.* Note: Photocopies of original handwritten letters. WP.

Patton, George S., Jr. *Letters: January 10, 1918 to December 29, 1918.* Note: Typewritten copies of original handwritten letters. WP.

Patton, George S., Jr. *Letters to His Wife, 1942–1945.* Note: Photocopies of original handwritten or typed letters. WP.

Patton, George S., Jr. *Military Notes on the Probable Nature of the Next War and the Tactics, Organization Etc, Necessary to Fight It;* [1920s] File of typed cards containing excerpts from many sources and including Patton's own thoughts. WP.

Patton, George S., Jr. *Notes on Bastogne Operations.* Third United States Army: n.l.: n.p., January 16, 1945. Note: Mimeographed typescript.

Patton, George S., Jr. Obituary. "George Smith Patton, Jr." *Assembly* 4 (January 1947): 8. USMA Association of Graduates.

Patton, George S., Jr. Selected Poems, 1916–1925. Note: Typescript in looseleaf binder, annotations by Beatrice Patton. WP.

Patton, George S., Jr. *War As I Knew It.* New York: Houghton Mifflin, 1947.

Patton, George S., Jr. "War Letters." *Atlantic Monthly* (November–December 1947): 47. WP.

Peffer, Nathaniel. *Must We Fight in Asia?* New York, London: Harper & Bros., 1935. Note: Inscribed "G.S. Patton, Jr. Fort Shafter, T.H. July 22, 1935." WP.

Pershing, John J. *My Experiences in the World War.* 2 vols. New York: Frederick A. Stokes, 1931. Note: Signed by author.

Petain, Henri Philipps; MacVeaugh, Margaret, tr. *Verdun.* New York: The Dial Press, 1930.

Petre, F. Loraine. *Napoleon's Last Campaign in Germany, 1813.* New York: John Lane Company, 1912. Note: Inscribed "George S. Patton, Jr."

Phillips, Thomas R., ed. *Roots of Strategy: A Collection of Military Classics.* Harrisburg, Pa.: The Military Service Publ. Co., 1941, c1940. Note: Inscribed and dated Nov. 1945. WP.

Picq, Ardant du; Cotton, Robert C. and Greely, John N., tr. *Battle Studies: Ancient and Modern Battle.* New York: The Macmillan Company, 1921. Note: Inscribed "G.S. Patton, Jr. Maj GSC. Schofield Bks. May 29, 1926."

Pirie-Gordon, H., ed. *A Brief Record of the Advance of the Egyptian Expeditionary Force Under the Command of General Sir Edmund H. H. Allenby, July 1917 to October 1918.* Compiled from official sources. 2nd ed. London: H.M.S.O., 1919. WP.

Plicka, Karel; Wirth, Zdenek. *Praha ve fotografii Karla Plicky.* V Praze: Ceesk a grafick a Unie, 1940. WP.

Porter, Horace. *Campaigning With Grant.* New York: Century, 1907, c1897. Note: Inscribed "G.S. Patton, Jr. Dec. 13, 1926."

Poseck, M. von; Howe, Jerome W., ed. *The German Cavalry, 1914 in Belgium and France.* Berlin: E. S. Mittler & Sohn, 1923. WP.

Pratt, Sisson C. *Saarbruck to Paris, 1870: A Strategical Sketch.* London: George Allen, 1914. (Special campaign series, no. 1.) Note: Inscribed "G.S. Patton, Jr. Dec 1936." WP.

Prescott, William Hickling; Kirk, John Foster, ed. *History of the Conquest of Mexico: With a Preliminary View of the Ancient Mexican Civilization, and The Life of the Conqueror, Hernando Cortes.* New and rev. ed. 3 vols. Philadelphia: Lippincott, 1875. WP.

Prescott, William Hickling; Kirk, John Foster, ed. *History of the Reign of Philip the Second, King of Spain.* 3 vols. Philadelphia: J. B. Lippincott Company, [1902] WP.

Preston, R.M.P. *The Desert Mounted Corps: An Account of the Cavalry Operations in Palestine and Syria, 1917–1918.* Boston, New York: Houghton Mifflin Co., 1923. Note: Inscribed "G.S. Patton, Jr. 1920." WP.

Prioli, Carmine A. *Lines of Fire: The Poems of General George S. Patton, Jr.* Lewiston, N.Y.: The Edwin Mellen Press, 1991.

Province, Charles M. *The Unknown Patton.* New York: Hippocrene Books, Inc., 1983.

Pulitzer, Albert. Sherman, Mrs. B. M., tr. *The Romance of Prince Eugene, An Idyll Under Napoleon.* 2 vols. London: E. Arnold, 1895. WP.

Randall-MacIver, David. *The Etruscans.* Oxford: The Clarendon Press, 1927.

Rees, Thomas Henry. *Topographical Surveying and Sketching.* Leavenworth, Kans.: Ketcheson Printing, c1908. Note: Inscribed "G.S. Patton, Feb 10, 1910" on back cover. WP.

Regia universita degli studi de Palermo. Roma: Casa Editrice Mediterranea, 1940. WP.

Rehtwisch, Theodor. *Geschichte der Freiheitskriege in den Jahren 1812–1815.* 3 vols. Leipzig: Georg Wigand, 1908. WP.

Rhodes, Charles D. *History of the Cavalry of the Army of the Potomac.* Kansas City, Mo: Hudson-Kimberly Publishing Co, 1900. Note: Inscribed "G.S. Patton, Jr., Maj GSC, June 1, 1926."

Ridgely, Mabel Lloyd. *What Them Befell: The Ridgelys of Delaware & Their Circle in Colonial & Federal Times, 1751–1890.* Portland, Maine: Anthoensen Press, 1949. WP.

Robertson, William. *From Private to Field-Marshal.* Boston, New York: Houghton Mifflin, 1921. Note: Inscribed "G.S. Patton, Jr. June 7, 1926."

Robertson, William. *Soldiers and Statesmen, 1914–1918.* New York: Charles Scribner's Sons, 1926. Note: Inscribed "G.S. Patton, Jr. Jan. 1928."

Robichon de la Guerinière, François. *Ecole de cavalerie contenant la connoissance, l'instruction, et la conservation du Cheval.* Paris: J. Collombat, 1733. WP.

Robinson, C. W.; Moore, John. *Wellington's Campaigns, Peninsula-Waterloo, 1808–1815; Also Moore's Campaign of Corunna (for Military Students).* 2nd ed. London: H. Rees, 1906? Note: Inscribed "George S. Patton, Jr., March 23, 1907."

Robinson, Oliver Prescott. *The Fundamentals of Military Strategy.* Washington, D.C.: U.S. Infantry Assoc., 1928. Note: Inscribed "G.S. Patton, Jr. March 1931." WP.

Roger, J. *Artillery in the Offensive.* Wood, John Shirley, tr. Paris: Berger-Levrault, 1922. Note: Typescript. WP.

Rohmer, Richard. *Patton's Gap: An Account of the Battle of Normandy, 1944.* New York: Beaufort Books, Inc., 1981.

Rommel, Erwin. *Infanterie Greif An, Erlebnis und Enfahrung.* Potsdam: L. Voggenreiter, 1937. Note: First published in United States as *Infantry Attacks,* Washington, D.C.: The Infantry Journal, June 1944.

Rose, J. Holland. *The Indecisiveness of War: And Other Essays.* New York: Harcourt, Brace and Company, Ltd, 1927. Note: Inscribed "Georgie from Fox. G.S. Patton, Jr. Apr. 7, '28."

Rose, J. Holland. *The Personality of Napoleon.* The Lowell Lectures for 1912. New York: G. P. Putnam's Sons, 1912.

Roseberry, Lord. *Napoleon: The Last Phase.* New York: Harper and Brothers, 1902. Note: Inscribed "Geo. S. Patton, Lexington, Va. Sept 8, 1903 from L. H. Strother."

Rowan-Robinson, H. *Some Aspects of Mechanization.* London: W. Clowes, 1928. Note: Inscribed "G.S. Patton, Jr. Dec. 12, 1928."

Ruskin, John. *The Crown of Wild Olive: Four Lectures on Industry and War.* New York: Longmans, Green and Co., 1906. Note: Given to G.S.P. Jr. by Beatrice Ayer in 1909.

Russell, Charles Edward. *Charlemagne, First of the Moderns.* Boston, New York: Houghton Mifflin, 1930. Note: Inscribed "G.S. Patton, Jr. May 12, 1930."

Sargent, Herbert Howland. *The Campaign of Santiago de Cuba.* 3 vols. Chicago: A. C. McClurg & Company, 1914. Vol. 2 only. Note: Inscribed "G.S. Patton, Jr. 1924."

Sargent, Herbert Howland. *The Campaign of Marengo.* Chicago: A. C. McClurg & Co, 1918. Note: Inscribed "G.S. Patton, Jr. Nov 1928."

Sargent, Herbert Howland. *Napoleon Bonaparte's First Campaign.* Chicago: A. C. McClurg & Company, 1895. Note: Inscribed "G.S. Patton, Jr. 1909" and "Reread Dec '25 Jan '26."

Sargent, Herbert Howland. *The Strategy on the Western Front, 1914–1918.* Chicago: A. C. McClurg & Co, 1920.

Saumur. *Ecole d'application de cavalerie. Notes on Equitation and Horse Training.* Washington, D.C.: G.P.O., 1910. WP.

Saxe, Maurice, Comte de. *Les rêveries, ou, mémoires sur l'art de la guerre.* A la Haye: Pierre Gosse, 1756. WP.

Sayre, Farrand. *Map Maneuvers and Tactical Rides.* 5th ed. Springfield, Mass.: Press of Springfield Printing and Binding Co., c1911. Note: Inscribed "G.S. Patton, Jr. Ft. Myer, Va., 1921." WP.

Schaffer, Ronald. *Wings of Judgment: American Bombing in World War II.* New York: Oxford University Press, 1985.

Schell, Adolph von. *Battle Leadership.* Fort Benning, Ga.: Printed by the Benning Herald, c1933. Note: Inscribed "G.S. Patton, Jr. July 28, 1934." WP.

Schlieffen, Graf Alfred von. *Gesammelte Schriften.* 2 vols. Berlin: E. S. Mittler und Sohn, 1913.

Schokel, Erwin. *Das Politische Plakat.* 2nd ed. Munchen: Zentralverlag der NSDAP, 1939. WP.

Scrapbook; Gen. George S. Patton, Jr. Note: Contains documents relative to military assignments of Gen. Patton from 1909 to 1910. Various calling cards attached to last page. WP.

Scrapbook; Gen. John J. Pershing. Note: Consisting of newspaper clippings, photographs, and other memorabilia concerning General John J. Pershing and events occurring during WWI, compiled by Anne Wilson Patton, younger sister of General George S. Patton, Jr. WP.

Scrapbook; Olympics 1912, Stockholm. Consists of photographs, newspaper clippings, and other memorabilia. WP.

Seeckt, Hans von; Waterhouse, Gilbert, tr. *Thoughts of a Soldier.* London: E. Benn, 1930. Note: Inscribed "G.S. Patton, Jr. Dec 20, 1930."

Seely, J.E.B. *Adventure.* New York: Frederick A. Stokes Company, 1930. Note: Inscribed "G.S. Patton, Jr. from Aunt Nannie May 9, 1930."

Segur, Count Philip de. *History of the Expedition to Russia Undertaken by the Emperor Napoleon in the Year 1812.* 2 vols. London: Treuttel and Wurtz, Truettel, Juan, and Richter, 1827.

Semmes, Harry H. *Portrait of Patton.* New York: Appleton-Centring-Crofts, Inc., 1955.

Shannon, Fred Albert. *The Organization and Administration of the Union Army, 1861–1865.* 2 vols. Cleveland: The Arthur H. Clark Company, 1928. WP.

Sherman, William T. *Home Letters of General Sherman.* Howe, M.A. De W. ed. New York: Charles Scribner's Sons, 1909. Note: Inscribed "G.S. Patton, Jr. 1909."

Sherman, William T. *Memoirs of General William T. Sherman.* 2nd, rev. and cor. ed. 2 vols. New York: D. A. Appleton, 1913 [c1886]. Note: Inscribed "G.S. Patton, Jr. Jan. 28, 1925."

Sherwood, Midge. *Days of Vintage, Years of Vision.* San Marino, Calif.: Orizaba Publ., 1982. WP.

Shirer, William L. *Berlin Diary: The Journal of a Foreign Correspondent, 1934–1941.* New York: A.A. Knopf, 1941.

Shumway, Harry Irving. *Albert, the Soldier King.* Boston: L. C. Page, 1934. WP.

Slessor, J. C. *Air Power and Armies.* London: Oxford University Press, 1936. Note: Inscribed "G.S. Patton Jr Apr 21 1937."

Sloane, William Milligan. *Life of Napoleon Bonaparte.* 4 vols. New York: The Century Co., 1896.

Smith, Frederick. *A Veterinary History of the War in South Africa, 1899–1902.* London: Brown, [1919]. WP.

Smith, Harry George Wakelyn. *The Autobiography of Sir Harry Smith, 1787–1819.* London: J. Murray, 1910. WP.

Société de Militaires et de Marins. *Dictionnaire historique des batailles, siéges, et combats de terre et de mer pendant la revolution française.* Paris: Menard et Desenne, 1818. 4 vols. WP.

Solis, Antonio de. *The History of the Conquest of Mexico by the Spaniards.* London: Printed for T. Woodward, 1724. "Done into English from the original Spanish . . . by Thomas Townsend, esq." WP.

Solovev, L. Z. *Actual Experiences in War: Battle Action of the Infantry; Impressions of a Company Commander.* Washington, D.C.: G.P.O., 1906. Note: Translation of: Ukazaniia Opyta Tekushche i Voinyna Boevye de Istviia Pekhoty. WP.

Southey, Robert. *History of the Peninsular War.* 3 vols. London: J. Murray, 1823–32. WP.

Spaulding, Oliver. *Pen and Sword in Greece and Rome.* Princeton, N.J.: Princeton University Press, 1937. Note: Inscribed "G.S. Patton, Jr. Feb 23, 1938."

Spaulding, Oliver Lyman; Nickerson, Hoffman; Wright, John Womack, joint authors. *Warfare: A Study of Military Methods From the Earliest Times.* New York: Harcourt, Brace, [c1925] Note: Inscribed "G.S. Patton, Jr. Maj GSC, Apr 8, 1926. Schofield Bks T.H."

Spears, Edward Louis. *Liaison, 1914: A Narrative of the Great Retreat.* London: W. Heinemann, [1930]. Note: Inscribed "G.S. Patton, Jr. Maj Cav, Christmas 1931."

St. Denis, Louis Etienne; Potter, Frank H., tr. *Napoleon From the Tuileries to St. Helena.* New York: Harper and Brothers Publishers, 1922. Note: Inscribed "G.S. Patton, Jr. from Aunt Nannie."

Steele, Matthew Forney. *American Campaigns.* Vol. 1. *Text.* Washington, D.C.: Byron S. Adams, 1909. (War Dept. document no. 324.) WP.

Steinheil, Marguerite (Japy). *My Memoirs.* New York: Sturgis & Walton, 1912. WP.

Stevenson, Burton Egbert. *The Home Book of Verse, American and English.* 9th ed. 2 vols. New York: Holt, [1953].

Strenger, A. D. *Insight Into the Nazi Industrial War Machine With Ideas and Suggestions Relating to Occupation, Chances of Germany's Inside Collapse, Prevention of Germany's Rearmament and the Post War Period,* c1943. Note: Presented by the author to Gen. Patton. Photocopy of typescript. WP.

Strutt, Joseph. *The Sports and Pastimes of the People of England.* A new ed. Hone, William, ed. London: T. Tegg, 1831. WP.

Sun Tzu. *Transcription of the Text of Sun Tzu on the Art of War: The Oldest Military Treatise in the World.* London: Luzac and Company, 1910. Reprinted by Major C. C. Benson, 1919. Signed "G.S. Patton, Jr." Note: Translated from the Chinese by Lionel Giles, M.A., Assistant in the Department of Oriental Printed Books and MSS. in the British Museum.

Swinton, E. D. "The Defence of Duffer's Drift." Reprint from *United Service Magazine.* London: n.p., n.d. Note: Inscribed "G.S. Patton, Jr. 1912." Bound with "A Summer Night's Dream," translated from the German by Captain Gawne. Introduction to both by Colonel R. A. Maurice, Professor of History, Staff College, England.

Tate, Allen. *Stonewall Jackson: The Good Soldier.* New York: Minton, Balch & Company, 1928. Note: Inscribed "G.S. Patton, Jr. April 1928."

Thaddeus, Victor. *Julius Caesar and the Grandeur That Was Rome.* New York: Brentano's, 1927. Note: Inscribed "G.S. Patton, Jr. from Aunt Nannie, Christmas 1927."

Thiebault, Paul Charles Francois Adrien Henri Dieudonne, Baron. *The Memoirs of Baron Thiebault (Late Lieutenant-General in the French Army).* Butler, Arthur John, tr. 2 vols. London: Smith, Elder, 1896. Note: Vol. 2 only. WP.

To the Memory of General George S. Patton, Jr., Stockholm 1945. Stockholm: n.p., 1945. Note: In looseleaf binder. "A collection of pictures taken during the stay of General George S. Patton, Jr. in Sweden 28 November–1 December 1945. To Mrs. Beatrice Patton." WP.

Totten, Ruth Ellen Patton. Manuscript and notes from interview with author. n.l.: n.p., August 1990. WP.

Treitschke, Heinrich Gotthard von. Hausrath, Adolph, ed. *Treitschke, His Doctrine of German Destiny and of International Relations,* together with a study of his life and work. New York, London: G. P. Putnam, 1914. WP.

Truscott, Lucian K., Jr. *Command Missions: A Personal Story.* New York: E. P. Dutton and Company, Inc., 1954.

"Ubique." *Modern Warfare: How Soldiers Fight.* London: Nelson, 1903. LC lists author as Parker Gillmore.

U.S. Army Expeditionary Force, 1917–1920. *Notebook for the General Staff Officer.* In six parts. General Staff College (U.S.). Paris: Imprimerie de Vaugirard, 1918. WP.

U.S. Army Service Schools. *Studies in Minor Tactics.* 3rd ed. Fort Leavenworth, Kans.: Staff College Press, 1909. WP.

U.S. Army. *Drill Regulations for Cavalry.* Washington: G.P.O., 1902. Note: "Patton" stamped inside cover. WP.

U.S. Army. Cavalry School. *Cavalry Combat.* Fort Riley, Kans.: The School, c1937. Note: Inscribed "G.S. Patton, Jr., Lt. Col. 9 Cav, Feb 11, 1938." WP.

U.S. Army. Cavalry School. *The Employment of Cavalry.* Washington, D.C.: War Department, 1922. (Training Regulations, No. 425–105.) Note: Mimeographed. WP.

U.S. Army. Cavalry School. *Methods of Combat for Cavalry.* Fort Riley, Kans.: Academic Division, The Cavalry School, 1938. WP.

U.S. Army. Cavalry School. *The Rasp.* Fort Riley, Kans.: The School, 1923. "The Cavalry Service Annual." Note: Partial holdings. WP.

U.S. Army. Command and General Staff School. *Problems. The Command and General Staff School, 1925–1926.* Fort Leavenworth, Kans.: General Service Schools Press, 1926. WP.

U.S. Army. Command and General Staff School. *Tactical Employment of Cavalry.* Fort Leavenworth, Kans.: The Command and General Staff School Press, 1936.

U.S. Army. Command and General Staff School. *Tactics and Technique of the Separate Branches.* Vol. 1. *The Division.* 3rd ed. Fort Leavenworth, Kans.: Command and General Staff School Press, 1925. Note: Inscribed "G.S. Patton, Jr." WP.

U.S. Army. Command and General Staff School. *Problems, One-Year Course 1935–1936.* Fort Leavenworth, Kans.: Command and General Staff School Press, 1936. Note: Inscribed "G.S. Patton, Jr. Dec. 31, 1936." WP.

U.S. Army. Corps of Engineers. Provisional Engineer Special Brigade Group. *Operation Report Neptune, Omaha Beach, 26 February–26 June 1944.* n.p., 1944.

U.S. Army. General Service Schools. *Problems in Troop Leading: An Infantry Division.* 2nd ed. Fort Leavenworth, Kans.: Army Service Schools Press, 1918. Note: Inscribed "G.S. Patton, Jr. Aug. 23, 1920." WP.

U.S. Army. General Service Schools. *Field Fortifications.* Fort Leavenworth, Kans.: The General Service Schools Press, 1926. Note: Inscribed "G.S. Patton, Jr. 1934." WP.

U.S. Army. General Service Schools. *The German Offensive of July 15, 1918.* (Marne source book.) Lanza, Conrad Hammons. Fort Leavenworth, Kans.: The General Service Schools Press, 1923. WP.

U.S. Army. General Service Schools. *Methods of Training.* Fort Leavenworth, Kans.: The General Service Schools Press, 1923. WP.

U.S. Army. General Service Schools. *Psychology and Leadership.* 2nd ed. Fort Leavenworth, Kans.: The General Service Schools Press, 1924. WP.

U.S. Army. Hawaiian Department. *Hawaiian Department Intelligence Issued by Military Intelligence Division, General Staff.* Fort Shafter: The Division, 1936.

U.S. Army. Infantry School; Lanham, C. T., ed. *Infantry in Battle.* Washington, D.C.: The Infantry Journal, 1934. Note: Annotated.

U.S. First Army. *Report of General John J. Pershing, August 10 to October 15, 1918. Report of Lieutenant General Hunter Liggett, October 16, 1918 to April 20, 1919.* Note: Inscribed "G.S. Patton, Jr."

U.S. Forces, European Theater of Operations. U.S. Army. General Board. *Report on the Organization of the Armored Division,* November 7, 1945. Mimeographed typescript. WP.

U.S. Military Academy. Association of Graduates. *Twenty-Fourth Annual Reunion of the Association of the Graduates of the United States Military Academy, at West Point, New York, June 9th, 1893.* Saginaw, Mich.: Seemann & Peters, 1893. WP.

U.S. Military Academy. Class of 1912. *34th Anniversary Number Bulletin of the Class of 1912.* West Point, N.Y.: The Academy, [1946]. Note: Inscribed to 2nd Lieut. George S. Patton, IV, From Brig. Gen. William H. Hobson, August 23, 1946. WP.

U.S. Military Academy. Department of Economics, Government, and History. *The United States Military Academy and Its Foreign Contemporaries.* West Point, N.Y.: n.p., 1943.

U.S. Military Academy. Department of History. *Summaries of Selected Military Campaigns.* West Point, N.Y.: n.p., 1971.

U.S. Mounted Service School. *The Army Horseshoer.* Fort Riley, Kans.: Mounted Service School Press, 1909. WP.

U.S. Mounted Service School. *The Army Horse in Accident and Disease.* 1909 ed. Washington, D.C.: G.P.O., 1909. (War Dept. document no. 347.) WP.

U.S. Mounted Service School. *The Successive Periods of Instruction in Equitation for Jumpers, Schooled Horses and Training Colts.* Fort Riley, Kans.: Mounted Service School, 1914.

U.S. Quartermaster's Department; Daly, Henry W. *Manual of Pack Transportation.* Washington, D.C.: G.P.O., 1917. (War Dept. document no. 565.) WP.

U.S. Seventh Army. *Report of Operations of the United States Seventh Army in the Sicilian Campaign, 10 July–17 August 1943,* 1943. WP.

U.S. Third Army. *After Action Report, Third US Army, 1 August 1944–9 May 1945.* n.l.: Reprod. jointly by 652nd Engineer (Topo.) Bn. Co. B, 942nd Engineer Avn. (Topo.) Bn., 1945? WP.

U.S. Third Army. *Inspection Standards and Instructional Guide for Officers and NCO's.* Munich: Headquarters, Third United States Army, 1946. WP.

U.S. Third Army. *Report on Third Army Activities, 9 May–7 October 1945.* n.l.: n.p., Nov 1, 1945. Note: Typescript. WP.

U.S. Third Army. *A Souvenir Booklet for the Officers, Enlisted Men and Civilians Who Made History With the Third U.S. Army in the European Theater of Operations, 1944–1945.* Bad Tolz, Ger., n.p., 1945. WP.

U.S. Third Army. Photograph album prepared by the 166th Signal Photo Company, 1945. WP.

U.S. War Department. *Cavalry Tactics.* In three parts. Washington, D.C.: G.P.O., 1864. WP.

U.S. War Department. *Combat Lessons, No. 8.* Washington, D.C.: G.P.O., 1942. WP.

U.S. War Department. *Manual of Equitation of the French Army for 1912.* Reprint ed. Chaffee, Adna R., tr. Fort Riley, Kans.: Mounted Service School Press, 1919. WP.

U.S. War Department General Staff. Military Intelligence Division. "Description of Operations in Eastern Campaign." Military Attache Report I.G. 6910 from *Frankfurter Zeitung,* July 27, 1941. n.l.: n.p., n.d. Patton Collection, Library of Congress.

U.S. War Department General Staff; Schuyler, Walter Scribner [and others]. *Reports of Military Observers Attached to the Armies in Manchuria During the Russo-Japanese War.* 5 vols. in 4. Washington, D.C.: G.P.O., 1906–07. (War Dept. document no. 273.) WP.

Upton, Emory. *The Military Policy of the United States.* 4th impr. ed. Washington, D.C., 1912. (War Dept. document no. 290.) Note: Inscribed "G.S. Patton Jr. 1909." WP.

Vaissiere, Pierre de. *Henri IV.* [Paris]: Hachette, [c1935] (Encyclopédie par l'image.) Note: Signed by author. WP.

Vauban, Sebastien Prestre de. *De l'attaque et de la défense des places.* Nouvelle ed., plus correcte que la précé-

dente, et enrichie de plusieurs notes nouvelles et instructives. A La Haye: P. de Hondt, 1743. WP.

Verdenskrig II, Skrevet af Sejrherrerne. Kobenhavn: Westermann, 1949, c1948. 1 bind. WP.

Verdy du Vernois, Julius Adrian Friedrich Wilhelm von; Swift, Eben, tr. *A Tactical Ride.* Fort Leavenworth, Kans., 1906. WP.

Vestal, S. C. (Samuel Curtis). *The Maintenance of Peace, or, The Foundations of Domestic and International Peace as Deduced From a Study of the History of Nations.* 2nd rev. ed. New York: Putnam, 1923, c1920. Note: Inscribed "G.S. Patton, Jr. Jan. 19, 1931."

Viollet-le-Duc, E.; Bucknall, Benjamin, tr. *Annals of a Fortress.* Boston: James R. Osgood, 1876. Note: Inscribed "G.S. Patton, Jr. Nov 27, 1916, Schofield Bks." WP.

Wagner, Arthur Lockwood; Craig, Malin [and others]. *Organization and Tactics.* 7th ed. Kansas City, Mo.: F. Hudson, 1906. Note: Inscribed "George Patton, Cadet U.S.M.A., Nov 6, 1908." WP.

Waldron, William H. *Tactical Walks.* New York: G. Harvey, c1918. (Harvey military series.) WP.

Warnery, Charles Emmanuel de. *Remarks on Cavalry.* London: Printed for the translator and sold by T. Edgerton, 1798. WP.

Watson, G. L. de St. M. *A Polish Exile With Napoleon: Letters of Captain Piontkowski.* New York: Harper & Brothers, 1912.

Watson, Thomas E. *Napoleon: A Sketch of His Life, Character, Struggles and Achievements.* New York: The Macmillan Company, 1906.

Wavell, Archibald Percival, Earl of. *Allenby, A Study in Greatness: The Biography of Field Marshal Viscount Allenby of Megiddo and Felixstowe.* New York: Oxford University Press, 1941. Note: Inscribed "G.S. Patton, Jr. Mar 28, '41."

Wavell, Archibald Percival, Earl of. *Generals and Generalship.* The Lees Knowles Lectures delivered at Trinity College, Cambridge in 1939. New York: Macmillan Company, [c1941].

Weigall, Arthur Edward Pearce Brown. *Alexander the Great.* New York: G. P. Putnam Sons, 1933. Note: Inscribed "G.S. Patton, Jr. from Beatrice, Mar. 1933."

Wells, Carveth. *Six Years in the Malay Jungle.* Garden City, N.Y.: Doubleday, Page, 1925.

Weygand, General Max. *Turenne: Marshal of France.* Boston: Houghton Mifflin, 1930.

Wheeler, Walter Raymond. *The Infantry Battalion in War.* Washington, D.C.: Infantry Journal, 1936. Note: Inscribed "G.S. Patton, Jr. January 1937." WP.

Whipple, Wayne. *The Story-Life of Napoleon.* New York: The Century Company, 1914.

White, John Baker. *Red Russia Arms.* London: Burrup, Mathieson, & Co., Ltd, 1932. Note: Inscribed "G.S. Patton, Jr. March 9, 1936."

Wilbur, William H. *Infantryman: The Fighters of War.* Washington, D.C.: n.p., 1944 or 1945.

Willcox, Cornelis DeWitt. *A French-English Military Technical Dictionary.* Washington, D.C.: G.P.O., 1910. (War Dept. document no. 95.) WP.

Williamson, James Joseph. *Mosby's Rangers: A Record of the Operations of the Forty-Third Battalion Virginia Cavalry.* New York: R. B. Kenyon, 1896. Note: Inscribed "G.S. Patton, Jr., Maj., 3 Cav. from B. Jr., Nov. 11, 1921."

Williamson, Porter B. *General Patton's Principles for Life and Leadership.* Tucson, Ariz.: Management and Systems Consultants, Inc., 1988.

Wintringham, T. H. *Mutiny: Being a Survey of Mutinies From Spartacus to Invergordon.* New York: Fortuny's Publisher, n.d. Note: Inscribed "G. S. Patton, Jr. Mar 28, '41."

Wolff and Tritschler, Paul, photographer. *Germany.* Beckmann, Eberhard, text and captions: U.S. Army Exchange Service, [1948?] WP.

Wood, Evelyn. *Achievements of Cavalry.* London: George Bell, 1897. Note: Inscribed "G.S. Patton, Jr. June 30, 1926." WP.

Woods, Frederick Adams. *Mental and Moral Heredity in Royalty.* New York: H. Holt, 1906.

Wrangel, Gustav, Graf. *The Cavalry in the Russo-Japanese War, Lessons and Critical Considerations.* Montgomery, J., tr. London: Hugh Rees, 1907. Note: Inscribed "G.S. Patton, Jr. Jan. 25, 1926."

Wright, Robert. *Life of Major-General James Wolfe.* London: Chapman and Hall, 1864.

Wyeth, John Allan. *Life of Nathan Bedford Forrest.* New York: Harper Brothers Publications, 1899. Note: Inscribed "G.S. Patton, Jr. 1916."

Wylly, H. C. (Harold Carmichael). *The Campaign of Magenta and Solferino, 1859.* London: G. Allen & Unwin, 1907. (Special campaign series, no. 4.) WP.

Yorck von Wartenburg, Maximilian Graf. *Napoleon as a General.* 2 vols. London: K. Paul, Trench, Trubiser and Co., Ltd, 1902.

Index

Army school system, 161
Army War College, 93, 94, 118, 120
Arnold, Edward, 7, 9
Arnold, Henry, H. ("Hap"), ix
Arthur, G., 60
Artillery
    and Devers' stress on firepower, 115
    Patton on use of heavy, 138
Aspinall-Oglander and Becke, 104
Atomic explosion, 88
Attack, 101
    breakthrough achieved by, 47
    continuous attack, 137
    as first stroke in war, 55
    frontal attack, 71
    in meeting engagements, 54
    orders for, 53
    to outflank enemy, 139
    Patton on, 46, 47
    Patton on enemy capability to, 147
    in Patton's letters of instruction, 136
    in Patton's static offense, 140
    as principle of war, 16
    and pursuit, 50
    rear attack, 47, 63, 89, 95, 111, 113, 118, 120, 122
    tank-infantry type of, 82
    in war of movement, 54, 57
    when too weak to defend, 147
Augusta, 146, 147
Ausabel, N., 99
Ayer, Ellen Banning (mother-in-law), 30
Ayer, Frederick (nephew), 92–93, 138
Azan, P., 88

Bad Wimpfen, Germany, 162
Balck, W., 35, 58
Baldock, T., 28
Baltic, H.M.S., 40, 95, 110
Banks, Nathaniel, 89
Bard, Thomas R., 13, 14
Barrès, 89
Bastogne, Belgium, 154
Battle of the Bulge, 135, 154–156, 162
Bavaria, Germany, 152
Belgium, 95
    maps of, 173–176
Belmont Park, New York, 34
Berlin, Germany, 119, 122, 144
Bernhardi, Friedrich von, 35, 54, 56, 59, 94, 96
Bible, 65, 157
Bill of Rights, 152
Bird, W.D., 67
Bismarck, Otto von, 73
Bjornstad, A.W., 69
Bland, H., 166
Bloem, W., 95
Blumenson, Martin, xi, 4, 125, 142
Boetticher, Friedrich von, 6
Boldness, as a military virtue, 14
    in acting quickly, 54, 138
    in cavalry patrols, 63
    Patton's notes on, in Fuller, 89
    in tank warfare, 45

in Virginia exercises, 53
Borcke, H. von, 110
Bourienne, L. de, 30
Bowman, S.M., 167
Brack, A. de, 82
Bradley, Omar, 138, 142, 149
    World War II leadership of, ix
    study of profession by, x
    as II Corps commander, 1, 131
Brady, C.T., 60
Breasted, J., 73
Brest, France, 139
British, 26
    accused by Patton of saving empire, 149
    accused by Patton of "war by committee," 148
    cavalry operations by, 95
    and Germany-first strategy, 126
    in North Africa, 131
    and Operation Torch, 131
    Patton biased against, 69
    Patton on competition with, 149
    Patton visits in Middle East, 147
    soldiers, Patton on, 156
    and use of American troops in World War I, 98
    as visionaries of armored warfare, 85
    and World War II bombing, 144
British War Office, 83
Brittany, France, 143, 148
Brooke, Alan, 130
Bryant, A., 157
Bryce, J., 35, 60
Buddecke, A., 27
Buel, C., 28
Burgundy, France, 167
Burnod, Gen., 88
Burton, R.G., 104
Bywater, H.C., 69
Byzantium, 110

Caen, France, 147
Caesar, Julius, 5, 89, 122, 148, 156, 158, 167
Cairo, Egypt, 148
Callwell, C.E., 58
Camp Meade, Maryland, 50, 54, 84
Canones, General, 111
Carlyle, Thomas, 16
Carthage, 77, 147
Casablanca, Morocco, 131, 158
Catalina Island, California, 4
Cavalry
    all-terrain capability of, 63
    and armored cars, 84
    branch of Patton, 18, 22
    charge of, 57, 58
    command and control of, mechanized, 119
    defeat of, by mechanized forces in maneuvers, 113
    doctrine of mobile warfare not appreciated by, 125
    fighting of, in all directions, 137
    mechanized cavalry organization, 84, 112, 119
    operations in France, 95
    Patton's blend of horse and tank, 87
    Patton's history of, 82
    Patton's learning from cavalry experience, 113